Teaching Chinese as a Foreign Language:
A Series for Instructors
国际汉语教师发展丛书

Teaching Chinese as a Second Language

Curriculum Design & Instruction

汉语作为第二语言教学
课程设计与教学实例

AF278374

主　编　温晓虹 (Xiaohong Wen)
副主编　毕念平 (Nyan-Ping Bi)

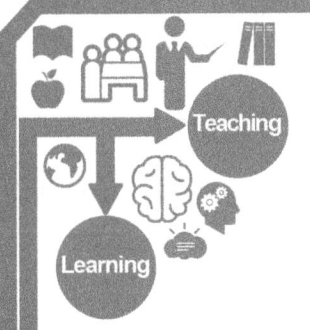

PHOENIX
TREE
PUBLISHING INC.

北京语言大学出版社
BEIJING LANGUAGE AND CULTURE
UNIVERSITY PRESS

Published by Phoenix Tree Publishing Inc.
& Beijing Language and Culture University Press
5660 N. Jersey Ave · Chicago, IL 60659

First Edition

Printed in China

ISBN: 978-1-62575-017-4

Library of Congress Control Number: 2015942165

Phoenix Tree Publishing Inc.
5660 N. Jersey Ave · Chicago, IL 60659
Phone: 773.250.0707 · Fax: 773.250.0808
Email: marketing@phoenixtree.com

For information about special discounts for bulk purchases, please contact the publisher at the address above.

Find out more about Phoenix Tree Publishing Inc. at
www.phoenixtree.com

Contents

1

Introduction

Theme-based Curriculum and Research-based Instruction

Xiaohong Wen（温晓虹）

Teaching Chinese as a Second Language: Curriculum Design & Instruction brings together a broad range of curriculum and instructional designs for Chinese language teachers, both novice and veteran. The volume features theme-based curriculum and student-centered instruction. It consists of eight themes with seventeen designs/ chapters written by fourteen classroom educators. All the designs have been field-tested and further improved based on students' feedback and teachers' reflections. The volume collects best practices to meet the demand from Chinese language instructors today, and projects the future of a field that is facing myriad opportunities and diverse challenges. The volume is state-of-the-art in terms of the theoretical framework upon which the designs are built, the current research-based instruction, and teacher training literature for concept-building and instructional creativity.

Most of the authors are leaders in the field, directing their Chinese or world language programs and/or serving on state or national boards on teaching Chinese as a second language (CSL) in the United States.

I. The Theoretical Framework

1. Learners and Learning

This volume draws upon a constructivist position on learning (Vygotsky, 1978), teaching theories such as "Backward Design" (Graves, 2000; Wiggins & McTighe, 2005), research on second language acquisition (Gass & Mackey, 2012), teacher education research (Darling-Hammond, 2010), and the "Standards for Foreign Language Learning in the 21st Century" from the American Council on the Teaching of Foreign Languages (ACTFL, 1999). We believe that students are active learners who construct concepts based on their learning experiences. They connect existing knowledge to new information and develop their understanding via language use.

Furthermore, learners acquire the Chinese language not merely through knowledge of grammar and vocabulary, but via social interactions where, while focusing on content, they notice language features, form and test their hypotheses, and readjust their understanding to match the competence of native speakers. In the process, students compare and share their ideas, and question or even challenge each other in collaborative learning.

2. Research-based Instruction

Chapters in this volume are developed based on an understanding of research from second language (L2) acquisition. Recent research on the acquisition of L2 and CSL has revealed important findings which have implications for Chinese language instruction. An incomplete list of examples follows. From the Monitor Model (Krashen, 1985), the concept of *i+1* is used as a reference for the relationship between the learners' language level and the linguistic input. In this volume, a great quantity of comprehensible input for listening and reading from various sources is provided in the curriculum. The Noticing Hypothesis (Schmidt, 2001, 2010) and the Input Processing Model (VanPatten, 2015) have shaped our understanding of what kind of input to provide and how to facilitate learning. Each chapter in the volume has a section, *teaching focus,* that presents carefully selected grammatical forms correlated to language function. The functions are described as "can-do" statements in the *learning objectives* section. The instructional input is designed with multimedia features aiming at arousing students' attention and stimulating their perceptions. In addition, based on the framework of the Operational Principles, summarized as "an intended underlying meaning is expressed with one clear invariant surface form" (Andersen, 1984), instructional input in the volume avoids introducing several different forms (e.g., several vocabulary items) at one time with one meaning reference and vice versa.

Equally important is the Output Hypothesis (Swain, 2005), which focuses on comprehensible output. Learners' production must be syntactically correct and contextually appropriate in order to be understood. Instruction must give learners myriad opportunities for them to use the target language meaningfully through speaking and writing (pushed output). The concepts of "pushed output" and performance-based assessment have been clearly reflected in all chapters. Students' performance can vary in format, time duration, and communicative modes, yet one thing remains consistent: they all negotiate meaning and genuinely communicate.

The skill acquisition theory (DeKeyser, 1997, 2015) also provides explanations of why it is essential to provide both comprehension and production activities. The theory states two important propositions. First, explicitly taught grammar can serve as declarative knowledge. Through repeated practice, declarative knowledge may develop into procedural knowledge, the knowledge that can only be employed to solve a particular problem in a situation. Procedural knowledge can be fine-tuned to reach automatic processing, which is fast and accurate. Second, procedural knowledge is domain-specific in comprehension and production. Therefore, skill-specific practice is the driving force for promoting performance accuracy and speed in different skill domains (Li, 2012). In this volume, abundant activities and input for practicing both comprehension and production skills are provided.

The processability theory (Pienemann, 2003, 2015) has influences on the curriculum organization and instructional input sequence. The processability theory explains the developmental stage and processing procedure of syntax and morphology. Structures that require fewer processing resources, e.g., simple Chinese verbal complement phrases (e.g., 你说得对, Design 8), should be introduced earlier than more complex ones (e.g., 这条裤子比那条贵一点儿, Design 8). An adjective functioning as a stative verb should be introduced earlier than an adjective modifying a noun because the former is less complex and thus acquired earlier than the latter (Zhang, 2004). In this book, adjectives that function as modifiers are absent in the designs of the lower proficiency levels, whereas their functions as both stative verbs and modifiers are used in all the upper proficiency levels.

II. Theme-based Curriculum Design

Meaningful learning develops through real-world tasks. In the second language curriculum, the "real world" can be interwoven and represented in themes. A theme-based curriculum provides continuity of content throughout different levels and courses. This is especially important in the current situation, where the backgrounds of Chinese language learners are becoming increasingly diverse. Teaching requires a balance between addressing individual needs and achieving learning objectives. This book adopts a theme-based curriculum.

When selecting themes, we emphasize three curriculum characteristics:

1) communication-focused with social engagement;

2) cross-culture-oriented with broad perspectives;

3) cognitively appropriate to learners' age group.

Consequently, these themes enable learners to connect different disciplines via language. The themes help learners make linguistic and cultural comparisons, and develop their learning strategies while functioning as a competent communicator. For example, the theme *dining* involves multiple areas such as geography and climate, diversity of regional diet and customs, cooking procedures, and dining etiquette. Another example is the theme of two cities (Chicago and Beijing). It incorporates a wide range of facts (e.g., from history to geography and from traffic to food cultures), useful topics (ranging from pastimes to schedules), and rich learning resources (such as comparisons of aspects of culture, sports, and daily life, as well as websites and multimedia communication). All the chapters, from the elementary to AP course levels, present a multifaceted spectrum tailored to students' learning. The book facilitates differentiated instruction, spiral curriculum, and curriculum articulation by having a same or similar theme address different proficiency levels or educational settings.

Within each design/chapter, the presentational sequence is based on "Backward Design" (Wiggins & McTighe, 2005); that is, the curriculum design starts by clearly identifying the end results. Evidence of learning/understanding should be defined prior to planning classroom instruction. First, a design begins with essential questions enabling teachers to ponder "what's worth understanding" in terms of content and skill acquisition, which in turn are reflected in unit goals. Second, the goals guide the establishment of intended learning outcomes, which are revealed by acceptable evidence, such as solving problems by applying knowledge in realistic settings. Third, learning activities (i.e., planning learning experiences through appropriate instructional techniques) must align with assessments and identified learning outcomes. Well-structured activities in a student-centered classroom bring maximal impact to the learning experience. Fourth, assessment tools are varied and pertinent to learning objectives. In this way, learners know the purpose of activities and the expected performance requirements. Each chapter, therefore, presents its concepts in the following steps:

1. Essential questions

2. Unit goals

3. Applications of the National Standards

4. Unit questions

5. Daily lesson outlines

6. Daily learning objectives

7. Analysis of learning difficulties and teaching focus

8. Teaching materials and resources

9. Instructional strategies, e.g., instructional input, scaffolding steps, and facilitating techniques

10. Class activities under the framework of task-based instruction

11. Assessment rubrics

III. Teacher Training and Need for a Curriculum and Instructional Design

1. Effectiveness of Teacher Training

Traditional teacher training books typically focus on content knowledge and the teaching methodology of "telling how". Teachers, however, frequently fail to apply such knowledge in their classrooms (Bartels, 2005). This book *shows* how teaching and learning can be efficiently intertwined by offering a discourse that stimulates reflection on one's own teaching effectiveness. Using the framework of the cognitive developmental theory (Piaget & Inhelder, 2000) and the socio-cultural theory (Taber, 2011; Vygotsky, 1978), this book embodies the constructivist nature of learning and teaching. It underscores tacit understandings and creation of new meaning through constant conceptualization. Since each theme is addressed by different authors and followed by an editorial critique, readers are encouraged to make comparisons and develop their own critical analyses.

The last two decades have witnessed rapid development of Chinese language education in the world. In the US, federal and local institutions have started various programs, such as AP Chinese Tests and Courses, Chinese Flagship Projects starting at the kindergarten level and continuing through college, STARTALK Programs aiming at increasing the number of Chinese language learners in high schools and teacher training, and Chinese immersion programs, which have emerged in many independent school districts throughout the country. Furthermore, Confucius Institutes and Classrooms have been established in many independent school districts and universities in the US. These institutions receive a great number of Chinese language volunteers and teachers from China. For these programs to succeed and for schools to meet sustained demands from students, parents, and communities, it is critical for the field to train teachers and provide institutions with well-qualified instructors.

Darling-Hammond (1998: 8) states that "teachers learn best by studying, doing, and reflecting; by collaborating with other teachers; by looking closely at students and their work; and by sharing what they see." In other words, teacher learning is connected with actual teaching. The book is accompanied by DVD clips of classroom teaching and students' performances, either in groups or individually, demonstrating how the classroom activities are conducted based on the designs. These concrete examples and hands-on experience in classroom instruction are valuable for teachers' reflection and peer learning.

2. Why a Curriculum and Instructional Design Is Needed?

A teacher's first task is to decide what to teach and how to organize the content into instructional deliveries that accommodate students' cognitive, linguistic, social, and emotional needs. A curriculum and instructional design is a scheme to organize learning content into a series of classroom activities to facilitate learning. It is developed based on a comprehensive analysis and understanding of students' needs, their learning styles and interests, and instructional approaches and techniques.

A curriculum and instructional design is fundamental for a new teacher, and indispensable to a veteran teacher. Although similar curriculum materials may be used repeatedly, teaching methods may vary each time. Consequently, a curriculum and instructional design must undergo a revision process to readjust to the present group of students. The process also has stimulating effects on teachers, who re-examine their previous teaching. Each time a curriculum and instructional design is revised, a teacher becomes better informed and more innovative in organizing the curriculum and instruction.

A curriculum and instructional design is particularly critical to a language course. A language course consists of a series of activities. Scaffolding strategies, the sequence of activities, and transitions from one activity to another are not arbitrary, but carefully arranged; a well-prepared plan gives a teacher confidence in the success of classroom performance.

Although all the authors share a similar theoretical framework and teaching principles, their designs vary in curriculum selection and focus, and especially in teaching style. Instructional strategies frequently have relevance to a particular group of students and to the educational setting. Readers are encouraged to understand the rationales and principles behind the selected curriculum and instructional methods, and creatively adapt any sections to fit into their own teaching and learning situations.

IV. Features and Usages of This Book

The designs in this volume are examples for teachers' reference when they design their own curriculum and instructional plans. States in the US require their K-12 language teachers to design curriculum and instruction according to the "Standards for Foreign Language Learning in the 21st Century" (ACTFL, 1999). Not only public schools but private and heritage schools also require their curriculum and instruction to align with current education theories. As stated previously, ACTFL's standards have served as guidelines in developing this volume. The theoretical underpinnings of the book cover multiple facets: current research in teaching and learning, second language acquisition, and teacher education.

Targeted readers

This volume serves as a practical guide for Chinese language teachers, both pre- and in-service teachers who take part in training or professional development programs sponsored by many institutions around the world. It is also intended as a textbook for pedagogy and methodology courses on teaching CSL at the postgraduate level. Furthermore, it can be a reference for teachers of other foreign languages because of its theoretical approach and research-based instruction: although the examples are in Chinese, the content and issues in the book are fundamental to foreign language education.

Terms

The term "Language Proficiency Level" at the beginning of each design is used in a broad sense, providing a relative reference without a standardized measurement. The *unit questions* and *learning objectives* sections emphasize communicative competence, that is, what students can do with the language. The ultimate goal is to help students become skillful communicators who can use the language to solve problems. The fundamental task for a classroom teacher is to create contexts and opportunities for students to engage in meaningful communication. The *learning objectives* section is followed by *learning difficulties / teaching focus* in each design. *Learning difficulties* refer to the linguistic difficulty and/or the complexity of the content. Predicting learning difficulties requires awareness of current research findings and learning theories, as well as insightful teaching experience. Each theme section is followed by an editorial *critique* intended to promote discussion and reflection.

Instructional input and strategies

Each chapter's *instructional strategies* section highlights teaching techniques in instructional steps. Well-designed input and varied scaffolding techniques are the key to instructional effectiveness. Input must provide language form, meaning, and function in context for students to acquire the form via language function. For example, noun classifiers are introduced in the context of talking about the number of family members (in the theme *family and birthday*) and ordering dishes in Chinese restaurants (in the *dining* theme). It should be noted that the teacher's questions are not only a part of instructional input, but also a significant teaching technique. Good questions require skill and careful preparation. In this book, teacher's questions as input are intended to connect students' prior knowledge, trigger their inquisitive minds, and promote their analytical skills.

The authors have innovatively employed a variety of strategies to make the activities learner-centered, fun, and meaningful. A learning task becomes easier and more engaging when it progresses step by step. One such approach is task-based instruction featured with scaffolding and targeted to developing students' problem-solving abilities. Major activities consist of pre-, in-, and post-phases. The first instructional steps (variously referred to by authors as "pre-tasks", "pre-activities", "warm-up activities", or instructional steps) prepare students to be ready both linguistically and cognitively. Comprehensible input is provided, and clear modeling with interactions between the teacher and students is demonstrated. During the in-activity/task, students frequently work in pairs or groups. The class becomes an authentic language and culture community in which ideas are exchanged and language forms are repeatedly practiced. In the post-activity/task, students are frequently required to present their work to the class, be it in the form of an interview, a skit, a survey report, or a narrative. Students usually have little difficulty in this task because they have just practiced and worked in groups.

Every chapter demonstrates a fundamental principle: spirally cycling from the easy to the difficult in terms of the curriculum sequence and instructional delivery. The process may range from guiding students in their readiness for the next step and conducting "drills" in meaningful contexts to engaging students in open-ended communicative tasks and using post-activities as formative assessments.

Assessments

Assessments, including rubrics for both oral and written performances, further represent the concept of "backward design" and student-centered instruction. Assessment rubrics are given to students at the beginning of the class to clearly show them what is expected and how their performances will be evaluated, as seen in King's, Ruan's, and Zhao's designs. Furthermore, students are encouraged to conduct peer evaluation, as demonstrated in the designs of Fu, King, and Ruan. In Fu's design, students are also encouraged to participate in developing the rubrics. Formative assessments are also conducted to provide continuous feedback to, and receive feedback from, students through class activities.

Several designs, especially at the higher proficiency levels, require students to develop unit projects individually or in groups. Such projects require students to research topic-related information and form their own understanding. Assessment of these projects is comprehensive by nature, encouraging students to build critical thinking and problem-solving skills.

Assessments in this book are developed under the practical guidance of ACTFL documents (e.g., Performance Guidelines for K-12 Learners, 1998; and ACTFL Integrated Performance Assessments, 2003) and the College Board's scoring guidelines for the AP Chinese oral presentation and writing.

Diversity

Diversity is one of the significant features of this book. Thematic content ranges widely, from historical to modern, and from global to local. Themes with distinctive Chinese characteristics include Chinese gardens, food/diet, dining etiquette, bargaining, transportation, family, birthdays, schedules, and leisure. The grammar content is varied, covering noun classifiers, compound sentences, verb complements, the *ba*-construction, and more. A wide range of language functions are covered, from making requests and declining invitations to making comparisons and synthesizing cross-cultural perspectives. Last but not least, our authors are diverse. Coming from the East and West coasts and from the north and the south, they represent the entire United States. Approximately fifty percent (50%) of the authors are working in public and private institutions. They also represent different ethnic backgrounds and working experiences. Their rich diversity has strengthened the volume with broad perspectives.

Website for multimedia resources

A website is provided to illustrate teaching steps and instructional strategies, as well as students' performance. The online multimedia materials serve samples to demonstrate how class activities are conducted based on the instructional designs in this volume. The web address is: http://www.uh.edu/class/mcl/chinese/teaching-chinese/.

V. Acknowledgements

With a book of this scope, there are many people deserving of thanks for their support in developing ideas and helping deliver the volume into the hands of Chinese language teachers and graduate students. I thank the contributors, who share the same learning and teaching philosophies and commitment to the book's excellence. They are extremely busy classroom educators, yet they found time to write and revise their chapters and respond to our numerous requests for revisions, frequently more than anticipated. I would also like to thank my dear colleague, Nyan-Ping Bi at the University of Washington, who accepted the position of co-editor and has done tremendous work especially in reviewing the manuscripts. My sincere thanks go to Dr. Maiheng Shen for her generous help with reviewing and to Hao Yun and the editors at Beijing Language and Culture University Press and Phoenix Tree Publishing Inc. for their meticulous work. I would like to extend thanks to the STARTALK Program from the National Foreign Language Center at the University of Maryland and the students who participated in the STARTALK Texas Teacher Program at the University of Houston. Both gave me much inspiration for this book. This project is supported by grants from the College of Liberal Arts and Social Sciences, the University of Houston.

References

ACTFL. (1999). Standards for Foreign Language Learning in the 21st Century. Lawrence, KS: Allen Press, Inc.

Andersen, R. W. (1984). The one to one principle of interlanguage construction. *Language Learning, 34*, 77-95.

Bartels, N. (2005). *Applied Linguistics and Language Teacher Education*. New York: Springer.

Darling-Hammond, L. (1998). Teacher learning that supports student learning. *Educational Leadership, 55(6)*, 6-11.

Darling-Hammond, L. (2010). Teacher education and the American future. *Journal of Teacher Education,* 61(1-2), 35-47. DOI: 10.1177/0022487109348024

DeKeyser, R. (1997). Beyond explicit rule learning: Automatizing second language morphosyntax. *Studies in Second Language Acquisition, 19*, 195-221.

DeKeyser, R. (2015). Skill acquisition theory. In B. VanPatten & J. Williams (Eds.), *Theories in Second Language Acquisition: An Introduction* (pp. 94-112). London: Routledge, Taylor & Francis Group.

Gass, S. M. & Mackey, A. (2012). *The Routledge Handbook of Second Language Acquisition*. London: Routledge, Taylor & Francis Group.

Graves, K. (2000). *Designing Language Courses: A Guide for Teachers*. Boston, MA: Heinle & Heinle.

Krashen, S. (1985). *The Input Hypothesis: Issues and Implications*. London and New York: Longman.

Li, S. (2012). The effects of input-based practice on pragmatic development of requests in L2 Chinese. *Language Learning, 62*, 403-438.

Piaget, J. & Inhelder, B. (2000). *The Psychology of the Child*. New York: Basic Books, Inc.

Pienemann, M. (2003). Language processing capacity. In C. Doughty & M. Long (Eds.), *The Handbook of Second Language Acquisition*. Malden, MA: Blackwell Publishing.

Schmidt, R. (2001). Attention. In P. Robinson (Ed.), *Cognition and Second Language Instruction* (pp. 3-32). Cambridge: Cambridge University Press.

Schmidt, R. (2010). Attention, awareness, and individual differences in language learning. In W. M. Chan, S. Chi, K. N. Cin, J. Istanto, M. Nagami, J. W. Sew, T. Suthiwan, & I. Walker (Eds.), *Proceedings of CLaSIC 2010*, Singapore, December 2-4 (pp. 721-737). Singapore: National University of Singapore, Centre for Language Studies.

Swain, M. (2005). The output hypothesis: Theory and research. In E. Hinkel (Ed.), *Handbook of Research in Second Language Teaching and Learning*. Mahwah, NT: Lawrence Erlbaum Associates.

Taber, K. S. (2011). Constructivism as educational theory: Contingency in learning, and optimally guided instruction. In J. Hassaskhah (Ed.), *Educational Theory* (pp. 39-61). New York: Nova.

VanPatten, B. (2015). Input processing in adult second language acquisition. In B. VanPattern & J. Williams (Eds.), *Theories in Second Language Acquisition: An Introduction* (pp. 113-134). London: Routledge, Taylor & Francis Group.

Vygotsky, L. S. (1978). *Mind and Society: The Development of Higher Mental Processes*. Cambridge, MA: Harvard University Press.

Wiggins, G. & McTighe, J. (2005). *Understanding by Design*. Upper Saddle River, NJ: Pearson Education, Inc.

Zhang, Y. (2004). Processing constraints, categorical analysis, and the second language acquisition of Chinese adjective suffix -*de*(ADJ). *Language Learning, 54(3)*, 437-468.

前言

主题式课程设计、研究型教学模式

Xiaohong Wen（温晓虹）

《汉语作为第二语言教学：课程设计与教学实例》向不同背景的汉语教师展示了一系列的课程与课堂教学设计方案。这些方案基于以学生为中心的教学理念，用主题课程和任务型教学策略来设计课程内容与教学活动。本书包括 8个课程主题，由 17 个设计方案组成，出自 14 位资深的一线教师之笔。本书的每个设计方案都经由作者在课堂中实际使用，又在教学实践的基础上，依据学生的反馈和自身的教学反思，进行了修订完善。当前，汉语教学领域正面临着多样的机遇与挑战。本书所展现的教学设计方案不仅是为了满足当前广大汉语教师的教学实际需求，更旨在揭示汉语教学领域的发展趋势以及应对策略，迎接汉语教学领域的挑战。本书课程设计方案所援引的理论框架、教学研究基础，以及教师培训等方面的文献，都是当今教学研究与语言习得研究的前沿成果，立足于引领对外汉语课程概念重建和教学创新。

本书的大多数作者都是当前美国对外汉语教学领域的领军人物，他们有的是汉语教学或者世界语言教学的科系负责人，有的效力于美国汉语作为第二语言教学（CSL）的各管理执行委员会。

一、本书所依据的理论基础

1. 本书秉承的基本理念

建构主义学习观（Vygotsky，1978）、教学的"逆向设计"（Backward Design）理论（Graves，2000；Wiggins & McTighe，2005）、第二语言习得研究（Gass &

Mackey，2012）、教师教育研究（Darling-Hammond，2010）以及美国 ACTFL 的《21世纪外语学习标准》（ACTFL，1999）都是编著本书的理论基础。基于以上课程设计理论与语言习得理论，本书秉承的基本课程设计与教学理念是：学生是主动的学习者；学习者以自己的学习经验为基础建构概念；学习者通过将自己已有知识与新信息相互联系进行学习；学习者通过语言的运用来实现对语言意义的理解；学习者不仅仅通过语法和词汇知识来学习汉语，更重要的是通过社会交际互动来习得汉语。在社会交际过程中，学习者实现对内容的理解与意义的表达，注意目的语的语言信息特征，对其形成假设，进而在后来的语言运用中继续观察检验这个假设，或弃或扬，不断向目的语发展。通过交际互动，学习者把自己的语言与输入的目的语进行比较，在内容上向交际者提出疑问、澄清观点、确定信息，并且在交流中调整自己对语言的理解与语言运用的能力，进而重建自己对语言信息特征的认识以习得语言。

2. 基于第二语言习得研究的教学设计

第二语言习得研究是本书的另一个重要理论基础。我们认为，第二语言习得研究以及汉语作为第二语言习得研究的前沿理论，应当适时地应用于当前的汉语教学实践中。在此仅列举几个二语习得研究理论在本书中的应用。从监控模式（Monitor Model）（Krashen，1985）看，该模式用"i+1"这一概念来说明学生的语言水平和语言输入之间的关系。在本书中，很多课程教学方案都设计了大量的、多源的、可理解的听读语言输入。再如，注意假设（Noticing Hypothesis）（Schmidt，2001、2010）和输入处理模型（Input Processing Model）（VanPatten，2015），探讨如何确定语言输入的内容、种类和输入的方式方法，以促进学习者语言的习得。基于此理论模型，本书的每一个教学设计都要求有"教学要点"这一环节，所选择的语法点紧密地关联对应其语用功能。对于课程"学习目标"的阐述，则运用了学生"能用语言实现怎样的意义功能"这一形式，来表明语言形式和语用功能之间的关系，以明确所要实现的"学习目标"。对于教学输入的设计，很多方案采用了多样化的多媒体方式，以激活学习者对语言特征的注意，刺激学习者的感知。此外，操作性原则（Operational Principles）（Andersen，1984）强调语言形式与功能一对一的教学导入，即在首次教学输入时，要把清晰的语言形式与意义功能之间的对应关系展现给学生，而不是要求学生一下子掌握很多的语言形式，而相对应的意义只是单一的（例如一下介绍很多同义词），也不是在讲解一词多义时把多项意义同时介绍给学生。

同样重要的还有输出假设（Output Hypothesis）（Swain，2005）理论。该理论着重研究可理解输出（comprehensible output）与强制性的输出（pushed output）。输出假设理论认为，学习者的语言输出要句法正确且语用得体，才能够为他人所理解。因此，语言教学必须为学习者提供大量的练习机会，让学习者通过说和写进行有意义的语言运用。"强制性输出"概念和基于表现的评价模式（performance-based assessment）都体现在本书的设计中。在本书各章节的学习评估方案中，虽然在学生语言运用的形式、时间、交流方式等方面评估内容各有不同，但是评估的内容和原则是高度一致的，即学习者都要进行有意义的沟通，进行真实意义上的交流。

技能习得理论（DeKeyser，1997、2015）解释了为什么要同时进行理解性的活动和产出性的活动。该理论有两个很重要的主张，第一，直接的语法讲授可以看作陈述性知识；通过反复练习，陈述性知识可以发展转化成为程序性知识，用以解决特定情境中的特定问题；程序性知识最终能够进行精细调适，进行快速而准确的自动加工处理。第二，程序性知识在理解和产出方面有着特定的域界，不同技能之间不能互通。特定技能训练能推动促进不同技能领域内的语言准确性和表达速度（Li，2012）。基于这样的认识，本书的教学设计方案中都提供了大量的语言输入与输出练习活动，以此训练学生理解力和语言输出能力。

可加工性理论（Processability Theory）（Pienemann，2003、2015）对于课程组织和教学输入顺序有着重要的启迪意义。该理论解释了句法和词法的发展阶段和加工过程。其对汉语教学的启示包括：先导入那些占用较少加工资源的结构，如动词补语中结构比较简单的形式（如"你说得对。"见实例8），然后再学习复杂的补语结构（如，这条裤子比那条贵一点儿"（见实例8））。再有，对形容词的教学先导入谓语形容词，然后再学习作修饰语的形容词，其原因是前者的加工处理过程没有后者复杂，因而比后者先习得（Zhang，2004）。因此，本书在初级水平阶段的课程设计中，不出现形容词作为修饰语的情况。而在语言水平进入中级阶段时，才导入了形容词作为修饰语的语法内容。

二、课程设计理念和思路

有意义的学习是通过完成真实世界的交际任务而实现的。在第二语言课程的教学中，主题课程能够为第二语言教学提供一个贯穿各个学习层次与各种学习内容的课程形态体系，使得"真实世界的任务"可以在课程的各个主题中不断呈现。当前，随着汉语学习者的背景日益多元化，层次更加多维，汉语教学的主题课程设置就变得更加重要和必要。本书的课程设计就是基于主题进行的。

对于汉语教学课程主题的选择，我们特别强调三个"注重"：

（1）注重交际性与社会参与；

（2）注重跨文化取向，视野广阔；

（3）注重适应学习者年龄阶段的认知特征。

立足于以上三个特征的主题课程，不仅能够帮助和促进学习者在语言的习得过程中进行学科联结与贯通、进行语言与文化的比较，同时也能促进、发展学习者的学习策略。例如，本书中"饮食"这一主题，涵盖了很多不同社会文化领域以及不同学科的内容，包括地理和气候，不同区域、不同种族的饮食习惯、风俗习惯，以及食物烹制方法和饮食礼仪，等等。再例如"双城记"（芝加哥和北京）这一主题，涉及了众多不同的学科领域（比如历史、地理、交通和饮食文化等）、各种实用的日常话题（比如休闲娱乐和日程安排），以及多种多样的学习资源（比如文化、体育、日常生活的多视角对比，提供网站资源和进行多媒体交流等）。本书各个教学设计方案，无论是针对小学的课程，还是针对高中的 AP 课程，都是为学生量身定做的多维度的主题设计。对于同样的或者类似的主题内容，本书又根据不同的语言熟练程度、不同的教育情境做了相应的分类处理，从而实现区分性教学，构建螺旋式课程，增强不同语言水平和课程之间的衔接。

每一个教学设计方案都是根据"逆向设计"（Wiggins & McTighe，2005）的顺序来进行的。每个课程设计首先明确该课程的学习结果；然后在具体的课堂教学设计之前，先说明学生应达到这一学习成果的依据与表现。具体来讲，第一步，课程的设计从教学基本问题开始。所谓教学基本问题，就是教师首先要考虑，在教学内容和语言习得方面"哪些是值得理解、学习的"。教学基本问题也是教师制定教学目标的基础。第二步，以教学目标为导向，设定预期学习成果。学习成果要用具体的学生表现作为依据来体现。如，学生在某个实际情境中运用已习得的语言技能来解决具体问题。第三步，设计与学习成果和评估内容相一致的学习活动。例如，通过适宜的教学手段和技巧，组织安排学生的学习活动。在以学生为中心的课堂上，设计完善的学习活动对学生获得学习经验具有重要作用，因而活动设计是本书每个教学实例设计编写的重中之重。第四步，设计形式多样、内容丰富、与学习目标和活动紧密相联的学习评估方案。通过学习评估方案，学习者可以明确了解课程学习活动的目的以及预期的语言学习要求。鉴于以上的四个基本教学设计步骤，本书的每个教学实例都按照以下顺序依次展开：

1. 教学基本问题

2. 单元目标

3. 国家外语标准的应用

4. 单元问题

5. 每日教学内容概括

6. 每课时的学习目标

7. 学习难点与教学重点分析（教学要点）

8. 教学材料和资源

9. 教学策略（如：教学输入、支持步骤和促进学习的手段）

10. 任务型教学的学习活动设计

11. 评价设计

三、教学设计与教师培训

1. 教师培训的有效性

传统的教师培训主要关注教学知识以及"教你如何做"（telling how）的教学方法指南，而实际上教师在课堂上却常常用不上这些知识（Bartels，2005）。本书另辟新径，通过展示完整的主题课程教学设计案例，展示教师如何通过反思教学的有效性，将教和学融合为一体。具体来讲，本书运用了认识发展理论

（Piaget & Inhelder，2000）和社会文化理论（Taber，2011；Vygotsky，1978），以建构主义的学习观和教学观为基础，将具体的课程设计和教学方案全面展现于教师读者面前（show how）。换句话说，我们强调教师培训要通过概念化学习来获得内在的理解和意义上的建构。因此，本书中的每一个主题都由两位或两位以上的作者分别撰写教学实例，各自呈现，而后又附上编者对各个设计从理论到实践的点评论述，以此激发和鼓励读者对于同一主题的不同教学设计方案做出比较与反思，并做出判断和分析，构建内在的理解和意义。

最近二十年，汉语教学在全世界范围内迅速发展。在美国，联邦政府和地方的各类机构近年来都启动了很多汉语教学项目，如汉语 AP 课程和汉语 AP 考试、幼儿园到大学的汉语旗舰项目、旨在增加初高中学校汉语学习人数和进行中小学教师培训的星谈计划（STARTALK）项目，以及在全美很多学区开始设立的汉语沉浸式教学项目等。不仅如此，美国的很多学区和大学开设了孔子学院或孔子课堂，有很多来自中国的汉语教学志愿者和中文教师在这些机构从事和开发汉语教学项目。我们认为，对汉语教师的有效培训，以及设立具有良好资质的汉语教师培训机构，是所有这些汉语项目能否取得成功的关键，也是这些项目能否满足来自学生、家长和社区各方面的持续需求的关键。

Darling-Hammond（1998：8）指出"教师的最佳学习方式是在做中学，在教学实践中学，在不断的反思、积累过程中学，在与其他教师合作及教学观摩中互相给予的反馈中学；在密切地关注学生，并对他们的创见与所取得的成绩做仔细的观察，而且把自己的观察思考与同事分享中学。"换言之，教师的学习必须和实际教学紧密相联。鉴于这样的认知，与本书配套的资源，有节选的DVD 教学实况，展现教师和学生的课堂教学活动，目的就是要向读者直观示范汉语课堂活动是如何以这些设计方案为基础而进行的。我们相信，课堂教学的实践案例和真实经验，对于教师的反思和互动学习有着重要的价值。

2. 为什么要做课程与教学设计？

教师的首要任务是确定教什么、如何教。换言之，就是要依据学生的认知、语言、社会情感等方面的需要，将语言教学内容组织到学生的学习过程之中。而课程与教学设计正是这样一个"组织"活动的过程。即教师依据学生的需求、学习风格和兴趣，以及教师对教学方法和技巧的综合分析与理解，通过课程与教学设计，将学习内容编织成一系列教学活动，引导学习者学习。

课程与教学设计对于新教师来说是最基本的工作，对于有经验的教师而言也同样必要。教师在教学中可能会反复教授相似的课程内容，但是依据以学生为中心的要求，为了适应不同的、变化的学生群体，所采用的教学方法每次都应有所不同。课程与教学设计必须是一个不断更新和修订的过程，以适应总是在变化的学生群体。同时，课程教学设计和修订过程也是一个进一步激发教师重新审视自己前期教学的重要时机。教师每修订一次课程与教学设计方案，对课程与教学的组织也就会有新的认知与理解，在以后的教学上就有可能发挥新创意。

课程与教学设计对于语言课来说尤为重要。因为，语言教学往往包含一系列的教学活动。不管是教学手段的运用，还是教学活动顺序的安排、转换与过渡等，都需要教师的精心安排，不能随意而为。经过精心准备和设计的教学活动能让教师轻松自信地进入课堂，有信心在教学中引导学生达到预期的学习成果。

不同的教学策略适用于不同的学生群体和具体的教学情境。尽管本书中所有的课程与教学设计都秉承了同样的理论框架和基本教学原则，但在具体的课程主题和教学内容上，特别是在教学策略方面，各位作者的设计和展现都各不相同，独具匠心。在此，我们也鼓励教师读者不仅要把握本书中课程设计背后的理论基础，同时也能根据自己学校、课堂的实际情况，对本书各教学设计内容，做出创建性的改进，以适应各自具体的教学情境和学生群体。

四、本书的特点与使用

本书编写的主要目的，是为广大的一线汉语教师在设计主题课程和教学方案时提供参考，包括理论基础的参考。本书的理论基础涵盖了语言教学多个方面的研究，比如当前语言教学和学习研究、第二语言习得研究以及教师教育的研究。目前，美国各州都要求基础教育的语言学科要依据《二十一世纪外语学习标准》（ACTFL，1999）进行课程与教学设计。根据这一要求，无论是公立学校，还是私立学校或中文学校的教师，其课程与教学设计都需要运用与当前的教育理论相一致的主流的课程教学方式。ACTFL 的标准是本书所依据的主要大纲之一。我们期待广大读者能通过本书的运用和学习，窥见并回溯主题课程与教学设计的诸多理论源头，汲取前沿的语言教学理论营养，用理论研究丰富并坚实自己的课堂教学实践。

对象读者

本书首先是一本具有很强实用性的课程教学指导书，可以作为一线教师的操作指南，也适用于在职或职前对外汉语教师的教师培训。另外，本书还可作为汉语国际教育专业研究生阶段类似"汉语作为第二语言教学的教学论、方法论、课程设计或教案分析"等课程的教材。此外，虽然本书所设计编写的案例是关于汉语教学的，但本书对课程基本问题和教学内容的讨论，都是基础性的，因此也可以作为其他外语语言教师的教学实践和课程研究的参考。

术语

本书每一个教学设计开头都用了"语言水平"这一术语，该术语在这里的内涵是广义的，是一个相对性的考量，没有经过标准化的测量。关于"单元基本问题"和"学习目标"，主要是强调学生语言交际能力目标，即学生用语言能够做什么，最终目的是帮助学生成为熟练的语言交际者，能够用目的语来解决实际问题。因此，教师的任务是创设语境和机会，让学习者能够参与到有意义的交际之中。紧跟着"学习目标"的是"学习难点"与"教学重点"。"学习难点"指语言的难度或者内容的复杂程度。教师需要了解并运用当前汉语教学的研究成果和语言习得理论，依据有效的教学经验来对语言难度做出判断。每个"主题课程教学设计"的最后都以编者的"评论"来小结，目的是为了促进读者的进一步讨论和反思。

教学输入和教学策略

"教学策略"部分是明确每个教学步骤中所采用的教学手段。精心设计的教学输入和多样化的教学手段是实现教学有效性的根本。教学输入要包括语言形式、语言意义和语言功能的合而为一，而且目的语的输入必须在语境中发挥其功能，使学生能通过语言功能实践习得语言形式、理解语言意义。比如，在谈论家庭成员数量（课程主题是"家庭与生日"）和在中餐馆点单的语境中（课程主题是"饮食"），我们引入名词前面的量词学习，有助于学生理解语言意义。应当指出，教师的提问既是教学输入的一部分，也是一项重要的教学手段。是否能提好问题要看教师教学技巧和教学准备是否充分。在本书中，作为教学输入的教师提问，有的指向链接学生的先前知识，有的是为了激发学生的探究精神，有的是为了提升学生的分析能力。

本书的很多作者在其教学方案设计中都提出了各种富有创新性的教学策略，这些策略不仅使得课程的学习活动更加体现以学习者为中心，也使得课堂学习活动更有趣，更富有意义；学习活动也因此更容易展开并吸引学生参与进来。其中，任务型教学活动是本书展现的一个主要教学策略。任务型教学活动的特征是用任务来作为学生学习的脚手架，让学生在达到任务目标这一过程中发展他们分析问题、解决问题的能力。任务型学习活动主要包括"任务前""任务中"和"任务后"三个组成部分。第一个阶段（不同的作者用"任务前""活动前""热身活动""教学步骤第一步"等说法）帮助学生在语言上和认知上做好准备，给学生提供可理解性的教学输入，明确如何进行互动活动。第二步，在活动 / 任务过程中，学生成对或者分组完成任务，课堂成为一个真实的语言和文化共同体，学生在共同构建的语境中进行交际互动，通过不同的途径，反复练习语言形式。第三步，在活动 / 任务后阶段，学生进行展示活动，方式可以是访谈、短剧、调查报告或者故事叙述等。一般来讲，因为学生已经分组练习并准备过了，在任务后阶段，通常不会有太大的困难。

教学策略开展的步骤和过程往往是多样化的：有的教学活动是在有意义的语境中进行"操练"；有的教学活动则组织学生进入到开放的交际任务之中；有的是引导学生通过阅读来准备下一个任务活动；有的则用任务后学习活动进行形成性的学习评估。无论表现形式和活动内容多么多样，教学策略和步骤设计都遵循一个基本原则：从易到难，以螺旋式的循环方式进行。

学习评估

无论是对于口语能力还是书面语能力，本书评估量表的设计和运用都体现了"逆向设计"和"以学习者为中心"的语言教学理念。比如，有的评估量表在开始上课时就提供给学生，以便让学生清楚地了解课程学习的预期目标和评估内容。本书中 King、Ruan 和 Zhao 的设计方案中就运用了这样的方式。再如，我们也鼓励进行学生之间的同伴评估，在 Fu、King、Ruan 等的设计方案中都体现了这一点。Fu 的教学设计中还邀请学生参与评估量表的制定。另外，也可以通过设计课堂活动来为学生提供持续不断的学习反馈，同时从学生那里不断获得教学反馈，从而进行形成性评估。

在高级水平阶段，有的教学活动要求学生个体或者学生小组集体开发单元项目，由学生自主开发和研究与主题相关的语言信息，形成他们自己的理解。

这种学习任务项目的评估往往是综合性的，涵盖语言能力的各个方面，能够综合评估学生的批判思维能力、创造力，以及问题解决能力。

指导本书各评估方案形成的主要参考指南是 ACTFL 的文献（如：Performance Guidelines for K-12 Learners，1998；ACTFL Integrated Performance Assessments，2003）以及大学理事会汉语先修课程的口语和写作的评分量表。

多元性

多元性是本书的一个重要特点。这里列举几个方面的例子。首先，本书课程设计的主题内容多样，涉猎广泛，包括了历史与现代、全球性与地域性的各类主题。比如具有鲜明中国地域性特点的主题，包括中国园林、饮食、就餐礼仪、讨价还价、交通、家庭、生日、日程表、休闲等等。其次，本书涵盖的汉语语法内容也是多样性的，从量词到复合句，从动词补语到"把"字句等。另外，本书课程设计所涉及的语言功能也很广：从提出要求到拒绝邀请，从跨文化比较到跨文化综合等。最后，非常重要的一点是我们作者的多元性。本书的14 位作者来自美国东西两岸、南北各地，代表了众多的区域。在美国公立或私立院校工作的教师各占一半。他们还代表着不同的民族，有着多样的文化背景。老师们把自己丰富的经验和多彩的背景带入书中，使得本书视野宽阔、内容丰富。

多媒体辅助资源

我们建立了教学多媒体辅助资源把数位作者的书面内容用多媒体方式展现出来。网站暂为：http://www.uh.edu/class/mcl/chinese/teaching-chinese/。

五、致谢

首先我要感谢各位作者，我们分享了共同的理论框架与第二语言的教学原则，我们更是齐心协力有着一定要把书稿写好的决心与投入。一年多来各位作者戮力而为，追求卓越。作为一线教师，他们极其繁忙，但是他们拨冗撰写，并对于主编的要求积极耐心地做出回应，多次进行修改。也要感谢华盛顿州立大学毕念平老师应邀成为本书的合作主编，在书稿评审的过程中做了大量的工作。更要感谢沈迈衡教授在审稿时的慷慨相助。感谢北京语言大学出版社、Phoenix Tree Publishing Inc. 郝运社长的支持与各位编辑辛勤细致的工作。感谢美国国家外语中心的 STARTALK 项目和参加休斯顿大学 STARTALK 教师项目的所有学生，他们给了我萌发此书的意念与决心。本项目得到了休斯顿大学人文与社会科学学院的资助，在此一并鸣谢。

（引用文献请见前页的英文介绍）

Theme 1
History and Modern Cities

Two Cities: Comparing Chicago and Beijing

Haiyan Fu (傅海燕)
Northside College Preparatory High School, Chicago, Illinois

Language Proficiency Level: Chinese 3/Intermediate Low - Intermediate High

Age Range: 15-17

Class Size: 25-30 students

Time Frame: 1 block schedule class (102 minutes) for each class, with two lessons in total

Essential Questions:

- What is special about me and what do I share in common with others?

- To what extent or in what ways do I connect to others in my community and in the world?

Sub-Unit Goals and Outcomes:

- Support students' development of their abilities to use simple but coherent language to express ideas/opinions on various aspects of daily life, compare differences and identify similarities of two cities, and interact with/challenge one another on topics concerned.

- Assess students' abilities to use simple but coherent language to express ideas/opinions on various aspects of daily life, compare differences and identify similarities of two cities, and interact with/challenge one another on topics concerned.

Standards: Based on National Standards for Foreign Language Learning

- **Communication:**

  -Interpersonal (1.1)

  -Interpretive (1.2)

  -Presentational (1.3)

- **Connection:**

  -Relate discussion topics to researched or learned information from social science subjects, such as world geography, historical events, consumer education, etc.

  -Evaluate the information received or present a topic with personal views.

- **Comparison:**

  -Aspects of city life such as weather, population, dining, pastimes, traffic, sports, etc. are compared between Chicago and Beijing.

- **Culture:**

  -Typical Chinese pastimes and hobbies such as 打太极拳, 跳传统/民族舞蹈, 逛公园 / 在公园锻炼 are discussed in the umbrella unit.

  -Rules/regulations about public facilities are discussed using authentic materials such as the 天坛 website and information from previous lessons in the unit.

  -Other aspects of life in Beijing such as traffic, population, and food learned from previous units.

- **Community:**

  -Students are encouraged to learn beyond the classroom.

Standards: Illinois State Foreign Language Standards

- 28.A. Understand oral communication in the target language.

  -2b; -4

- 28.B. Interact in the target language in various settings.

  -2a; -3a; -4b

- 28.D. Use the target language to present information, concepts, and ideas for a variety of purposes to different audiences.

  -2b

- 29.E. Understand geography of various target language societies.

  -3

Unit Questions:

- Can students talk about the selected topics in a coherent manner?
- Can students compare a variety of aspects of city life?
- Can students comprehend one another when interacting in the target language?
- Can students challenge one another on topics of discussion in the target language?
- Can students relate their own ideas on topics of discussion?

Lesson Outlines:

Context of the Sub-Unit:

- Chicago public schools have a school year of 40 weeks. Every five weeks is a progress report cycle in the official grading system. For convenience, all Chinese courses are broken down into 5-week units.

- This featured unit is a sub-unit of one 5-week unit. It covers a week (two block schedule classes) of lesson planning, emphasizing how to develop speaking proficiency via interaction with comprehensive assessment.

- The Theme of the Unit: 芝加哥与北京

- **Week 1:** 大都市的休闲生活

  Learning Focus: Introduction to the new unit; final project requirements and

5

rubrics; identify interesting spots in Chicago; review topics related to city life.

- **Week 2:** 芝加哥

  Learning Focus: Four-word expressions, such as 数一数二，五花八门 , and compound sentences.

- **Week 3:** 北京

  Learning Focus: Online resources and authentic reading.

- **Week 4:** 芝加哥与北京 —— 谈不同、找相同

  Learning Focus: Comparison and oral assessment.

- **Week 5:** 你的最爱 —— 介绍一个好去处

  Learning Focus: Individual project and assessment.

The Profiled Week 4 Sub-Unit Lesson Outlines (2 days of classes; 102 minutes per class)

Talking about differences and similarities of the two cities 北京 - 芝加哥——谈不同、找相同

Day 1: Let's do it together! 大家合作

Day 2: Let's see who does it better! 竞赛

Learning Objectives:

Students will be able to:

Day 1

- Work together to talk about characteristics and personal views of Beijing and Chicago (interpersonal);

- Work together to compare Compare characteristics and personal views of Beijing and Chicago (interpersonal);

- Ask about characteristics and personal views of Beijing and Chicago (interpersonal);

- Suggest possible questions when making comparisons between cities (interpersonal).

Day 2

- Collaborate with a partner to prepare for a presentation on given topics (interpersonal);

- State characteristics and one's opinion of the selected topics of city life (presentational);

- Compare the selected topics on city life (presentational);

- Request/challenge other speakers to elaborate on certain assertions (interpersonal).

Teaching Focus:

Comprehensive use of all previously learned sentence patterns and vocabulary

Speaking:

- Express logically developed and well-thought-out ideas (presentational)

- Ask spontaneous and intelligent questions (interpersonal)

Grammar (Review/Recycle/Spiral):

- Compound sentences (Students identified nine compound sentences to use; see attached Course Material 1)

- Comparisons (Students identified four ways to compare; see attached Course Material 2)

- Interrogative sentences

- Word order of a statement:

  Subject + (Time/Place/Manner) + Action: 老年人早上在公园跟朋友一起打太极拳。

Vocabulary (Comprehensive Use):

- Four-word expressions (四字成语) (See attached Course Material 3)

- Vocabulary (See attached Course Material 4)

Learning Difficulties:

- Word order: Due to possible interference from their native language (English), students may make mistakes with basic Chinese word order.

- For compound sentences, students may make mistakes with 要是……就…… by putting a subject after 就: *要是有时间，就芝加哥人去湖边。Also with 先……然后……: *先我去北京然后去上海。

Of all the four comparison sentence patterns (see attached Course Material 2), students make the most mistakes with the 比 sentence: *北京人比芝加哥人很多得多。To prevent this kind of mistake from happening, two simple steps are taken:

1. Avoid translating – When students are given preparation time before delivering an oral report, only individual words are allowed as talking points;

2. Prompt with a mental alert – Write the sentence pattern on the board: if a student uses it incorrectly, point at the visual on the blackboard so that student may immediately self-correct.

Teaching Difficulties:

- Keeping a large number of students engaged when an individual student is speaking;

- Teaching students at various levels of proficiency in one class.

Teaching Materials and Resources:

- Printed handouts (See Course Materials 1, 2, 3, 4, 5 attached at the end of this lesson plan)

- Authentic materials:

  http://www.tiantanpark.com/cn/a

  Photos of Chicago and Beijing

- Stacks of colored paper cards, markers, and worksheets

- PowerPoint slides

- Internet access (optional)

- *Chinese Essentials* Book 1

Instructional Strategies:

To address development of coherent speech:

The key to any coherent discourse begins with clear thinking. A solid speech, regardless of depth or sophistication, contains a beginning, middle, and an end. To help students talk coherently, teachers rely on designing coherent instructions:

1. Selecting Instructional Goals:

Presentational and Interpersonal Communication: The topic of this lesson is to compare two cities. Each student is expected to talk about one aspect of the comparison at paragraph length for 1-2 minutes. Then the audience must spontaneously ask three questions to interact with their fellow speakers during the course of this event.

Major Linguistic Components: Four-word expressions (四字成语), four ways of comparison, and compound sentences have been developed during the previous lessons and emphasized as the required elements in the assessment rubrics.

2. Scaffolding Learning:

It is important that new vocabulary is introduced based on the students' needs, and through use; that new sentence patterns are developed one at a time and accumulated to express more sophisticated ideas; that new information is integrated through a variety of means; and that new inquiries are expanded upon in statements.

3. Engaging All Students:

To further enhance differentiated instruction, an extended list of vocabulary is provided.

Certain students' weaknesses or difficulties are to be identified and problems solved on the spot and right after class.

Many language tasks/projects are designed to include cooperative learning, where individual roles and obligations are clearly defined, recorded, and assessed.

4. Involving Students in Assessment:

The required elements and rubrics are communicated to the students as a rule of classroom practice. The students participate in making the rubrics, and they provide the language they feel strongly about.

5. Developing Critical Thinking:

Chicago Public Schools' new teacher evaluation system emphasizes students asking "good" questions in class. To break the stereotype that students in world language classrooms with limited language skills only use "baby talk", world language teachers need to rationalize and secure critical thinking skills in our practice.

Teacher modeling is crucial. A teacher in the language classroom needs to not only model the use of the target language to initiate inquiries, but also use questions to press students to think critically for deeper meanings. To start, a simple question "为什么" or "为什么不" will serve the purpose. Also, always guide the students to think out of the box: "还有什么可能性？还有什么其他的选择？" Furthermore, acknowledge, and thus encourage, good questions at all times.

This is the reason why there is a built-in session of the teacher modeling question forms in the warm-up session and a "required but spontaneous Q&A" after each oral presentation.

The byproduct of this design (required free Q&A) is that students are fully engaged when others are presenting.

Day 1

Learning Objectives:

Students will be able to:

- Work together to talk about characteristics and personal views of Beijing and Chicago (interpersonal);

- Work together to compare characteristics and personal views of Beijing and Chicago (interpersonal);

- Ask about characteristics and personal views of Beijing and Chicago (interpersonal);

- Suggest possible questions when making comparisons between cities (interpersonal).

Instructional Steps:

Part I – Housekeeping: Daily Routine (5 minutes)

1. Teacher takes attendance while students practice characters either on the board or at their desks to prepare for daily dictation.

2. Formative Assessment – Dictation (10 minutes)

   1) Students write their names and the date in Chinese on the dictation sheet.

   2) Teacher says 10 phrases selected from the reading by the students from the previous class: 踢毽子, 忙碌, 轻松, 热闹, 温馨, 聚, 愉快, 丰富, 免费, 优惠, and students write them down. It will be helpful that teacher repeats the phrases in sentences as they appear in the reading:

   人们在那儿散步、跑步、踢毽子、跳舞、打拳、唱歌、唱戏。他们三三两两或者成群结队地一起活动，慢中有快、动中有静，既忙碌又轻松，既热闹又温馨。为什么这样说呢？因为人们每天聚在一起，交了不少朋友，除了锻炼，还有社交。身体好了，心情愉快了，生活也丰富了。天坛不是一个免费的公园，去那儿要买票。不过月票、季票和年票都不太贵，老年人还有优惠。

   3) Students swap papers and quickly check each other's writing, circling mistakes and signing their names at the bottom.

   4) All papers are collected and submitted to teacher.

   (Practicing the characters or using new vocabulary in written homework serves as part of the homework. Also, an extra phrase will oftentimes be selected as a bonus point for grading as an incentive to practice more characters.)

3. Review – Check Homework (10 minutes)

   (The previous day's homework was to write about Beijing. Integrating new vocabulary and compound sentences is a requirement.)

   1) Teacher asks students if there are questions concerning the homework.

   2) Students read a neighbor's written homework and select a good sentence or something they would like to share with the class.

   Sample Sentences:

1）除了最有名的北京小吃以外，北京还有各种各样的美食，比如说烤鸭、饺子等。

2）虽然北京的公园里早上非常热闹，有很多活动，比如唱歌、跳舞、打太极拳，可是早上去公园锻炼的人常常是老人。年轻人因为要上班，所以不喜欢早上去公园锻炼。

4. Homework Collection

Part II – Main Content: Comparing Two Cities

Pre-Activity 1 (10 minutes)

1. Teacher-student (T-S) and student-student (S-S) interaction (Interpersonal)

   Purpose: To brainstorm topics of comparison.

   我们现在知道了芝加哥和北京都是非常大、特别有意思的城市。谁能说一说这两个城市有哪些地方差不多？又有哪些地方不一样呢？比如说：

   Students name the topics for comparison, and teacher projects class notes onto the big screen. If topics from previous learning are overlooked, teacher gives hints: 芝加哥的东西贵还是北京的东西贵呢？谁知道？

2. Summarize the notes and list 12 topics:

   ① 城市（人口、地理等）② 天气 ③ 交通 ④ 活动 ⑤ 物价 ⑥ 公园
   ⑦ 名胜古迹 ⑧ 历史 ⑨ 名人 ⑩ 运动 ⑪ 动物 ⑫ 饭馆和食品

   (Class notes are to be posted at the end of day on Google Drive to share with the whole class.)

Pre-Activity 2 (10 minutes)

Teacher-student (T-S) and student-student (S-S) interaction (Interactive)

Purposes:

- To establish parameters of the language task;
- To set to work collaboratively on content of the comparison;
- To provide a sample to scaffold learning.

1. Organize students into groups of 3-4; each group has a computer to work with.

2. Communicate format, requirements, and rubrics for the oral presentation due next class.

3. Teacher discusses with the class briefly but very clearly the format and required grammatical elements of the oral presentation. Teacher also invites students to review the oral presentation rubrics that have been established for Chinese 3. (Show quick visual now and post details online after class.)

> **Format:**
>
> Two-minute oral presentation on one randomly chosen topic
> Two on the spot questions for Q&A sessions
>
> **Required Elements:**
>
> Use of compound sentences – see Course Material 1
> Use of all four ways of comparisons – see Course Material 2
> Use of four-word expressions (四字成语) – See Course Material 3
>
> **Five Categories to Be Assessed:**
>
> Content – Five facts
> Pronunciation and tones
> Fluency and speed of speaking (absolutely no reading)
> Accuracy (grammar)
> Logic of speech

4. Warm-up activity – Scaffolding before group work (Interpersonal)

我们选了这么多可以比较的题目，怎么比呢？请每个小组的同学一起想一想每个题目的 "talking points"，然后我们一起来说说。

Teacher asks students to pick a topic as a working sample: 物价

> 比物价（5 facts）
> 买房 / 租房
> 日常生活：吃饭、穿衣
> 休闲：看电影、运动
> 你觉得

Teacher projects class notes onto the big screen while students are talking. Teacher guides the conversation.

Activity 1 (15 minutes)

For Learning Objectives 1 and 2

Purpose: To organize ideas and lay out talking points.

1. Students sit together in groups. Each group is given four topics to work with. Students follow the sample to create talking points for each topic (interpersonal);

2. Students post group-generated talking points on a class Google document to share (interpersonal and presentational);

3. The whole class reviews the final document and comments on it (interpersonal).

Activity 2 (15 minutes)

For Learning Objectives 3 and 4

Purpose: To review sentence patterns and brainstorm questions.

Students sit in groups as before. Teacher asks each group to create two lists: learned compound sentences and four ways of comparisons (interpersonal);

Each group generates 10 possible questions on various topics for comparison, then shares them with the class (interpersonal).

Post-Activity (15 minutes)

Purpose: To assess correct use of the sentence patterns and questions.

1. Review and reinforce: Teacher shows the required compound sentences (Course Material 1) and four ways of comparison chart (Course Material 2) on the projector so that students can revise their lists (interpretive);

2. Assessment: Teacher asks the students which patterns tend to be problematic; students give examples of correct use of the sentences (interpretive and presentational);

3. Teacher draws students' attention to:

   "要是……，S 就 Verb" (就 can only be placed before a verb, not a subject);

   "S 先 Verb，然后 Verb" (先 can only be placed after a subject not before);

   "A 比 B Adjective by How Much (很 cannot appear before the adjective)";

"A 跟 B 一样 (Adjective)" (Use "跟 / 和", not "比").

4. Assessment: Teacher asks each student to share with the class one question that they think is the best (presentational).

Summarize and give homework assignments (5 minutes)

Teacher does the following:

1. He/She repeats performance assessment requirements and rubrics;

2. He/She reminds students what all course materials and supporting documents are, and where to find them;

3. He/She gives homework assignment: Ask students to prepare for oral presentation and assessment.

   By this time, teacher has communicated with students at least three times the tasks that they must perform on their own with sufficient support. If that is not enough, ask students to verbalize one or more times.

Part III: Communication after Class

Teacher makes sure that all students have access to the course materials and related documents for learning after school. Besides printed materials, teacher may also post all course materials, class notes, and homework assignments online. If any students do not have Internet access, a hard copy has to be provided.

Google Drive Postings

Homework:

Prepare to talk about 12 topics about Beijing and Chicago. Your presentation will be for two minutes on one of the 12 topics, chosen at random. You will also improvise two questions in total during the interactive part of the presentation.

Your speech must include use of all four categories of comparison patterns, some four-word expressions, and some compound sentences.

Refer to the postings on the Google Drive "Chinese 3/compare 2 cities" folder for your presentation.

Posting 1: Comparison Topics

Comparison Topics for next class speaking assessment:
① 城市（人口、地理等）② 天气 ③ 交通 ④ 活动 ⑤ 物价 ⑥ 公园
⑦ 名胜古迹 ⑧ 历史 ⑨ 名人 ⑩ 运动 ⑪ 动物 ⑫ 饭馆和食品

Posting 2: Sample Questions

问题：

北京在哪儿？芝加哥在哪儿？

北京是首都吗？人口有多少？人口多元化吗？芝加哥呢？

芝加哥很现代化，北京有那么现代化吗？

为什么你说北京没有芝加哥现代化？

芝加哥和北京还有什么一样和不一样的地方？

相同点还有哪些？请举例。

不同点还有哪些？请举例。

请再比较一下北京和芝加哥的交通（地理、历史、文化、经济等）。

Posting 3: Required Sentence Patterns[1]

复句：

1. 因为……所以……

2. 要是……，（S）就 V……（如果……，（S）就 V……）

3. 虽然……，可是 / 但是……

4. 不但……而且

5. 又……又……

6. 一边……一边……

7. 除了……以外，……也（Inclusive）/ 都（Exclusive）……

8.（S）先……，然后……，（再）……

9. 有时候……，有时候……

---

1 Postings 3 and 5 have been repeatedly used throughout Chinese 2 and 3. Students should be familiar with them by now, but still may need to be reminded from time to time in order to use them for more sophisticated language tasks.

Four Ways to Provide Comparison (visual on board)

摆事实	谈看法	比不同	找相同
例子： 芝加哥是一个大城市。 北京也是大城市。	例子： 我觉得芝加哥大，可是北京更大。	例子： 北京比芝加哥大（得多）。	例子： 北京跟芝加哥一样四季分明。

Posting 4: Four-Word Expressions

首屈一指	数一数二	风景如画	三三两两	三五成群	五花八门
车水马龙	四面八方	七嘴八舌	讨价还价	十全十美	多姿多彩

Posting 5: Speaking Rubric

Speaking Rubric

Evaluation	Does Not Meet Requirements	Meets Requirements	Exceeds Requirements
Content	Fewer than 5 facts	5 facts with details	More than 5 with additional information
Pronunciation and Tones	Major flaws and incomprehensible at times	Minor flaws but quite comprehensible	No flaws
Fluency	Unnecessary pauses; speaks with visual cues	Artificial flow; no reading	Native-like, natural flow; no reading
Speed of Speaking	Slow	Natural speed	Natural speed
Logic of Speech	Random sentences	Organized point by point with supporting details	Organized speech with supporting details and natural transitions
Accuracy	Contains grammatical errors	No grammatical errors	Self-expression and creative use of sentence patterns

Differentiated Instruction:

- Allow Student A extra time for preparation and speaking

- Provide Student B with handout that has *pinyin* for key vocabulary

Teacher Self-assessment:

- What went well?

- What would need more review in the next class?

- Did the activities help students learn effectively?

- What should be done differently?

Day 2

Learning Objectives:

Students will be able to:

- Collaborate with a partner to prepare for a presentation on given topics (interpersonal);

- State characteristics and one's opinion of the selected topics of city life (presentational);

- Compare the selected topics of city life (presentational);

- Request/challenge other speakers to elaborate on certain assertions (interpersonal).

Teaching Materials and Resources:

- Handouts: List of compound sentences

- A basket with X number of hidden topics (X = # of students, with some topics repeated)

- Visual of four ways of comparison on blackboard (highlight the "比" sentence)
- Computer projector

Teaching Focus:

Students speak individually as well as interact with one another in target language.

Instructional Steps:

Part I – Housekeeping: Daily Routine and Pre-Activity (5 minutes)

1. Teacher takes attendance;

2. Students each pick a partner to prepare for the presentation (see procedures below);

3. Students pick up the compound sentences handout;

4. Teacher explains the procedures and restates the requirements and rubrics once again briefly and clearly.

Format:

Two-minute oral presentation on one randomly chosen topic
Two questions for on the spot Q&A sessions

Required Elements:

Use of compound sentences – See Course Material 1
Use of all four ways of comparison – See Course Material 2
Use of four-word expressions – See Course Material 3

Five Categories to Be Assessed:

Content – five facts
Pronunciation and tones
Fluency and speed of speaking (absolutely no reading)
Accuracy (grammar)
Logic of speech

Part II – Main Content: Comparing Two Cities

Warm-up Activity 1 (10 minutes)

For Learning Objective 1

Purpose: Students prepare for oral presentation with support from a partner (interpersonal).

Instructional Procedures:

1. Teacher prepares a basket in which there are folded slips that bear the 12 topics for today's comparison presentation. There are 2-3 slips with the same topics and a total number of slips equal to the number of the students in class.

2. List of the 12 topics and the order for presentation:

   ① 城市 (人口、地理等) ② 天气 ③ 交通 ④ 活动 ⑤ 物价 ⑥ 公园
   ⑦ 名胜古迹 ⑧ 历史 ⑨ 名人 ⑩ 运动 ⑪ 动物 ⑫ 饭馆和食品

3. Students come into the classroom, draw a topic at random, and are automatically paired with another student who happens to pick the same topic. The two students work together to prepare for the oral presentation.

4. While students are working together, teacher writes the four ways of comparison on the blackboard as a visual reminder.

Warm-up Activity 2 (2 minutes)

Purpose: Teacher models the Q&A to scaffold the oral presentations.

- Teacher emphasizes that asking relevant questions is also part of today's assessment. Each student is required to improvise two questions. 每人必须问两个问题。

- Tips on how to ask good questions: 怎么问问题？

  1. 注意听。
  2. 问有意思的问题。可以问的问题有很多，比如：为什么你觉得北京没有芝加哥现代化？你是怎么知道的？对这个问题你有什么看法？

Main Activity (70 minutes)

For Learning Objectives 2, 3, 4

Purpose: To assess students' speaking performance.

Teacher-student (T-S) and student-student (S-S) interaction (interactive and presentational)

1. Students take turns talking for two minutes about the topic they picked, then ask two relevant questions during on the spot Q&A sessions.

2. Teacher serves as the time manager and occasional grammar reminder, but only when the "比" sentence is stumbled on. Usually, if students make a mistake, teacher points at the sentence pattern demonstrated on the blackboard to draw attention, and students will correct themselves immediately.

3. Teacher assesses each presentation and interaction with quick notes or check marks on the rubrics.

4. Teacher pays full attention to all student speakers, uses eye contact and facial expressions to show agreement and encouragement during the whole process, and expresses emotions through body language, short comments such as "很好！有意思！是吗？", laughter, etc., in order to make these presentations and interactions a true communicative experience for everyone.

Sample Presentation and Exchanges:

Student A:

Talking Points:

- 历史长短
- 城市现状
- 历史故事
- 历史人物
- 我的看法

Sample narration:

今天我要比较的题目是历史。这个题目很难。你们知道美国的历史不太长，只有二百多年，可是中国的历史特别特别长，几千年。中国的历史比美国长得多得多得多得多。因为美国的历史短，芝加哥的历史也短。因为中国的历史长，北京的历史也长。芝加哥不是美国的首都。北京不但是中国的首都，而且是中国第二大城市，可是以前不是。芝加哥数一数二的最有名的历史故事是芝加哥的大火。北京最有名的历史故事五花八门，可是常常在天安门。芝加哥有名的历史人是林肯，还有奥巴马。北京有名的历史人我不太知道，Chairman Mao？ Jet Li？虽然芝加哥的历史没有北京的长，可是我觉得芝加哥的历史比北京的有意思。

Q & A

Student B: 什么？为什么你说芝加哥的历史比北京的有意思？可是芝加哥历史太短了。

Student A: 因为我家住在芝加哥，我爱芝加哥。

Student B: 那不应该是原因。

Student A: 好吧。因为我了解芝加哥所以我觉得芝加哥有意思。我不了解北京。

Student C: 为什么你说 Jet Li 是北京有名的历史人？他不是历史人。

Teacher: 历史人物。Jet Li 算不上一个历史人物。

Student A: Jet Li 可能不是历史人物，可是很多美国人知道他。

Teacher: 非常好，谢谢，下一个。

Post-Activity (5 minutes)

Purpose: To summarize today's lesson and connect with the next sub-unit.

Summarize and Give Homework Assignment (5 minutes)

Teacher does the following:

1. He/She makes general comments and generously appraises what students have done well;

2. He/She draws attention via projector to guiding questions and writing rubrics of Final Unit Project;

3. He/She reminds students what and where to find all course materials and supporting documents;

4. He/She gives homework assignment: Ask students to work on written draft (handwritten or typed) by answering questions.

Part III: Communication after Class

Teacher makes sure that all students have access to the course materials and related documents for learning after school. Besides printed materials, teacher may also post all course materials, class notes, and homework assignments online. If any students do not have Internet access, a hard copy has to be provided.

Google Drive Postings

Posting 1: Class Notes

Class Notes: Suggested questions for the next part of the project:

1. 休闲活动有哪些?

2. 经常在哪些地方活动?

3. 什么时间是最好的时间?

4. 都有什么人参加这些活动?

5. 需要什么器械/设备(东西)?

6. 怎么做? 为什么大家都参加活动?

7. 要不然,怎么样?

Homework:

　　Revise the draft of your own place of interest

Reminder:

　　Project due date

Posting 2: The End of Unit Project

The End of Unit Project (Written and Oral) 介绍一个好去处

简介:

1. 大概情况

2. 地方/方位

3. 吸引人的 Attractions/ 特色

4. 注意事项(公共场所)

5. 历史、故事

6. 你的故事: 为什么去那儿?

7. 开放时间

---

8. 门票

9. 交通

Posting 3: Writing Rubric

Evaluation	Does Not Meet Requirements	Meets Requirements	Exceeds Requirements
Functional Language Use	Lack of four-word expressions	Some proper use of four-word expressions/ mostly imitation of the sample	Creative and proper use of four-word expressions
Functional Language Use	Lacks proper use of compound sentences	Proper use of frequently used compound sentences	Uses a variety of compound sentences correctly
	Lack of comparison	Some use of comparisons	Uses a variety of comparisons in both positive and negative forms
Technical Aspects of Writing	Text is developed without proper beginning-middle-end format	Text is developed with proper format	Text is developed with proper format and creative/interesting features
	Information is not provided in a recognizable sequence and with adequate details	Information is provided in a recognizable sequence and with some details	Information is provided with specific/additional details
	Sentences have major grammatical errors (suggesting computer generated text)	Sentences have a few minor grammatical mistakes	Rare grammatical errors
	Not all in characters; too many characters are mistakes (or typos)	All sentences are in characters; a few characters contain writing mistakes	All characters are correct without mistakes in writing

Teacher Self-assessment:

- What went well?

- What would need more review in the next class?

- Did the activities help students learn effectively?

- What should be done differently?

Course Handouts:

Course Material 1 (List of compound sentences)

Compound Sentences:
1. 因为……所以……
2. 要是……，（S）就 V……（如果……，（S）就 V……）
3. 虽然……，可是 / 但是……
4. 不但……而且……
5. 又……又……
6. 一边……一边……
7. 除了……以外，……也（Inclusive）/ 都（Exclusive）……
8.（S）先……，然后……，（再）……
9. 有时候……，有时候……

Course Material 2 (List of four ways of comparison)

Four Ways to Provide Comparison (visual on blackboard)			
摆事实	谈看法	比不同	找相同
例子： 芝加哥是一个大城市。 北京也是大城市。	例子： 我觉得芝加哥大，可是北京更大。	例子： 北京比芝加哥大（得多）。	例子： 北京跟芝加哥一样四季分明。

Course Material 3 (Four-word expressions)

Sample Text

美丽的城市——芝加哥

芝加哥是美国中西部首屈一指的大城市。那里有全国数一数二的博物馆、科学馆和天文台，最有名的是风景如画的密歇根湖。

在湖边，你会看到三五成群的人们：有的人跑步，有的人骑自行车，有的人打球，夏天还有许多人游泳。

如果你喜欢逛街和买东西，密歇根大道上五花八门的商品更是不可以错过。在这里，你每天可以看到车水马龙的街道和从四面八方来的游客，他们在店里七嘴八舌地讨价还价，非常热闹。

要是你有兴趣爬上 Sears Tower，你可以试试看。不过你得用上九牛二虎之力，等站在上面的时候，你可能害怕得手脚发软，心里七上八下的，完全六神无主了。

虽然芝加哥不是一个十全十美的城市，但是它却是一个多姿多彩、多元化的美丽城市。

生词表

① 首屈一指：to come first on the list/ 芝北预科中学是芝加哥首屈一指的中学。

② 数一数二：one of the top ones/ 他是全校数一数二的数学天才。

③ 三五成群：in small groups; in threes and fives/ 午饭的时候，学生们三五成群地在花园聊天。

④ 四面八方：from all sides; all around; all directions/ 参加这次比赛的人来自全国四面八方。

⑤ 五花八门：all kinds of / 商店里的东西五花八门，什么都有。

⑥ 六神无主：scared out of your mind/ 我吓怕得六神无主。

⑦ 七嘴八舌：everyone talking at the same time/ 下课时，同学们七嘴八舌地说个不停。

⑧ 七上八下：to be flustered, perturbed or upset/公车迟到了，他的心里七上八下的。

⑨ 九牛二虎：extreme effort/ 我用了九牛二虎的力气，才把电视机搬进来。

⑩ 十全十美：perfect/ 天下没有十全十美的事。

⑪ 风景如画：scenic beauty/ 这公园有山有水，真是风景如画。

⑫ 逛街：shopping/ 我最喜欢逛街了。

⑬ 车水马龙：busy street/ 街上车水马龙，非常热闹。

---

⑭ 讨价还价：to negotiate a price/ 姐姐买东西时，最喜欢讨价还价了。

⑮ 手脚发软：to be so scared that you are powerless/ 只要看到老鼠，我就手脚发软。

⑯ 却是：but; yet; however; while/ 我以为今天会下雨，结果却是个大晴天。

⑰ 多姿多彩：colorful/ 这次活动，真是多姿多彩。

⑱ 多元化：variety; pluralism/ 芝加哥是个多元化的城市。

(Made by Hong 2010)[2]

Course Material 4 (Vocabulary list)

主要词汇：

休闲　芝加哥的好玩儿的地方

市中心

立体电影院（3D）　平面 2D　博物馆 / 美术馆　文化中心　商场 / 百货公司

超市　湖边　新千年公园　植物园　海军港　露天音乐厅　教堂　摩天大楼

免费动物园　夏令营　森林保护区

多元文化

背景

夜生活

在湖边你可以

　　　　跑步　走路　散步　骑自行车

　　　　做义工

　　　　游泳　玩儿水　玩儿沙子　野餐　看风景

忙碌　热闹　五颜六色　拥挤　吵闹　肮脏　干净　（黑）暗　（明）亮

四面八方　世界各地　现代化　自然景观

(All vocabulary is selected by students during class)

2　C. Hong was a student teacher in 2010. She made this text based on an old version of class materials and texts.

Course Material 5 (Texts for Chicago and Beijing)

Sample Reading 1

芝加哥是一个大城市，是美国第三大城市，在美国的中西部。（不在美国的东部，也不在西部。）

芝加哥不是美国的首都。（美国的首都是华盛顿。）

芝加哥地区有五百万人口，人很多，人口多元化。

芝加哥是一个非常重要的国际城市。政治、经济、文化和教育都很发达。

芝加哥的历史不长，只有几百年。但是芝加哥非常漂亮，也非常现代化，还有很多有趣的去处。

芝加哥有很多免费对外开放的公园，其中最方便去的就是密歇根湖边。

Sample Reading 2

北京是中国的首都，在中国的北方，是中国第二大城市。

北京现在的常住人口差不多有两千二百万。

北京是一个非常重要的国际城市，是中国的政治、文化和教育中心。

北京是一个古老的城市，有三千多年的历史，所以北京有很多名胜古迹。

北京是一个非常漂亮的城市。除了著名的故宫、颐和园以外，还有很多其他的皇家公园，比如天坛、地坛、日坛、月坛等。

北京现在也是一个特别现代化的城市。

傅老师是在北京出生、在北京长大的。傅老师的父母现在还住在北京。

天坛是古代皇帝祭天的地方。北京的天坛离市中心不太远，现在是一个很大的公园。一年到头，从早到晚，天坛都有许许多多的游客，有的是从全国各地来参观的，有的是从世界各国来游览的。但是天坛的早上是一天中最有意思、最热闹的时刻。

每天天一亮，就有很多人去天坛锻炼身体，多数

是老年人。人们在那儿散步、跑步、踢毽子、跳舞、打拳、唱歌、唱戏。他们三三两两或者成群结队地活动，慢中有快、动中有静，既忙碌又轻松，既热闹又温馨。为什么这样说呢？因为人们每天聚在一起，交了不少朋友，除了锻炼，还有社交。身体好了，心情愉快了，生活也丰富了。

天坛不是一个免费的公园，去那儿要买票。不过月票、季票和年票都不太贵，老年人还有优惠。

Haiyan Fu（傅海燕）, author of *Chinese Essentials: What and How*, has been teaching Chinese to speakers of other languages professionally since 1982. She teaches at Northside College Preparatory High School in Chicago. She has research interests in second language acquisition, teaching methodology, and learning resource development.

A Significant Historical Figure: Qin Shihuang

Xiaolin Chang (常小林)
Lowell High School, San Francisco, California

Language Proficiency Level: AP Chinese/Intermediate High

Age Range: 15-18

Class Size: 25-30 students

Time Frame: 50 minutes per day, with about 10 lessons in total for the entire unit

Essential Questions:

- What could be learned about a country's history by examining a historical figure's contributions?

- How could historical events impact modern daily life?

Unit Goals:

Students will be able to:

- Describe the significance of Qin Shihuang;

- List Qin Shihuang's contributions, in both written and oral presentations;

- Use the expression 在……方面 to state their opinions more formally.

Standards: Based on the National Standards for Foreign Language Learning

- **Communication:**

  -Interpersonal (1.1): conversations; e-mail writing

  -Interpretive (1.2): reading

  -Presentational (1.3): presentations

- **Connection:** Learning Chinese history.

- **Comparison:** Looking at influential people in US history.

- **Culture:** Learning about Chinese characters, the Great Wall, etc. through studying Qin Shihuang.

- **Community:** Learning more about Chinese history at the local Asian Art Museum.

Learning/Teaching Focus for Instructional Sessions:

- Can students identify in which dynasty Qin Shihuang played a significant role?

- Can students name Qin Shihuang's contributions to the unification of China?

- Can students use the phrase 在……方面 to express what they know about Qin Shihuang's historical impact on different areas of Chinese society?

Lesson Outlines:

Day 1: Introduction to Qin Shihuang's name, dynasty, and his efforts to unify China.

Day 2: Reviewing and reading, checking students' understanding of learned content, and helping them learn more specific vocabulary and expressions.

Day 3: Grammar practice focusing on 在……方面 and how to use this structure in sentences and discourse.

Day 4: E-mail practice and cultural presentation preparation; practice interpersonal writing with the learned materials.

Day 5: Cultural presentation: Practice presentational skills using the learned topic.

Day 6: Listening practice and reading: Practice comprehension skills related to Chinese history.

Days 7-8: Students' PPT presentations: Create opportunities for students to organize their research results for their presentations.

Day 9: Lesson quiz: Design a quiz or quizzes depending on how much time is available. They could be oral, written, or reading quizzes.

Day 10: Additional information related to Qin Shihuang or more discussions about Chinese history: Chinese proverbs, movies, or any extra stories about Qin Shihuang.

Learning Objectives:

Students will be able to:

Day 1

- Identify in which dynasty Qin Shihuang lived;

- Tell what China was like before it was unified by Qin Shihuang;

- Name some of Qin Shihuang's contributions to the unification of China.

Day 2

- Demonstrate their knowledge by answering questions about what they have learned about Qin Shihuang;

- Recognize newly learned vocabulary items and pronounce them correctly.

Day 3

- Use the 在……方面 structure in sentences and discourse;

- Translate sentences from English to Chinese and Chinese to English using the newly learned structures.

Day 4

- Comprehend an e-mail requesting information about important historical figures;

- Reply to an e-mail and give suggestions regarding important historical figures.

Day 5

- Organize information gathered about Qin Shihuang;

- Give an oral presentation about Qin Shihuang with accurate information, pronunciation, and intonation, which will also demonstrate oral presentation skills such as formatting, organization, etc.

Day 6

- Choose correct answers about Qin Shihuang from listening comprehension practice;

- Correctly pronounce new vocabulary words and identify their English meaning.

Days 7-8

- Use PPT to show the class their extended knowledge of important historical figures;

- Collaborate with classmates to work on group presentations;

- Demonstrate oral presentation skills by sharing their PPT with the class.

Day 9

- Show what they've learned from this lesson by recapping Qin Shihuang's historical impacts in their oral presentations.

Day 10

- Tell additional stories related to Qin Shihuang, such as Chinese proverbs derived from Chinese history related to Qin Shihuang, or learned from a movie about Qin Shihuang.

Suggested Lesson Plan

Day 1 (Sample Lesson)

Learning Objectives:

Students will be able to:

- Identify in which dynasty Qin Shihuang lived (interpretive);

- Tell what China was like before it was unified by Qin Shihuang (presentational);

- Name some of Qin Shihuang's contributions to the unification of China (presentational).

Teaching Focus:

Introducing Qin Shihuang and his contributions to the unification of China

Learning Difficulties:

There might be too many new vocabulary items for students. The historical background of Qin Shihuang's unification of China might be too difficult for some students to understand.

Teaching Materials and Resources:

- Pictures of the Great Wall

- PPT slides about Qin Shihuang (Google Images is a good source of pictures)

- A list of key vocabulary (Co-reference: see the Chinese text below)

- *Integrated Chinese* Level 2 Part 2 by Yuehua Liu and Tao-chung Yao (Lesson 18)

- 《中国历史常识》"中国第一位皇帝——秦始皇" by 国务院侨务办公室 / 中国海外交流协会, 高等教育出版社

Instructional Strategies:

Set-up Stage (10 minutes)

1. Ask students warm-up questions such as:

    1) How far back does the history of China go? 中国历史有多长？

    2) What do you know about the Great Wall? 你听说过长城吗？

    3) Do you know any important people in Chinese history? 你知道中国历史上的要人吗？

    These questions can be in Chinese or English. The purpose is to get students interested and engaged. At this point, students might not have enough vocabulary to share their knowledge of the topic.

2. Show pictures/slides of the Great Wall. Each student says one sentence about it. They can repeat what is already said if they do not have anything new to add or do not know what to say. The teacher can start with:

> 长城很长。
>
> 长城很高。
>
> 长城的历史悠久。
>
> 长城建在高山上。
>
> 长城很壮观。
>
> 长城很美丽。
>
> 长城是两千多年以前建的。
>
> 修长城时死了很多人。
>
> 修长城是为了保卫国家。
>
> 去中国一定要去爬长城。

Teacher can model one or two sentences, and then ask each student to say one sentence. Depending on the class size, students may take turns and say one or more sentences. If students have difficulty thinking of sentences, teacher can give them a hint by asking questions about the Great Wall. If possible, teacher can assign homework the previous day, asking students to do research on the Great Wall.

Comprehensible Instructional Input (20 minutes)

1. Based on the Chinese language text below, share facts about the Great Wall with students. The following questions serve as advance organizers:

   1) 长城是什么时候修建的？

   2) 长城是谁修建的？

   3) 谁把长城连接起来了？

   4) 为什么修长城？

   5) 修长城用了多长时间？用了多少人力？死了多少人？

   Teacher can ask students to share their knowledge of the Great Wall. After the introduction to the Great Wall, teacher starts the presentation on Qin Shihuang.

2. Introduce Qin Shihuang to students. Teacher starts the presentation by asking:

   1) 谁是秦始皇？

   2) 谁听说过秦始皇？

   Teacher's presentation about Qin Shihuang includes the following:

   1) Give students a brief history of 战国七雄 and show them a map of 战国七雄 using Google Maps.

   2) Introduce Qin Shihuang PPT (Google Images)

      Teacher can find pictures on Google Images such as: http://china-mike.com/wp-content/uploads/2011/03/chinese-characters-writing-evolution.gif to give students a visual aid to understand why Qin Shihuang had to do what he did.

Guided Practice (20 minutes)

1. Give students a copy of the vocabulary list. The list can be as-is; ask students to look up definitions on their own after class, or the teacher can give the *pinyin* and definitions depending on time and students' language proficiency. If time is an issue or most students are non-heritage, provide the definitions and *pinyin*. Tell students when the vocabulary quiz will be and how they will be tested.

2. In groups, have students study vocabulary together. Make sure they know the meaning of all the words, and know how to pronounce the bold-faced words.

Vocabulary:

秦始皇　秦国　公元前　通过　战国　七雄　强国　灭　统一　统治　称为
巩固　在……方面　政治　设立　郡县制　划分　直接　任免　统管
经济　度量衡　标准　货物　长度　容量　重量　货币　促进　交流
车轨　运输　文化　下令　种植　烧　批评　活埋　焚书坑儒　军事　打
败　修筑　安定　保护　暴君　残暴　产生　不良

3. Show the PPT about Qin Shihuang again. One slide at a time, groups of students describe in Chinese the information presented in the slides.

4. Independent practice and assessment: Show the PPT of Qin Shihuang and ask individual students to say one or two sentences about Qin Shihuang and his contributions.

Independent Practice

Homework: Read 中国第一位皇帝——秦始皇 and answer the comprehension questions below. (This reading sample was simplified from an article in *Common Knowledge about Chinese History*《中国历史常识》published by 高等教育出版社)

中国第一位皇帝——秦始皇

　　公元前 770 年秦国只是一个小国，后来变得越来越强大，成为一个强国。秦王嬴政用了十年的时间，先后消灭了六个国家，在公元前 221 年统一了中国。

　　秦王希望能永远统治中国，称自己为"始皇帝"，历史上称他为"秦始皇"。

　　秦始皇统一中国后，做了很多巩固统一的事情。

　　首先，在政治方面，秦始皇把全国划分为 36 郡，郡下面设县。秦始皇直接任免每个郡的郡守，每个县的县令，用这样的方法来统一管理全国。

　　在经济方面，秦始皇首先统一了度量衡。以前各国的度量衡都不一样。秦始皇把全国的度量衡改成同一个标准。人们在购买货物时，在长度、容量和重量等方面都用同样的标准。秦始皇还统一了货币，人们用同样的货币买卖东西，促进了各个地方的经济交流。另外，秦始皇还统一了车轨，加快了货物的运输与交流。

在文化方面，秦始皇统一了文字。以前每个地方都有自己的文字。秦始皇统一了中国以后，因为各个地方使用的文字不同造成文化交流上的很多不便，所以秦始皇下令统一文字，促进了文化交流。不过在文化方面，秦始皇也做了一些坏事。他统一中国以后很怕有人反对他的统治，于是除了医药、种植等方面的书籍以外，把其他的书都烧了。后来有些读书人批评秦始皇的一些做法，秦始皇就活埋了四百多名读书人。烧书和活埋读书人这两件事在中国历史上叫作"焚书坑儒"。

在军事方面，秦始皇打败了匈奴，修筑了长城，安定了北方，保护了统一后的中国。

秦始皇统一了中国，是中国第一个皇帝。他在历史上有很重要的作用。但秦始皇又是一个暴君，他的残暴统治也对中国历史产生了不良影响。

Comprehension Questions

1. Who is Qin Shihuang?

2. In terms of the political system, what did Qin Shihuang do?

3. In terms of the economy, what did Qin Shihuang do?

4. Why is it so important to have the same money?

5. What did Qin Shihuang do to protect unified China?

Note: These questions will be answered by students in English first (interpretive). After practice reading, teacher asks the questions again in Chinese, and students are expected to answer them in Chinese (interpersonal).

Day 3 (Brief Outline)

Activity 1 (20 minutes)

Purpose: Instructional input on the language forms 在……方面，在……上（in terms of... ）

1. Teacher first shows PPT slides of the content studied the previous day. Each slide has both a sentence with 在……方面 and a picture for comprehensible input; see the first four sentences below.

2. Teacher models the sentences orally. Students follow the teacher as a class, then individually.

3. Teacher-student interaction: Teacher asks a student questions (在文化方面/上，秦始皇做了什么？ 在军事方面，秦始皇做了什么？ etc.) and the student answers by using 在……方面/上. Then students ask each other questions, as a class divided into two groups, or in pairs.

4. Class presentation on the dialogue just practiced by students in pairs or groups.

Examples:
1) 在政治方面，秦始皇统一了中国。
2) 在文化方面，秦始皇统一了文字 / 焚书坑儒。
3) 在军事方面，秦始皇修建了长城 / 打败了其他六国。
4) 在经济方面，秦始皇统一了货币 / 度量衡。

Activity 2 (15 minutes)

Purpose: To relate specific content from the previous activity on 秦始皇 to students' general life by using the language form 在……方面/上.

1. See the instructional input (the four sentences below). Teacher shows the sample sentences to students and explains the linguistic elements which may pose difficulties for comprehension.

2. Pair work: Pass out the sentences below and ask students to read for comprehension.

3. Student interview: All students are required to stand up and walk to the front of the room to find partners with whom they have not talked this week. Each student will ask three students two questions by using 在……方面/上 based on the sentences they just practiced in pairs.

4. Report the interview: Teacher asks two or three volunteers to report their interview results to the class.

1) 在听力方面，他没有什么太大的问题；在写作方面，他有点儿吃力。
2) 在工作方面，他很努力；在生活方面他很马虎，常常丢三落四的。

3) 在学习方面，他的成绩还不错；在体育方面，他不喜欢运动，所以成绩
稍微差点。

4) 在性格方面，他很活泼；他姐姐比较严肃。

Activity 3 (15 minutes)

Purpose: To consolidate understanding and usage of the expression 在……方面/上.

1. The previous instructional input on the expression 在……方面/上 was limited to the sentential initial position. Based on the previous two main activities, the instructional input will extend to a more flexible position of 在……方面/上 by placing it either before or after a subject and always before a verb.

2. Teacher provides sentences below by PPT and leads a discussion of the differences between this group of four sentences and the previous eight sentences: 这四个句子跟以前的八个句子在形式（form）上有什么不同？ Students' meta-linguistic awareness and meta-cognitive strategies are encouraged.

3. After discussion, teacher sums up the language form and functions of 在……方面/上.

4. Class practice: Have students individually (or in pairs if the task is difficult) do the following exercise.

选择正确的短语，填入句子中。

在生活方面　在工作方面　在体育方面　在听力方面

在性格方面　在说话方面　在学习方面

1）他_____很努力，每次考试都能考到很好的成绩。

2）她_____不是太好，因为她从小身体不好，不能像别的小朋友那样
锻炼身体。

3）最近我们_____遇到了一些困难，周末都得到公司开会解决问题。

4）我的老师_____对我们的帮助很大，现在我看电影的时候比以前
听懂的多。

5）_____，她对自己的要求很高，从来不乱花钱买不需要的东西。

6）_____，他和他弟弟完全不一样，他比较内向，他弟弟比较爱讲话。

7）因为她练习得不多，所以她＿＿＿＿＿还不太有信心。每次发言时，她都有点紧张。

Homework:

1. Students will review and finish the task of filling in the blanks above if they did not have time to do so in class.

2. Students will prepare for an in-class discussion on Day 4. The topic of the discussion is "Who is a very influential person in American history?" Put students in groups of 2-3. They will choose one person and describe their significance using 在……方面. Provide students the vocabulary if needed. Students report back to the class with a group PPT presentation using 8-10 slides.

Rubric for PPT Presentation (Total Points: 10)

Rating	Excellent 5	Good 4	Adequate 3	Poor 2-1
Content Delivery (Group Points)	Information accurate; well organized	Information mostly accurate; good organization	Some information errors; poor organization in some parts	Many information errors; poor organization for the entire presentation
Language Competency (Individual Points)	Excellent pronunciation and grammar; clear voice	Sporadic errors in pronunciation and grammar; mostly clear voice	Some errors in pronunciation and grammar; voice not clear	Many errors in pronunciation and grammar; voice not clear

Day 4 (Brief Outline)

Activity 1 (25 minutes)

Purpose: To practice interpretive and presentational skills via reading and replying to an e-mail.

E-mail practice:

The following e-mail response practice could be done in a language lab with a time limit or assigned as homework. Teacher discusses this with students before they do the task.

1. Reading strategies practice:

1) Look for key words: Teacher helps students find the key words via techniques such as putting distinct stress on key words in boldface while reading the passage loud.

2) Look for requests: Teacher leads students to focus on linguistic clues such as 能不能……?

3) Look for meaning via language forms (the underlined sentences below) by asking students questions such as 李文和谁好久没有联系了？老师让学生做什么？, etc.

发件人：李文

邮件主题：PPT 报告

张明：

　　你好！

　　好久没有和你联系了。你学习怎么样？忙不忙？我们现在在历史课上学对人类文明有影响的人物。老师让我们选一个历史名人，做一个报告，哪个国家的都可以。我想选一个中国历史名人介绍给我的同学们。听说你在学中国历史。能不能给我推荐一个人？还有，你对怎样在班上做好一个报告有什么建议？

　　希望能很快收到你的建议。谢谢！

李文

2015.1.24

---

2. Writing skill practice:

1) Clearly specify the requirements for the reply. Provide students with the following list of points to which they are required to respond:

- Greet and tell Li Wen about your school work.

- Recommend an important person in Chinese history.

- Explain why this person is recommended.

- Suggest how to make a good PPT presentation.

2) Discuss linguistic organizers and connectors for students to use. The list may include as follows:

既然……，那就 V……

你看……怎么样？

之所以……，是因为……

就我所知，……

3) Provide a sample for students to discuss or critique. It is necessary to use a couple of student samples to critique before or after they finish the task. The advantage of showing the sample before the task is that students know what will be expected.

Activity 2 (25 minutes)

Purpose: To further practice oral presentational skills on a significant person in Chinese history.

Prepare a cultural presentation: Qin Shihuang

When students practice recording cultural presentations, the following points may be useful for pedagogical consideration:

1. There is no time limit for students' first practice recording.

2. Allow students to make several recordings and submit the one which satisfies them.

3. Ask a couple of students to present their work in person to the class. Teacher and other students critique the presentations.

Teacher's Sample of Cultural Presentation

秦始皇是中国第一个皇帝。他在公元前221年统一了中国。统一后，秦始皇做了很多重要的事情，为中国的统一和发展做出了很大的贡献。

在经济方面，秦始皇统一了车轨，方便了各地的交通和经济交流；他还统一了货币、度量衡，对促进经济发展也起了很大的作用。

在文化方面，秦始皇统一了文字，方便了各地人们之间的交流。

在军事方面，为了保护中国不受北方的侵犯，秦始皇还修了长城。

在政治上，秦始皇把中国分成36个郡，方便了他的中央集权统治。

秦始皇也是一个暴君，做了一些坏事。比如历史上有名的"焚书坑儒"。他烧了很多书，杀了四百多个读书人。在修长城的时候还累死了很多人，民间故事像"孟姜女"讲的就是这样的故事，一直流传到今天。

秦始皇是中国第一个皇帝，也是中国历史上一个重要的人物，对中国的影响很大。

Sample Topics for Supplementary Materials:

故事：荆轲刺秦王、孟姜女哭长城

成语：图穷匕见、焚书坑儒

Xiaolin Chang (常小林) has been teaching AP Chinese and serving as the World Language Department Chair at Lowell High School in San Francisco. In the professional development field, she was on the committee of the Chinese section for the National Standards for Foreign Language Learning for K-12. Her professional experience in AP Chinese Development includes being a member of the AP Chinese Language and Culture Exam Development Committee and the Professional Development Advisory Group, co-author of the Pre-AP Summer Institute manual, and one of the syllabi contributors to the AP Chinese Teacher's Guide. She also serves as a College Board AP Chinese workshop consultant.

Critique

Two Cities: Comparing Chicago and Beijing – Haiyan Fu
A Significant Historical Figure: Qin Shihuang – Xiaolin Chang

A good curriculum and instructional plan integrates effective implementation of National Standards for Foreign Language Learning in the classroom, methods that help learners acquire communicative skills, and classroom management in a student-centered environment. The two designs in this section, *Two Cities: Comparing Chicago and Beijing* by Haiyan Fu and *A Significant Historical Figure: Qin Shihuang* by Xiaolin Chang, are such examples. Each chapter provides rich pedagogical information and detailed advice that is beneficial not only to Chinese language teachers but to classroom teachers of other subjects as well.

In applying the national and state standards, Fu's primary concerns are how to effectively facilitate students' learning, and how to assess their language performance. The designs show that keeping standards-guided "instructional purposes" in mind for every class activity is critical.

With clear and focused goals, Fu carefully designs classroom activities that scaffold students' learning and performance. For example, in the section "Instructional Strategies", Fu offers both rationale and methods of five important components of instruction design. They are conceptualized and integrated with scaffolding steps to optimally facilitate learning:

1. Selecting instructional goals that will be assessed via learning outcomes

2. Facilitating learning through scaffolding where a variety of teaching techniques are required, such as questioning, feedback, reviewing, and spiraling

3. Engaging all students via differentiated instruction and cooperative learning

4. Conducting student-centered assessments where students can participate in deciding the test contents and format

5. Developing critical thinking skills by triggering students' curiosity and promoting their logical thinking, as well as provoking them to ask interesting (有意思的) questions and alternatives such as "还有什么可能性？"

Activities presented in the second part of Fu's design vividly detail how these concepts and techniques are executed. Students perform real-world tasks regarding daily life topics ranging from history and geography to traffic, food cultures, and leisure. Step-by-step instruction fosters students' learning in a standards-guided, communication-oriented, and performance-based classroom.

In Chang's design, the stage is set by asking questions that trigger students' curiosity. Content-based activities immediately engage students in studying historical facts on the Great Wall and Qin Shihuang. Students create meaning from their readings, and construct their knowledge via discussion. History, culture, and biography are internally linked by the Chinese language that students are using as a tool for their discoveries.

Drawing upon their teaching experience, both authors insightfully select instructional focuses that include not only language forms, but appropriate contexts in which students map forms to meaning and function. Fu's design provides pedagogical grammar, pinpointing errors that English-speaking learners frequently make, such as the word order of adverbs and the comparison construction. Chang's design uses e-mail as a tool to help students develop their specific learning strategies at the discourse level, with suggestions such as "Look for requests", "Look for key words", and

"Look for meaning via language forms". Guiding students in the use of meta-cognitive skills is crucial in helping them learn how to learn. Both designs present skillful combinations of language form, content, and function to encourage students to use language correctly and appropriately. Furthermore, both authors have created curriculum materials which are pedagogically sound, authentic, and innovative.

Chang constantly offers classroom management strategies and instructional tips throughout her design. In a similar manner, Fu also provides a "Housekeeping: Daily Routine" section that offers practical skills by showing how to create a good class tone and rapport between the instructor and students. For example, the requirements for assignments to students should be well-planned and detailed, and the instructor's speech should be brief and very clear. In such an instructional setting, students become autonomous in their learning, with a clear understanding of their work and responsibilities. To visualize the concepts and practice, interested readers may also see Fu's teaching demonstration, published by Annenberg Learner at http://www.learner.org/channel/libraries/tfl/chinese/fu/.

Both designs raise concerns worthy of discussion. Fu's design is rich in content with myriad information related to linguistic, cognitive, social, and emotional aspects. Her students meet the challenges competently, as demonstrated in the *Sample Presentation and Exchanges* section of her design. It is important for readers to first clearly see the rationales and principles behind her designed activities, and then adapt these to their own instructional situations. The vocabulary requirements of Chang's design seem to be at a very high level of difficulty in comparison with the rest of the content and exercises given to students. Balancing new and infrequently used vocabulary in a content-based curriculum remains a challenge in both curriculum design and instructional implementation.

Theme 2

Chinese Gardens

Chinese Gardens

Xing King (金星)
The Bishop's School, La Jolla, California

Language Proficiency Level: Advanced (AP Chinese Language and Culture)

Age Range: 16-18 (high school students)

Class Size: 12 students (but any size class is fine)

Time Frame: An ongoing project requiring 9-10 days, 50 minutes per day

Essential Questions:

- What culturally distinctive elements do typical Chinese gardens employ?

- What are the differences between Chinese gardens and gardens from Western cultures in terms of garden layout, perspective, garden elements, plant arrangement, etc.?

- What is the significance of the Chinese cultural perspective "harmony between nature and human beings" (天人合一)?

- How does 天人合一 influence traditional Chinese garden design and landscaping?

Unit Goals:

Students will be able to:

1. Identify Desired Results (Wiggins & McTighe, 2005)

- What should students know, understand, and be able to do about this project?

- What enduring understandings are desired?

Consider:

- Learning goals and objectives

- Examine content standards

- Review expectations

- Students' interests

2. Determine Acceptable Evidence (Wiggins & McTighe, 2005)

- What is the acceptable evidence in terms of students' understanding as a result of this project?

- How are students' linguistic skills, including the skills of interpersonal, interpretive, and presentational communication, assessed to determine if they reach the AP level of Chinese?

Consider a range of assessments:

- Formative

- Summative

3. Plan Learning Experiences and Instruction (Wiggins & McTighe, 2005)

- How do teaching and learning experiences equip students to demonstrate their understanding of Chinese gardens and related concepts?

- What materials and resources are best suited to accomplish these goals?

- What technologies do students use to facilitate their learning?

Learning Objectives in Relation to the National Standards for Foreign Language Education:

(ACTFL Standards for Foreign Language Learning in the 21st Century)

- Students acquire a base of vocabulary on Chinese gardens and develop interpersonal communication skills through discussions of the culturally distinctive elements of Chinese gardens. (1.1 Interpersonal Communication)

- Students develop interpretive skills through reading articles and watching video clips about Chinese gardens. (1.2 Interpretive Communication)

- Students present Chinese garden models they design or artwork they draw, and write two Chinese essays. (See Student Learning Outcomes for details) (1.3 Presentational Communication)

- Students gain knowledge of traditional Chinese garden design and landscaping, practical daily life functions, naming conventions, and symbolism of Chinese gardens through Internet research on both English and Chinese language websites. (2.1 Practices of Culture, 3.2 Acquiring Information)

- Students gain knowledge of cultural products of Chinese gardens and their relationship with the Chinese cultural perspective of "harmony between nature and human beings" (天人合一) through online research as well. (2.2 Products of Culture)

- Students make connections with other subjects, such as art, English, geography, history, and/or religion by designing a garden model or drawing a garden that encompasses the most important aspects of Chinese gardens. (3.1 Making Connections)

- Students compare the linguistic difference between the traditional Chinese character for garden 園 and the English word "garden". (4.1 Language Comparison)

- Students discuss the major characteristics of Chinese gardens and compare and contrast them with those of gardens from other cultures in terms of garden layout, perspective, garden elements, plant arrangement, etc. (4.2 Cultural Comparison)

- Students may apply what they learn from this project to their own garden design in the future. (5.2 Lifelong Learning)

Learning Outcomes:

Student's final products include:

1. A 2D or 3D architectural rendering of a traditional Chinese garden following culturally appropriate naming conventions;

2. A proposal to an imagined board of trustees of the National Arboretum in

Washington, D.C. with an explanation of why their garden design should be adopted, and a comparison or contrast of his/her garden design with that of Western cultures;

3. An explanation of their understanding of the Chinese cultural concept of harmony between nature and human beings（天人合一）;

4. An essay that presents the pros and cons of their design to convince the trustees that the student's choice would be the best one for the National Arboretum.

Learning Assessments:

Two rubrics (Tables 1 and 2) are given and explained at the beginning of the unit so that students understand the expected learning outcomes. These two rubrics are similar, but have different focuses, one on oral presentation and the other on writing. Use either or both of them.

Table 1: Chinese Garden Presentation Grading Rubric *			
Task Completion 60%	**Excellent 6-5**	**Average 4-3**	**Poor 2-0**
	• Thorough and detailed presentation • Well organized and coherent • Ample and accurate cultural information	• Presentation may lack detail • Some parts may be inconsistent • Some cultural information may be inaccurate	• Presentation does not have detail • Information lacks organization and coherence • Inaccurate cultural information
A: 与中国文化相符的名称			
B1: 假山假石			
B2: 水景水池			
B3: 亭台楼阁，走廊，木桥			
B4: 花草树木			
B5: 诗画艺术			

Delivery 20%	Excellent 20-15	Average 14-9	Poor 8-0
	• Natural pace with minimal hesitation or repetition • Accurate pronunciation (including tones), with minimal errors	• Consistent pace with intermittent hesitation and repetition • Errors in pronunciation (including tones), which do not necessitate special listener effort	• Labored pace with frequent hesitation and repetition • Errors in pronunciation (including tones) necessitate constant listener effort
Language Use 20%	Excellent 20-15	Average 14-9	Poor 8-0
	• Appropriate vocabulary and idioms • Good range of grammatical structures	• Appropriate vocabulary with errors that do not obscure meaning • Grammatical structures with errors that do not obscure meaning	• Inappropriate vocabulary with errors that obscure meaning • Grammatical structures with errors that obscure meaning

Table 2: Chinese Garden Writing Grading Rubric *			
Task Completion 60%	Excellent 6-5	Average 4-3	Poor 2-0
	• Writing is complete, thorough, and detailed • Well organized and coherent • Sentences connected with appropriate use of transitional elements and cohesive devices	• Writing may lack detail • Some parts may be inconsistent • Sentences loosely connected	• Writing does not have detail • Information lacks organization and coherence • Disjointed sentences

A: 与中国文化相符的名称			
B1: 假山假石			
B2: 水景水池			
B3: 亭台楼阁，走廊，木桥			
B4: 花草树木			
B5: 诗画艺术			
C: 中国园林和西方园林的不同 (double points)			
D: 天人合一的概念 (double points)			
Delivery 20%	Excellent 20-15	Average 14-9	Poor 8-0
	Consistent use of register appropriate to situation	Includes several lapses in otherwise consistent use of register appropriate to situation	Frequent use of register inappropriate to situation
Language Use 20%	Excellent 20-15	Average 14-9	Poor 8-0
	• Appropriate vocabulary and idioms • Good range of grammatical structures	• Appropriate vocabulary and idioms with errors that do not obscure meaning • Grammatical structures with errors that do not obscure meaning	• Minimal appropriate vocabulary • Little or no control of grammatical structures

Reference: The College Board 2013 AP® Chinese Language and Culture 2013 Scoring Guidelines http://media.collegeboard.com/digitalServices/pdf/ap/apcentral/ap13_chinese_scoring_guidelines.pdf

Note: The above rubrics are adopted and modified from the College Board's official scoring guidelines for the AP Chinese oral presentation and writing. Each rubric is divided into three categories: task completion, language use and delivery. In the writing rubric, 'register' means the degree of formality. It is necessary to learn how to assess students' work holistically in these three categories and to train students to reach their utmost potential during the AP Chinese Language and Culture Exam.

Peer Evaluation – A writing evaluation from peers provides students with an instant feedback encouraging collaboration and constructive criticism among students. It is also divided into the same three categories as the grading rubric for writing.

Table 3: Peer Evaluation – Writing				
Circle "Yes", "Some" or "No" based on your evaluation.				
Task Completion	1. Addresses all aspects of prompt thoroughly and completely?	Yes	Some	No
	2. Well-organized and coherent with clear progression of ideas?	Yes	Some	No
	3. Sentences connected with appropriate use of transitional elements and cohesive devices?	Yes	Some	No
	4. Area(s) for improvement	Specify:		
Language Use	1. Appropriate vocabulary and idioms? Example:	Yes	Some	No
	2. Good range of grammatical structures? Example:	Yes	Some	No
	3. Area(s) for improvement	Specify:		

Delivery	1. Consistent use of appropriate register?	Yes	No
	2. Any lapses?	Yes	No
	3. Area(s) for improvement	Specify:	

Curriculum Materials and Resources:

1. Printed materials:

- *Suzhou Gardens* 苏州园林 , Zhang Xinsheng, China Intercontinental Press

- Classical Gardens 古典园林 , pp. 203-205, Kiosks, Towers and Pavilions 亭台阁楼 , pp. 206-207, *Common Knowledge about Chinese Culture*

- Ancient Pagodas 古塔 , pp. 208-209, Ancient Bridges 古桥 , pp. 210-212, *Common Knowledge about Chinese Culture*

2. Technologies and websites:

- See the website http://tbschineselanguagelab.weebly.com

3. Show:

- 远方的家—沿海行：第28集—苏州 http://www.youtube.com/watch?v=U7k RB3eKFNc

Lesson Outlines:

1. The Essential Questions and desired understanding for this project are briefly introduced so that students understand what will be learned and why.

2. Students read an article about Chinese gardens in Chinese, watch a Chinese video on Suzhou, and view a series of pictures of typical gardens from both the Chinese and Western traditions. Students acquire cultural knowledge and conduct research about the different philosophical, religious, literary, and artistic thoughts embedded in the design of those gardens.

3. Each student creates a Chinese garden model or draws a Chinese garden and writes an essay to an imagined board of trustees of the National Arboretum in Washington, D.C.

4. Every student role-plays as a member of the board of trustees of the National Arboretum and casts a vote for one of the designs.

5. Each student writes another essay trying to convince the rest of their classmates that their choice would be the best one for the National Arboretum.

Learning Difficulties:

Since this topic is not a daily life topic, in the beginning students may find it challenging to understand some Chinese cultural concepts, such as 天人合一, due to their limited vocabulary and knowledge.

Instructional Strategies and Syllabus:

Pre-Day 1 (Icebreaking Reading)

Homework Assignment:

Assign an article to students as an icebreaking reading before the unit starts. Suggestion for such a reading is *Suzhou Gardens* 苏州园林 by Zhang Xinsheng, China Intercontinental Press.

Day 1: Typical Chinese Gardens

Introduce the essential questions and learning outcomes for this unit. Distribute the grading rubrics. (Tables 1 and 2)

Activity 1 (Interpretive Communication, Practices of Culture, Products of Culture, Acquiring Information, 20 minutes)

Play the video 远方的家—沿海行：第 28 集—苏州. Before watching the video, have students pay attention to typical Chinese garden elements, such as kiosks, towers, pavilions, bridges and pagodas.

Activity 2 (Interpersonal Communication, Products of Culture, Acquiring Information, 5 minutes)

Show pictures of typical Chinese gardens, which can be easily found from the websites listed at http://tbschineselanguagelab.weebly.com/learning-resources. html. When viewing the photos, point to the typical Chinese garden elements, such as 假山假石，池塘，静湖，亭台楼阁，长廊，木桥，诗，画，etc. and help students pronounce these words.

After the above two activities, students should have an idea of what a typical Chinese garden looks like.

Activity 3 (Interpersonal Communication, 10 minutes)

Vocabulary building. facilitate students to use vocabulary in context at the sentence level with the aid of garden pictures.

1. Choose a typical Chinese garden picture from a website.

2. Point to the picture and ask students the following questions:

  Q：这是一幅什么图片？

  (A：这是一幅中国花园／园林的图片。)

  Q：这幅图片上有些什么？

  (A：这幅图片上有假山假石／池塘／静湖／亭台楼阁／长廊／木桥。)

  Q：这幅图片上还有一些什么？

  (A：这幅图片上还有松树／梅花／兰花／竹子／荷花／诗和画。)

Figure 1. Design Characteristics of a Typical Chinese Garden 中国园林设计特色

1. Conception: harmony between nature and human beings（概念：天人合一）

2. Culturally appropriate names（与中国文化相符的名称）

3. Major components（主要组成部分）：

  a. rockery and stones（假山假石）

  b. ponds, calm lakes 池塘，静湖

  c. pavilions, terraces, halls, bridges（亭台楼阁，长廊，木桥）

  d. flower and tree arrangements（花草树木）

  e. poetry and paintings（诗画艺术）

Plants used throughout the garden include pines（松树）, plums（梅花）, orchids（兰花）, bamboos（竹子）and chrysanthemums（菊花）. The garden features flowers including peonies（牡丹）for wealth and lotuses（荷花）for purity.

Note: Provide support for students when they do not know the words in Chinese.

Activity 4 (Interpersonal Communication, 15 minutes)

Vocabulary Practice:

1. Divide students into groups after they have familiarized themselves with the relevant vocabulary.

2. Have students discuss the question: 中国园林有哪五个主要组成部分？The discussion allows them to repeatedly speak and hear new words and phrases in context.

3. Check with each group and provide feedback and corrections on pronunciation, tones, vocabulary and grammar usage when needed.

Homework Assignment: Have students find three famous Chinese gardens and prepare a show-and-tell. (See Figure 2.)

Figure 2. Sample Grading Rubric for Day 1 Homework Assignment

Find three famous Chinese gardens. This homework should include a picture, the name, the geographical location, and a brief history of each garden, and show at least two of the five culturally distinctive elements in each garden. The history of each garden can be in English, but all other sections of the assignment must be in Chinese.

Grading Rubric:

	Possible Points	My Points
Names	15	
Locations	15	
History	15	
Pictures	15	
Major components	15	
Total points	75	

Day 2: Differences between Traditional
Chinese and Western Gardens

Activity 1 (Interpersonal and Presentational Communication, 20 minutes)

Show-and-tell activity. Have students share the famous Chinese gardens.

Instructional Strategy: Effective learning requires a deep understanding, and cannot be done by memorization. Therefore make sure that students thoroughly understand what they present. In order for students to gain insight into their learning and understanding, frequent feedback is critical: students need to monitor and actively evaluate their learning. Immediately after the show-and-tell activity, ask students questions such as the following. This follow-up activity can be done in groups or with the whole class.

1. 中国有哪些有名的园林？

2. 这些园林主要在中国的哪些地方？

3. 请谈谈给你印象最深的园林的历史。

Activity 2 (Interpersonal and Presentational Communication, 5 minutes)

Repeat the question students discussed the day before: 中国园林一般有哪五个主要组成部分？ Have students answer the question by writing Chinese characters on a piece of paper or using Socrative – an educational app for iPad and turn it in as evidence of learning and formative assessment. One student may be selected to put all five elements on the board; their answers finally will lead to 中国园林一般有：1. 假山假石 2. 池塘, 静湖 3. 亭台楼阁, 长廊, 木桥 4. 花草树木 5. 诗画艺术.

Activity 3 (Cultural Comparison, 25 minutes)

Encourage students to predict what question will be raised next. Prediction keeps students focused on new content, adds curiosity, and helps them apply prior learning to new situations. Following the essential questions, scaffold students to complete the following steps.

1. With the teacher's guidance, students may ask 中国园林和西方园林有哪些不同？

Instructional Strategy: It is important to provide students with visual and contextual clues to make learning more meaningful and successful. Students with limited verbal competence focus on visual and concrete lesson components to assist in their comprehension.

2. Show students a few garden websites that have photos of gardens in both Chinese and Western traditions.

3. New vocabulary building:

   Point to the roses in an English garden and say 玫瑰花.
   Point to an oriental plant in a Chinese garden and say 梅花 / 菊花 / 荷花 / 兰花.
   Point to a large lawn in a Western garden and say 草坪.
   Point to a winding path in a Chinese garden and say 弯弯曲曲的路.
   Point to a straight path in a Western garden and say 笔直的路.
   Have students repeat the words after you.

4. Let students distinguish gardens of different cultures. For example, they may say 这是英国园林，因为园里种了各种不同颜色的玫瑰花 when they see a photo of an English rose garden; 这是中国园林，因为园里开满了梅花 / 菊花 / 荷花 / 兰花 when they see a photo of a garden with oriental plants; 这是东方园林，因为园里有木桥，桥下是小池塘 when they see a photo of a garden with a wooden bridge over a little pond; and 这是西方园林，因为园里有一片大草坪 when they see a photo of a garden with a big lawn in the center.

5. Display pictures of a typical Chinese garden and a typical Western garden side by side. Facilitate students to use vocabulary in context at the sentence level and the transitional element 而 with the following questions and answers.

   Q: 中国园林里一般种的是什么花？西方园林里呢？

   A: 中国园林里一般种的是梅花 / 菊花 / 荷花 / 兰花，而西方园林里一般种的是玫瑰花。

   Q: 中国园林的园路是怎么样的？西方园林的呢？

   A: 中国园林的园路是弯弯曲曲的（曲径通幽），而西方园林的园路一般是笔直的（绿树成荫）。It is a good idea to introduce idioms.

   Q: 在中国园林里可以看到什么？在西方园林里呢？

   A: 在中国园林里可以看到木桥和池塘，而在西方园林里可以看到草坪。

   The discussion will gradually build up and eventually lead to a more synthesized question such as 在花草树木、园路、园景等方面，中国园林和

西方园林有哪些不同？

Instructional Strategy:

To be effective, this learning activity should train students from lower-level skills of identification and classification to higher-level skills of comparison and synthesis.

Chinese garden culture and its Western counterpart belong to two different schools. The table below is provided for teacher's reference.

Table 4		Western Garden Style	Chinese Garden Style
1	布局	有规律的	变化、自然的
2	树木	对称的种植	自然形成
3	花草	有规律的花坛图案	盆栽花卉、植物的自然形状
4	水景	动态水景如喷泉、瀑布	静态水景如小溪、池塘和静湖
5	园路	笔直的	弯弯曲曲的
6	雕塑	人物和动物石雕	巨大的石头和假山
7	园景	园景固定	强调创造天人合一的自然感觉

Homework Assignment:

Assign a written paragraph comparing Chinese gardens to Western gardens using 在……方面／上，是……的，而，强调 and 表现. The paragraph should contain at least 6 sentences.

Day 3: Chinese Culturd Concept 天人合一

Activity 1 (Interpersonal Communication, Cultural Comparison, 5 minutes)

Review the concepts and sentences.

1. Let students individually review the concepts and sentences they learned the day before by going over their notes.

2. Divide students into small groups to talk about differences between Chinese and Western gardens.

Activity 2 (Language Comparison, 5 minutes)

To make learning more interesting, compare the linguistic differences between the traditional Chinese character for garden 園 and the English word "garden". The character 園 can be explained in the following way. 口 is 围墙. 土 looks like buildings, and represents pavilions. 口 in the middle can be seen as a pond. The part below 口 looks like trees. The etymology of "garden" is the German word "gart", meaning enclosure. The modern definition is "an enclosed area where herbs, fruits, flowers or vegetables are cultivated." (Adopted from "Chinese Garden", Dr. Dali Tan, *CLASS AP Chinese Curriculum Scenarios*)

Activity 3 (Cultural Practices, Cultural Products, 40 minutes)

Introduce the Chinese cultural concept 天人合一 .

1. Ask students 天是什么? 人是谁? 合一是什么意思?

2. Guide students to come up with relevant answers, such as 天是大自然 (nature), 人是人类 (human beings), 合一就是和谐 (harmony).

3. Have students discuss the questions 中国人喜欢在花园里做什么? 为什么?

   Instructional Strategy: To effectively facilitate the discussion, help students recall the Chinese cultural products or practices from the pictures they saw or the video they watched using the sentence structure A 对 B 有好处 / 有益 . They may say:

   "中国花园里种了很多花，闻闻花香，对人们的鼻子有好处。"

"中国花园里有池塘，池塘里游着金鱼，听听流水声，对人们的耳朵有好处。"

"池塘上有小木桥，在园里散步，站在小桥上，欣赏水里的金鱼，可以放松，对人们的身体有好处。"

"看看绿色的树木，对人们的眼睛有好处。"

"在园里弹琴、练书法，对人们的手有好处。"

"在亭子里休息、看书、作诗、思考，对人们的大脑有好处。"

"呼吸园里的新鲜空气对人们的健康有益。"

3. Have students synthesize what they discussed and guide them to analyze the relationship between cultural products/practices and the cultural perspective of 天人合一 by asking them "在中国人看来，人和自然有什么关系？" This part of learning requires students' higher-level thinking skills of synthesis and analysis. Guide students to find out that Chinese people view human beings as a small part of nature and strive for a harmonious relationship with nature.

4. Encourage students to brainstorm and speculate on other Chinese philosophical ideas that influence their garden design. If possible, bring students to a Chinese garden where they can listen to the sound of water, see the green leaves of trees, breathe the fresh air, smell the flowers and appreciate the perspective of 天人合一 . Students may attach sense and meaning to the new learning.

Homework Assignment:

Have students jot down design ideas and draft a proposal to an imagined board of trustees of the National Arboretum in Washington, D.C., which has plans to add a Chinese garden to its grounds. The proposal explains why this garden design should be adopted by the National Arboretum.

Remind students first to go over the rubrics given on Day 1 before working on their assignment, and to bring their completed assignment to the next class session.

For details of Day 4, Day 5, and Day 6, check the website http://tbschinese languagelab.weebly.com.

Day 7: Project Presentation and Peer Evaluation

The written proposal is due.

Activity 1 (Interpretive and Presentational Communication, 40 minutes)

Garden design presentation. Before students' presentations, do the following:

1. Go over the grading rubric (Table 1) with students, making sure that everyone understands it.

2. Have students listen carefully to each presentation and choose the best garden design to write an essay about.

3. Let students go on stage one after another to present their garden model or drawing.

   With the presentation rubric (Table 1) in hand, take notes while listening to each student's presentation. The notes will help recall students' performances when grading their presentations later. Wait until after the presentation is done to comment on student's performance.

Activity 2 (Interpersonal Communication, 10 minutes)

Peer review and evaluation. Have each student find a classmate to be their partner and discuss each other's proposal using the Peer Evaluation – Writing (Table 3).

Homework Assignment:

Assign students an essay discussing and analyzing the pros and cons of their chosen design. Remind them that the essay has to try to convince the rest of the trustees that the student's choice would be the best one for the National Arboretum.

Day 8: Board Meeting and Peer Evaluation

Activity 1 (Interpersonal and Presentational Communication, 40 minutes)

Board Meeting. Before the meeting, tell students that during the meeting everyone will:

1. Role-play as a member of the board of trustees of the National Arboretum;

2. Cast a vote for one of the designs;

3. Explain to the board why their choice of garden design is the best.

Activity 2 (Interpersonal Communication, 10 minutes)

Peer review and evaluation. After the meeting, have each student find a partner and discuss each other's essays using Peer Evaluation – Writing (See Table 3).

Homework Assignment:

Have students revise their proposal and essay based on the peer evaluations. Sample student essays can be accessed at http://tbschineselanguagelab.weebly. com/student-products.html.com.

Day 9: Summative Assessment

This comprehensive assessment provides students with an opportunity to demonstrate their cultural knowledge of Chinese gardens and their interpersonal speaking skills by having a one-on-one conversation with the teacher. There are six questions (Figure 3). Each time it is a student's turn, they will have 20 seconds to speak.

The questions below are just for teacher's reference. Use College Board's AP Chinese Scoring Guidelines to assess students' communication skills for Interpersonal Speaking: Conversation at http://media.collegeboard.com/ digitalServices/pdf/ap/apcentral/ap13_chinese_scoring_guidelines.pdf.

Figure 3. Sample Test – Conversation Questions

1. 你好，你知道中国有哪些有名的园林？

2. 这些有名的园林大部分建造在中国的哪些地方？

3. 要是你可以去一个中国园林看看，你最想看哪一个？为什么？

4. 中国园林和西方园林有哪些不同的地方？

5. 在中国人看来，人和自然有什么关系？

6. 要是在你住的城市里修建一个花园，你觉得应该修建什么样的花园？为什么？

Acknowledgements:

I wish to thank CLASS for providing *AP Chinese Curriculum Scenarios*. Based on the scenario "Chinese Garden" sent to me via email by Dr. Dali Tan in August 2009, I have developed the current project-based learning unit. The results of four years of field tests indicate that the learning activities provide students with a hands-on learning opportunity for the cultural concept of 天人合一 and reflect the National Standards for Foreign Language Learning. Many thanks to my AP Chinese and Culture classes (2011, 2012, 2013 and 2014) for their participation and comments during the development of this project.

References:

American Council on the Teaching of Foreign Languages. (1996). Standards for Foreign Language Learning: Preparing for the 21st Century. http://www.actfl.org/sites/default/files/pdfs/public/StandardsforFLLexecsumm_rev.pdf.

Wiggins, G. & McTighe, J. (2005). *Understanding by Design* (Expanded 2nd Edition). Association for Supervision and Curriculum Development, Alexandria, VA 22311-1714 USA.

Sample Student Product 1 – Garden Model 静心园

Sample Student Product 2 – Garden Drawing 和平园

Xing King (金星), a faculty member of the Bishop's School, has been teaching Chinese of all levels. She presented her research project "Integration of Technology in the AP Chinese Curriculum" in various national conferences and "Chinese in the World" in the Professional Development Night of the AP Reading 2010. She conducted a one-day AP Chinese workshop to secondary school teachers in Washington/Portland area in 2010. She has been serving as a Content Leader for AP Chinese Readings since 2007 and a member of the College Board's SAT Test Development Committee since 2011.

Chinese Gardens

Henry Ruan (阮勇强)
Lower East Side Preparatory High School, New York City, New York
Hofstra University, Long Island, New York

Language Proficiency Level: Advanced Low – Advanced Mid

Age Range: 17-18 (high school students)

Class Size: 20-25 students

Time Frame: 45 minutes per period, 6 periods

Essential Question:

How do garden designs reflect the aesthetic values of a culture?

Unit Goals:

To help students develop their abilities to interact with speakers of Chinese on the topic of Chinese gardens and related topics, to introduce key aspects of Chinese gardens, and to appreciate the beauty and design of Chinese gardens, as well as their relationship with other Chinese art forms.

Standards: Based on the National Standards for Foreign Language Learning

- **Communication:**

  -Interpersonal (1.1)

  -Interpretive (1.2)

  -Presentational (1.3)

- **Connection:** Relate Chinese gardens to Chinese classical painting, poetry, literature, and possibly architectural design (e.g., 颐和园).

- **Comparison:** Various styles of gardens, including Chinese and Western gardens (such as those in the Forbidden City and the Palace of Versailles).

- **Culture**: Gardens as a way of life in traditional Chinese society.

- **Community:** Build learners' interest in Chinese gardens and related art forms, such as Chinese calligraphy, classic painting, and Chinese poetry; initiate learning on the topics to further understanding and exchange views with others.

Unit Questions:

- Can students describe the key aspects of the imperial garden of the Forbidden City?

- Can students share their opinions of Chinese gardens?

- Can students compare a Chinese garden with a Western garden?

- Can students present a project on Chinese gardens?

Lesson Outlines:

In the previous lessons, students learned about subjects such as landmarks in China, Chinese architecture, classical Chinese poetry, Chinese calligraphy, and Chinese paintings, so they have some basic knowledge about these topics. To prepare students for this new unit, teachers may provide a few websites or YouTube video clips about Chinese gardens, as well as pictures of beautiful local gardens. Since some public schools block YouTube, YouTube videos can be downloaded by using http://www.keepvid.com at home. A few personal pictures would definitely raise interest levels among students.

Day 1:
A Virtual Tour of the Imperial Garden of the Forbidden City

Learning Objectives:

Students will be able to:

- Discuss with others, orally and in writing, the imperial garden of the Forbidden City (interpersonal);

- Introduce the key aspects of the imperial garden of the Forbidden City to other students or family members (presentational).

Learning Difficulties/Teaching Focus:

- Use descriptive vocabulary and expressions in an appropriate context.

- Review the use of conjunctions and comparative sentences:

  1. 承接关系：首先……，然后……，最后…… ；于是……

  2. 并列关系：一方面……，一方面…… ；一边……，一边…… ；既……，又……

  3. "比"的用法：A 比 B Adjective（得多，一点）

- Use the sentence structures/vocabulary applicable to the imperial garden. The following websites may be found helpful in teaching:

  http://www.kinabaloo.com/fcs.html（故宫御花园）

  http://ipsm.hner.cn/czpd/kczy/shang/yw/2/07/rj-kebiao/2/kzzl2.htm（紫禁城园林植物）

  http://v.youku.com/v_show/id_XNjM4OTM5Nzg4.html?from=y1.2-1-87.4.19-1.12-1-2-18

  http://v.youku.com/v_show/id_XMjg0OTI2OA==.html

  http://v.youku.com/v_show/id_XNTMyMTEy.html

Day 2: A Brief Introduction to Chinese Gardens in Suzhou

Learning Objectives:

Students will be able to:

- Outline the unique characteristics of southern-style gardens in China (interpretive);

- Explain the key components of a Chinese garden (interpersonal and presentational).

Learning Difficulties/Teaching Focus:

- Outline themes and main ideas in reading.

- Use comprehension strategies such as guessing, looking for key words, inferring meaning, and prediction.

- Review the use of conjunctions and comparative sentences:

  1. 递进关系：不但……，而且……

  2. 因果关系：因为……，所以……

  3. "更" 在比较句中的用法

- Discuss the characteristics of traditional Chinese gardens with classmates orally or in writing in a focused and organized way (讨论中国园林的特点：亭、台、楼、阁，一步一景，大自然的缩影).

Useful Websites:

http://www.youtube.com/watch?v=BeBYlxZJZmM

http://www.youtube.com/watch?v=6o9CO6wGPnw

Day 3: A Discussion of the Palatial Gardens of Versailles

Learning Objectives:

Students will be able to:

- Highlight the key ideas from a reading about the palatial gardens of Versailles (interpretive);
- List the characteristics of Western gardens as observed from the assigned reading (interpretive);
- Describe key elements of Western gardens (presentational).

Learning Difficulties/Teaching Focus:

- Describe Western gardens with specific vocabulary and expressions in complete and complex/compound sentences.
- Use comprehension strategies such as guessing, looking for key words, inferring meaning, and prediction.
- Use conjunctions and comparative sentences appropriately:

  1. 转折关系：虽然……，但是……

  2. 假设关系：如果…… 就……

  3. 比较句型：Subject＋更喜欢＋Object，因为……

- Present a topic/argument with evidence in a convincing way.

Day 4 (Sample Day): A Comparison of Chinese and Western Traditional Gardens

Learning Objectives:

Students will be able to:

- Highlight key aspects of Western gardens (interpretive);

- Compare two types of gardens, the palatial gardens of Versailles and the imperial garden of the Forbidden City, by listing two major similarities and differences (interpretive and presentational);

- Present and support personal views on the topics with concrete evidence (presentational).

Learning Difficulties/Teaching Focus:

- Compare major characteristics of Chinese and Western gardens using comparative sentence structures and conjunctions.

- Write a short paragraph in well-connected sentences with conjunctions and comparative sentences.

Teaching/Learning Aids:

- Teacher references for garden imagery and comparisons:

  http://www.chateauversailles.fr/jardins-parc

  http://wenku.baidu.com/view/0029815177232f60ddcca145.html

- Providing visual tools is important. Let students use the following sites to create flashcards and practice writing Chinese characters. These cards should be posted in the classroom and word quizzes should be conducted during each lesson to check the mastery of vocabulary words.

  http://file.chinese.cn/FCM_EN/index.html 生字卡片

  http://cop.yes-chinese.com/hanban/tzg/ 写字笔划

- Internet access or downloaded video clips as referenced below in the Curriculum Materials and Resources section

- Computer/projector/smartboard

- Two rubrics for assessment (see Appendix 1 and Appendix 2). Teacher distributes them to students before class begins.

Curriculum Materials and Resources:

- Vocabulary cards, expression cards, and picture cards of Versailles and the Forbidden City. Vocabulary, expressions, and pictures can also be projected on the smartboard. Two rubrics should be distributed to students as they walk in the classroom.

- The following YouTube video clips may be used as reference:

  https://www.youtube.com/watch?v=sVeDz5YBSYA

  http://www.tudou.com/programs/view/uhf4JeHTXxM/

  https://www.youtube.com/watch?v=pZEqYVTpESE (2:30)

  http://www.chinadmd.com/file/uoxticasiip3oixsa3crpvec_2.html

- The YouTube videos can be downloaded by using http://keepvid.com. Copy the URL of the desired video to the site, and select the size/format of the video to download.

Instructional Strategies:

In this unit, each lesson provides tools and means to prepare students to reach the unit goals and to answer the unit essential question. Students are exposed to topics related to Chinese gardens through learning activities of vocabulary-building and the introduction of the imperial garden of the Forbidden City, the gardens of Suzhou, and the palatial gardens of the Palace of Versailles. Before Day 4, students learned major characteristics of Chinese and Western gardens, and they have pictures and vocabulary lists dealing with both styles of gardens. The lists and pictures are posted in the classroom where students can easily refer to them. This sample lesson could be used, with modifications, as a template for comparisons of other types of gardens at different proficiency levels. Teachers may consider using different teaching materials for this lesson, such as reading texts or video clips from other sources.

As planned and shown here, language components such as conjunctions and comparative sentences are reviewed and practiced before this lesson.

- 并列关系：不是……，而是……；一边……，一边……
  一方面……，一方面……；既……，又……
- 转折关系：虽然……，但是……
- 因果关系：因为……，所以……；由于……；因此……
- 假设关系：如果……，就……
- 递进关系：不但……，而且……
- 承接关系：首先……，然后……，最后……；于是……

Instructional Steps:

Warm-up (2 minutes)

Purpose: To prepare students for the vocabulary of the new lesson.

1. Teacher leads students as a group to recall the vocabulary and expressions learned in the previous lessons by displaying images of Chinese and Western gardens on the classroom wall.

2. Teacher asks individual students to write those words in Chinese characters, or *pinyin* if they cannot recall the characters, on large flashcards/paper.

3. Teacher asks students to form pairs and help each other with the characters on their flashcards.

4. Teacher tells students to have their cards ready for the next activities.

Activity 1 (10 minutes)

Purpose: To use the vocabulary and expressions gathered during the warm-up to comment on the palatial gardens of Versailles, based on a video clip selected from the list available in the Curriculum Materials and Resources section.

Pre-Activity

- Before showing the chosen video clip, teacher shows two pictures of Versailles:

  http://www.guidatours.com/images/Image/Grandes%20eaux%20musicales.jpg

  http://www.fodors.com/images/itineraries/versailles-garden.jpg

- Teacher asks students to describe the pictures in sentences by using the vocabulary from the flashcards.

- Lead-in Example (conversational style):

      Teacher: 凡尔赛宫的建筑怎么样?

      Student: 凡尔赛宫的建筑很高大。

      Teacher: 那凡尔赛宫的草坪呢?

Student: 凡尔赛宫的草坪很宽阔。

Example for practicing connecting sentences:

Teacher: 请用"不但"和"而且"把这两个句子的意思再说一遍。

Student: 凡尔赛宫不但建筑（很）高大，而且草坪（很）宽阔。

Example for a descriptive sentence:

凡尔赛宫不但有高大的建筑，而且有宽阔的草坪。

In-Activity

- Teacher writes the question of the activity on the board: 你最喜欢哪一幕 / 哪个景？ 写出最喜欢的一幕，并讲一个理由。

- Show the selected clip.

- While students are watching the clip, teacher may show vocabulary cards to students next to the video screen. These cards are prepared in advance by the teacher.

- After watching the clip, students are given two minutes to write their answers individually in their notebooks, using sentence structures like 我最喜欢（影片中的）……, 因为……. Students are also encouraged to reference the words and expressions shown on the vocabulary cards provided by the teacher when answering the questions and/or describing the scenes seen in the clip.

- Teacher calls on volunteers to share their answers with the class orally. Teacher also reminds students that their answers will be used in the activities to follow.

- Teacher then has students walk around the classroom to find at least two classmates who share the same favorite scene by asking 你最喜欢哪一幕 / 哪个景？ They compare their answers to make a group report on their common scene. Teacher calls four or five different group representatives to write their answers on the board.

    1. Examples of vocabulary:

    凡尔赛宫　花园　草坪　平整　水池　建筑　宏伟壮观　色彩鲜艳

    2. Examples at the sentence level:

    凡尔赛宫的建筑宏伟壮观。

    凡尔赛宫的草坪宽阔美丽。

3. Example of connected sentences:

凡尔赛宫不仅建筑宏伟壮观，而且草坪也宽阔美丽。

An oral review of the use of connectors, such as 又……又……, ……既……又……, 虽然……但是…… and comparative sentences using A 比 B + Adjective（大，漂亮）may be included in this activity before having students write their answers on the board.

Example 1:

> Teacher:凡尔赛宫大不大，漂亮不漂亮？
> Student:凡尔赛宫很大，很漂亮。
> Teacher:"凡尔赛宫很大，很漂亮。"还可以怎么说？
> Student:凡尔赛宫又大又漂亮。

Example 2:

> Teacher:凡尔赛宫的宫殿建筑怎么样？
> Student:宫殿建筑又宏伟，又壮观。
> Teacher:还可以怎么说？
> Student:宫殿建筑不但宏伟而且壮观。
> Teacher:还可以怎么说？
> Student:宫殿建筑既宏伟又壮观。

Post-Activity

Teacher leads students in reading aloud the sentences on the board in order to review where newly introduced vocabulary and expressions are positioned in sentences and how they function in context. This is to prepare students for the next activity.

Activity 2 (13 minutes)

Purpose: To describe the palatial gardens of Versailles by outlining their key characteristics, which will be compared with those of the imperial garden of the Forbidden City.

In the lesson on Day 1, students learned the major characteristics of the imperial garden. They used a worksheet that dealt only with the imperial garden; in this lesson, the worksheet expands to include the key aspects of the palatial gardens of Versailles.

Pre-Activity

Distribute worksheets. Teacher assists students in paraphrasing the items on the worksheet, and makes sure that students understand the meaning of each item. The following list of questions can be distributed to students:

1. 外表：我们可以看到些什么？ 什么形状？ 什么色彩？

2. 整体设计：凡尔赛宫花园的主要组成部分是什么？

3. 色调：凡尔赛宫花园的基本颜色是什么？ 主要的颜色是什么？

4. 建筑材料：凡尔赛宫花园主要用了什么建筑材料？

5. 园林要素：凡尔赛宫花园有哪些园林要素？ 在凡尔赛宫花园里，我们还可以看到些什么？

6. 细节：有哪些特殊的植物？ 雕塑有多大？ 雕塑名称是什么？

7. 其他：This is the part that allows students to put anything they like as long as they can explain in Chinese.

In-Activity

1. Teacher has students work on the worksheet individually for two minutes. Based on the content of the previous activity displayed on the board, students select the vocabulary to fill in the worksheet first, and highlight distinct characteristics of the palatial gardens of Versailles.

2. Students share their answers in groups of four by asking each other the questions from the Pre-Activity. They may ask other questions which are not listed in the Pre-Activity. They then fill out the worksheet with the answers they get from other members in the group.

3. With the blank worksheet projected on the board, teacher calls seven students to tape large flashcards into the corresponding blanks of the worksheet, based on their own selections from Step 1. Another similar list for Chinese gardens should be posted in the classroom. Students are able to refer to that list, which provides clues so that students use the vocabulary repeatedly in the class. Here is a filled-out worksheet sample.

描述的方面	凡尔赛宫花园
外表 / Appearance	色彩鲜艳
整体设计 / Design	雕塑、水池、喷泉
色调 / Color Tone	绿色、白色
建筑材料 /Building Material	石（大理石）
园林要素 /Elements	喷水池、草坪
细节 /Details	雕塑、植物
其他 /Others (specify)	

4. Teacher projects or writes the following expressions and sample questions on the board. Each group is required to complete two answers and post their answers on the board.

- ……由（person/institution）……建造

  Example:

  Teacher: 法国的凡尔赛宫是由谁建造的？

  Student: 凡尔赛宫是由路易十四建造的。

- Subject + 以……闻名于世

  Example:

  Teacher: 凡尔赛宫以什么闻名于世？

  Student: 凡尔赛宫以宏伟的建筑闻名于世。

- Subject + 以……为主

  Example:

  Teacher: 西方园林以建筑、雕塑为主，还是以花草为主？

  Student: 西方园林以建筑为主。

5. Pair students up and have them conduct a similar question-and-answer session to communicate with each other.

Post-Activity

1. Let students reflect on the activity by asking them to write down one question they still have about the palatial gardens of Versailles.

2. Usually, a few students will come up with questions first. Let them share their questions in the class, followed by a short discussion. For example, students may ask "为什么西方园林中要放一座雕像？西方园林中的水池有什么作用？建造这样的宫殿园林需要多少工人？", etc.

3. Students may freely respond to the above questions, and may also have different answers. Encourage students to spend time after class finding answers to the questions.

4. After the discussion, teacher may ask the students who haven't yet written any questions to either write one question or give an answer to one of the questions.

Note to Teachers:

These questions and the discussion help build the knowledge base for future lessons. Teacher may guide or help answer the questions accordingly. There are times when teachers are not able to answer; be frank and straightforward about them. Encourage students to find the answers on their own and award them with extra credit.

Activity 3 (20 minutes)

Purpose: To discuss and compare the palatial gardens of Versailles and the imperial garden of the Forbidden City, building upon Activity 2 and the lesson of Day 1.

Pre-Activity

Teacher reviews what the class did on Day 1 by reading the part of the worksheet done on that day and the one done during Activity 2 of this lesson (Day 4). Students may now add more vocabulary to the worksheet if they want. Below is a sample of the completed worksheet:

描述的方面	凡尔赛宫花园	故宫御花园
外表 /Appearance	平整宽阔、气派非凡	豪华秀丽、精致考究
整体设计 /Design	园林很大	宫殿群为主、御花园很小
色调 /Color Tone	绿色、白色	绿色、红色
建筑的材料 /Building Material	石（大理石）	木、石
园林要素 /Elements	喷水池、草坪	水池、假山、亭子
细节 /Details	雕塑、植物	雕龙刻凤
其他 /Others (specify)		

Teacher writes the following questions on the board:

1. 故宫御花园和凡尔赛宫花园有什么相同的地方？

2. 故宫御花园和凡尔赛宫花园有什么不同？

Teacher demonstrates the sample sentence structures that students may use to answer the questions:

1. 故宫御花园和凡尔赛宫花园相同的是……

2. 故宫御花园和凡尔赛宫花园不同的是……

It should be noted that teachers and students are not limited to using just these sample sentence structures.

- A 与 B 有着截然不同的 + Noun

  Example: 凡尔赛宫与故宫有着截然不同的风格 / 设计 / 布局。

- A 比 B + Adjective，但是……

  Example: 凡尔赛宫的林园比故宫的御花园大得多，但是故宫的御花园比凡尔赛宫的林园更有意思，因为里面有亭子和假山。

In-Activity

- Students are divided into groups of 3-4. Each group examines their completed worksheets and use a Venn diagram to list similarities and differences.

- Each group discusses and writes down at least two similarities and two differences in complete sentences.

- Each group needs to record their group answers on poster paper.

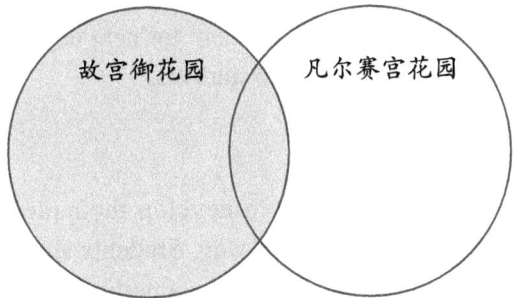

(The overlapping area should contain the similarities.)

Samples for possible answers:

Similarities: (A 和 B 都……)

凡尔赛宫花园和故宫御花园都很漂亮。

Differences:

凡尔赛宫和故宫截然不同，凡尔赛宫的宫殿很大，故宫的宫殿小，但是很多。

Comparisons:

凡尔赛宫比故宫宽阔，因为凡尔赛宫的花园有很大的草坪，故宫御花园虽然没有草坪，但是有漂亮的亭子和假山。

- All groups post their worksheets/posters on the board or on the walls.

- Call on two groups to sum up their findings. The group with the most details get a star/extra credit.

- Students also use the rubric provided in Appendix 1 to evaluate their fellow students' presentations.

Post-Activity

Ask students to walk around and review the writings of each group. This also facilitates the wrap-up activity – Exit Ticket.

The teacher uses the rubric provided in Appendix 1 to grade students' work.

Exit Ticket

Let students write a complete sentence describing one similarity or difference, or one aspect of the topics learned in the lesson.

Teachers may use this formative assessment for next day's lesson and to re-teach any part that is not well-learned by the students.

Homework Assignment:

This assignment requires students to develop their ideas and organize their thoughts in a logical and convincing way. Students should be able to provide evidence while presenting an argument or supporting their opinion. A rubric for this assignment is provided in Appendix 2.

1. 你喜欢凡尔赛宫花园，还是故宫御花园？为什么？

   (Write a paragraph with at least two reasons, using as many conjunction words as you can. The conjunction words were given to you and practiced in class.)

2. 东西方皇家园林主要差别在什么地方？举例说明。

   (Write a paragraph with one or two differences, using as many comparative structures as you can.)

In the assignments, students are encouraged to include information found outside the classroom. They are required to elaborate upon their responses instead of merely providing brief answers. If a student would like to include information found online or in a book, a reference should be provided at the end of the assignment. The content of these assignments can also be used in the unit project or term project.

Performance-Based Assessment:

Teachers should keep in mind the learning objectives set forth above. The activities, classwork, worksheets, and homework assignment are considered formative assessments. Teachers should be aware of the fact that every instance of students providing an answer or displaying a piece of writing can be considered teaching feedback, and therefore part of formative assessment. Teachers should adjust the teaching pace and/or material based on these assessments. At the end of the unit, a project and/or a unit test should be given to students as a means of summative assessment.

Day 5: Field Trip

Students visit a Chinese garden locally or online. Outline the key characteristics of the garden.

Learning Objectives:

Students will be able to:

- Describe the (virtual) tour using Google Earth or Google Maps (presentational);

- Present one personal view about the garden with convincing evidence/reasons (presentational).

Learning Difficulties/Teaching Focus:

- Use topic-specific vocabulary appropriately and accurately.

- Use conjunctions and comparative sentences in discourse.

Day 6: Presentation

Students will present their projects on Chinese gardens. They may include a tour guide component in the project.

Learning Objectives:

Students will be able to:

- Relate the art in Chinese gardens to other Chinese art forms (interpersonal);

- Use digital tools to present one favorite Chinese garden (presentational).

Learning Difficulties/Teaching Focus:

- Write short paragraphs to state opinions supported by details and elaboration.

- Use literary techniques in a descriptive narrative, such as metaphors, similes, personification, etc.

Appendix 1: Rubric for Activity 3

	5	4	3	2	1
Vocabulary	Correct use of over 10 new words	Mostly correct use of over 10 new words	Correct use of less than 10 new words	Use of new words with errors	Use of vocabulary with many errors
Content	Comparison with 2 differences and 2 similarities; well-connected sentences	Comparison with 3 differences and similarities; connected sentences	Comparison with 2 differences and similarities; fairly connected sentences	Comparison with one difference or similarity; disjointed sentences	No effort in comparison
Pronun-ciation	Fluent, correct, and accurate pronunciation	Mostly correct and accurate pronunciation	Fair pronunciation with errors that don't obscure meaning	Fair pronunciation with errors that obscure meaning	Poor pronunciation with many errors
Character Writing	A few minor errors	Over 5 errors	Over 10 errors	Many errors, but still understandable	Many errors; hard to understand

Appendix 2: Rubric for the Written Homework Assignment

	5	4	3	2	1
Meaning	Clear and focused, with one or two strong, relevant reasons	Focused, with one or two relevant reasons	Fairly focused, with one relevant reason	Confusing, with irrelevant reasons	Not understandable

	Rich, accurate, and precise use of vocabulary	Accurate and precise use of vocabulary	Mostly correct use of vocabulary, meaning is clear	Use of vocabulary with errors that obscure meaning	Poor use of vocabulary
Vocabulary					
Conven-tions	Consistent use of standard conventions of Chinese	Consistent use of standard conventions of Chinese, with a few minor errors	Fair use of standard conventions of Chinese, with a few errors	Inconsistent use of conventions of Chinese, with errors that cause confusion	Little use of standard conventions of Chinese

Henry Ruan (阮勇强) has over 20 years of teaching experience, teaches at a public high school in New York City, and supervises student teaching as an adjunct professor at Hofstra University in Long Island, New York. His passion is making classroom teaching more engaging and meaningful to students through the use of technology and new pedagogical approaches. He offers teacher training workshops on Chinese language teaching and classroom management at several colleges and universities, and has also presented on these topics at national and statewide professional conferences. From 2008 to 2012, Dr. Ruan served as a member of the AP Chinese Curriculum Development Committee of the College Board.

Critique

Chinese Gardens – Xing King
Chinese Gardens – Henry Ruan

"Chinese Gardens" is one of the theme-based scenarios provided to AP teachers by the Chinese Language Association of Secondary-Elementary Schools (CLASS). Although both designs in this section have the same title and share the same cultural philosophy, the authors, Xing King and Henry Ruan, use different theoretical frameworks and thus their designs differ in content and approach. King bases her work on the theory of Backward Design, the process of which consists of three crucial steps: identifying desired results, determining acceptable evidence, and planning learning experiences and instructions. In answering "what is worth understanding?", King proposes four essential reflections that guide her curriculum design:

1. Culturally distinctive elements characterizing typical Chinese gardens;

2. Comparisons of Chinese and Western gardens;

3. The significance of the Chinese cultural perspective regarding the relationship between human and nature;

4. How this perspective influences Chinese garden design and landscaping.

King carefully selects learning evidence-based projects and homework products. These products/projects represent real-world tasks, creative and fun for students. Each question in the *Unit Goals* section directly facilitates students' successful completion of the projects. King's curriculum starts with the end results, and rubrics are given to students at the beginning of the class. In planning learning experiences and instruction, King innovatively creates a series of easily conducted activities. For example, an activity links elements of a garden to people's multiple perceptions via a sentence structure: A 对 B 有好处 / 有益 (Activity 3) to help students understand the concept of 天人合一. The activities are scaffolding for learning steps, where students map language form and meaning in context to express their opinions and personal appreciation of nature. The design enhances the experiential part of learning, associating students' perceptions with language and language use.

Both King's and Ruan's designs are highly content-based and integrate the richness of Chinese culture. For example, King synthesizes the elements of Chinese gardens into five facets so that students can easily categorize, describe, compare, create meaning of, and assign value to Chinese garden design.

Ruan's design reflects the theory of Advance Organizers, i.e., that instruction helps students organize new incoming information based on what they have learned. In this way, learning becomes connected and meaningful. The design provides an example of structured instruction in which one activity leads to the next. Each of Ruan's activities consists of three phases: pre-, in-, and post-activities. The activities themselves are scaffolding, helping learners achieving higher competency levels step by step. Activities start with vocabulary, which is practiced in sentences through conversations. Strategies and instructions are also provided for students' projects in order to facilitate comparisons between the palatial gardens of Versailles and the imperial garden of the Forbidden City. The diagram (in Activity 3) provides a clear and cleverly designed chart, useful for students in summarizing the similarities and differences between the garden designs of two cultures.

Ruan provides an extended list of curriculum materials and resources, as well as teaching/learning aids which benefit both students and teachers. Students are encouraged "to learn beyond classroom walls" in an authentic language and culture community.

There may be a concern regarding consistency in the learning objectives in Ruan's design. The objectives of Day 1 seem a bit too challenging for a first day of the unit, which might start off better by engaging students' existing experience with gardens in their city, or even at home. The consistency between objectives and activities is also worth noting. Two objectives for the Sample Day include the interpretive mode, in which case pertinent meta-cognitive comprehension strategies and sample input text in the target language would be desirable and necessary. The term, "standard conventions of Chinese", in assessing written work may be too general to use. Lastly, the relationship between infrequently used vocabulary items and simple activities at the sentence level may lack some balance.

The sessions of project presentation and peer evaluation are indispensable in both designs since "Chinese Gardens" is a project-oriented theme with rich cultural features and cross-cultural differences. Project presentation and peer evaluation can take up much class time, as indicated in Xing's design. This time is worth spending, but programs may not be able to afford it, especially when class sizes are large. It is important for readers to understand the rationale and theoretical underpinnings of the projects, and thus adopt the current designs creatively.

Theme 3

Dining

Chinese Food Culture

Jeannine Fan Subisak (范良琦)
Columbus Academy, Gahanna, Ohio

Language Proficiency Level: Intermediate Mid

Age Range: 16-17 (11th grade students)

Class Size: 15-20 students

Time Frame: 110 minutes for each lesson, with 7 lessons in total for the unit

Essential Question:

How can a nation's geography impact its people's food sources and food preferences?

Unit Goals:

To help students develop the language skills to order dishes in a Chinese restaurant, describe the main characteristics of the four major Chinese cuisines, narrate cooking steps, critique a signature dish found online from a restaurant in China, and conduct a food drive for a rural school in China.

Standards: Based on the National Standards for Foreign Language Learning

- **Communication:**

  -Interpersonal (1.1): Order dishes according to the number of guests, such as 四菜一汤 , and converse about the four major Chinese cuisines (四大菜系).

  -Interpretive (1.2): Listen to instructions about making dumplings (饺子), watch a video on the cooking steps of the dish of scrambled eggs with tomatoes (西红柿炒蛋), research dishes served in restaurants in China and determine those dishes' origin, and find authentic recipes from websites like 美食杰 , 中国厨师网 , and 中国菜谱网 .

  -Presentational (1.3): Comment on the taste of dishes, describe the similarities and differences in Western and Chinese dining customs, give detailed instructions for making 西红柿炒蛋 , describe the main characteristics of 四大菜系 , present the process of making an authentic Chinese dish, write a critique of a dish, and make a flyer for a food drive.

- **Connection:** Research the topics of Chinese geography, agricultural products, customs practiced celebrating major traditional festivals, etc., and discuss nutritional values and *yin* and *yang* in a balanced meal.

- **Comparison:** Compare different dining customs in Western and Chinese food cultures, compare southern and northern cuisines in China such as 南甜北咸 , 南稻北麦 , and regional cuisines.

- **Culture:** Use vocabulary of commonly used condiments and ingredients in making Chinese food, e.g., 酱油, 香油, 葱, 姜, 蒜, discuss 四大菜系 – 鲁菜, 川菜, 粤菜, 苏菜, introduce common staple foods and popular dishes such as 饺子, 包子, 馒头, 米饭, 西红柿炒蛋, and discuss characteristics of being 色、香、味俱全 .

- **Community:** Make authentic Chinese dishes to share with the class, and design a flyer for a food drive to serve families in rural schools in China.

Unit Questions:

- Can students order Chinese dishes for a group of guests to share?

- Can students identify the main characteristics of the four major Chinese cuisines?

- Can students describe the cooking steps for making dumplings?

● Can students narrate the cooking steps of an authentic Chinese dish?

● Can students apply their language skills and cultural understanding to make a flyer for a food drive?

● Can students research dishes served in a restaurant in China and write a food critique based on the customers' postings?

Lesson Outlines:

Day 1: Ordering dishes and comparing Western and Chinese dining customs

Day 2: Stating the different geographic features relating to 南甜北咸, 南稻北麦 and 四大菜系

Day 3: Identifying food associated with traditional Chinese festivals, and stating steps for making 西红柿炒蛋

Day 4: Making dumplings

Day 5: Designing flyers for a food drive service project

Day 6: Enjoying and commenting on the dishes students made at home and watching students' cooking videos

Day 7: Unit review and summative assessment of 四大菜系 (see Appendix 1)

Learning Objectives:

Students will be able to:

Day 1

● Comment on the flavor of dishes (interpersonal);

● Ask and state choices of dishes when ordering food to share with a number of guests (interpersonal);

● Describe the similarities and differences in Western and Chinese dining customs (presentational).

Day 2

● Ask and state the impact of China's geography on regional cuisines (interpersonal);

- Ask and state the characteristics and representational dishes of four major Chinese cuisines (interpersonal);

- Narrate the commonly used condiments, ingredients, and cooking methods used in making Chinese food (presentational).

Day 3

- Ask and state dietary restrictions when ordering dishes (interpersonal);

- Summarize food associated with festivals and special occasions (presentational);

- Describe the steps in making scrambled eggs with tomatoes (presentational).

Day 4

- Recap the steps of making dumplings (presentational);

- Ask whether instructions have been followed correctly during dumpling-making (interpretive);

- Describe the shape and taste of dumplings, and if the experience of making dumplings is enjoyable (presentational).

Day 5

- Predict food that's needed for poor rural school children and their families (presentational);

- Summarize the dishes needed for donations in each meal for the food drive service project (presentational).

Day 6

- Ask questions about and give comments on the Chinese dishes students practiced making at home (interpersonal);

- Compare cooking methods and ingredients from the cooking videos students made (interpretive).

Day 1 (Sample Day)

Learning Objectives:

Students will be able to:

- Comment on the flavor of dishes (interpersonal);

- Ask and state choices of dishes when ordering food to share with a number of guests (interpersonal);

- Describe the similarities and differences in Western and Chinese dining customs (presentational).

Teaching Focus:

Vocabulary: Scaffolding the vocabulary learned from previous lessons and adding new words in the content of four major cuisines 四大菜系 in preparation for the next class.

- Dishes: 雪花丸子, 北京烤鸭, 麻婆豆腐, 水煮鱼, 清蒸鱼, 西红柿炒蛋, 炒青菜, 豆腐汤

- Common Chinese dishes seen in Chinese restaurants in the US: 春卷, 炒饭, 炒面, 饺子 / 锅贴, 馄饨, 青椒牛肉, 宫保鸡丁, 糖醋肉, 蛋花汤, 酸辣汤

- Beverages: 可口可乐, 百事可乐, 雪碧, 龙井, 乌龙

- Measure words: 道, 碗, 盘, 杯

- Cooking methods: 炒, 炸, 蒸, 煮, 烤

- Tastes and flavors: 酸, 甜, 苦, 辣, 油, 清淡

- Dietary restrictions: 对……过敏, 海鲜, 奶制品, 花生, 味精, 不吃 X 肉, 吃素

Grammar and sentence patterns:

- Toning down complaints using "有 (一) 点儿 + adjective"; indicating comparison using adjective + (一) 点儿

- 又 adjective/verb, 又 adjective/verb

- Comparative sentences using "A + 不如 + B (+ adjective)"

- It depends...: 这就要看……了

Learning Difficulties:

Students have a tendency to replace 有（一）点儿 with 一点儿, i.e., it is incorrect to say 清蒸鱼一点儿不新鲜. They also make mistakes by positioning the adverb 又 in the wrong place in the 又……又…… pattern. For instance, it is incorrect to say 这家饭馆儿的火锅，又肉很新鲜，又菜很辣.

Teaching Materials and Resources:

Pre-recorded ScreenFlow video for teaching new vocabulary and reviewing food-related vocabulary learned previously

- Movie: *Eat Drink Man Woman*《饮食男女》
- PPT for dish vocabulary in Chinese characters with dish images
- Sheets with dish vocabulary and matching dish images
- Pieces of paper to write down dish choices in a restaurant skit
- Textbook: *Integrated Chinese* Level Two, Part One
- PPT for dishes served in a formal Chinese dinner

Instructional Strategies:

Preview (Complete this assignment at home before Day 1, 20 minutes)

Flipped classroom instruction is a part of the teaching method for this unit. Before Day 1, students are assigned to watch a 12-minute ScreenFlow video clip for vocabulary in this unit. In the clip, the teacher touches upon topics such as main ingredients and nutrition values of the dishes introduced. For instance, snowflake meatballs (雪花丸子) using ground pork; kung pao chicken (宫保鸡丁) containing peanuts; both mapo tofu（麻婆豆腐）and water fish（水煮鱼）being potentially super spicy; 清蒸鱼 requiring very fresh fish; characters 西 and 番 in tomato 西红柿 and 番茄 suggesting non-native origin; adding ginger in 炒青菜 to balance *yin* and *yang*.

This unit rides upon the skills learned from Lesson 3 in *Integrated Chinese*, Level Two. Students are asked to complete the assignment, which is designed to check if students finished watching the pre-assigned video homework and to assess if they understand the content of the clip. There are different versions of matching questions on the worksheets to prohibit plagiarism. Another option is to post vocabulary and questions on Quizlet, and have matching questions randomly rearranged for every student.

A. Matching the names with their definitions.

1. _____ 雪花丸子　　　A. Sweet and sour pork

2. _____ 宫保鸡丁　　　B. Scrambled eggs with tomatoes

3. _____ 麻婆豆腐　　　C. Kung pao chicken

4. _____ 糖醋肉　　　　D. Snowflake meatballs

5. _____ 西红柿炒蛋　　E. Mapo tofu

B. Translation.

I would like to order three dishes, a plate of steamed fish, half a roast duck and a bowl of spicy and sour soup. In addition, I would like to have a pot of oolong tea.

C. List your dietary restrictions.

Answers: [for teacher's reference only]

A. 1. D 2. C 3. E 4. A 5. B

B. 我们想点三道菜，一盘清蒸鱼，半只烤鸭，一碗酸辣汤。另外，来四杯乌龙茶。

C. 例：我对花生过敏。

Housekeeping

Ask students to exchange homework assignments and make corrections, then collect papers.

Warm-up (S-S, Interpersonal, 10 minutes)

To enrich students' understanding of Chinese cooking experience and food culture, they are to watch a clip of the movie *Eat Drink Man Woman*《饮食男女》 (0:28-4:24), in which the retired Chef Zhu prepares dinner for the weekly family gathering. Pair the students and give them the following questions before they view the clip.

1. 电影里的朱师傅做菜的方法跟你家人的做菜方法有什么不同？

2. 他用了哪些肉？

3. 请你说说朱师傅做了一些什么菜。

Teacher shows the clip twice, the second time pausing the clip to indicate the cooking methods 炸，蒸，炖，etc., and usage of fresh meats like 有头有尾的鱼，鸡，鱿鱼，五花肉. Teacher then points out the dishes Chef Zhu makes, including steamed buns（包子），braised pork（扣肉），deep fried fish（炸鱼），stewed chicken（炖鸡），and details like cutting skills（刀法）and the presentation of dishes. Mention that although a common household wouldn't go to an extreme to make such dishes daily, authentic cooking involves a variety of methods and fresh ingredients, and does call for stir-fry and beyond. Students then perform Q&A for the above questions.

Activity 1 (In preparation for Objective 1, 20 minutes)

Purpose: To review the vocabulary that matches the images.

1. Use PPT to review old and new vocabulary words to reinforce the assignment done the night before. The PPT slides are grouped in four categories as follows. Each dish name comes with an identical image that was shown in the video assignment. Show the images one by one and call on students randomly to name them.

   1) Show the cooking method(s) for each dish, such as 炒，炸，蒸，煮，红烧 and 炖.

   2) Tastes and flavors such as 酸，甜，苦，辣，油 and 清淡.

   3) Review the measure words while going over each dish, such as 一盘红烧鱼，一碗鸡汤.

   4) Review and expand dish names based on cooking methods, ingredients, etc. For example: 炒小白菜，炒蛋，炒饭；麻婆豆腐，青菜豆腐汤，什锦豆腐.

2. Divide students into Groups A and B. Give students in Group A a sheet of paper filled with dish names and give students in Group B a sheet of paper with matching dish images (see the sample below). Each group creates a deck of cards by cutting the sheet into small cards and shuffling them. The teacher then pairs one Group A student with one Group B student. They take turns saying the dish name in Chinese, matching the pictures, and claiming the pair of cards.

The student who fails to name the dish or mismatches the cards loses a turn. Students play the matching game until they cannot make any more matches. The winners are those who claim the most pairs of cards. Teacher goes over PPT again for a quick review.

Group A: Sheet for Dish Names

水煮鱼	蛋花汤	宫保鸡丁	青椒牛肉	清蒸鱼
糖醋肉	雪花丸子	炒青菜	饺子 / 锅贴	西红柿炒蛋
炒面	春卷	炒饭	麻婆豆腐	北京烤鸭

Group B: Sheet for Dish Pictures

Activity 2 (For Objective 1, 30 minutes)

Purpose: To apply 一点儿 in commenting on the taste of dishes.

In-Activity 1: practice grammar points "有(一)点儿 + **adjective**" and "**adjective** + (一)点儿"

Teacher first points out "有一点儿 + adjective" has a tone of complaining, such as 有一点儿甜 indicating something being a bit too sweet for one's taste, while "adjective + (一) 点儿" indicating comparison, such as 甜一点儿 meaning relatively sweeter. Students form two lines facing the classroom board. Teacher calls out a sentence containing these grammar points for the first student in each line to respond (see below for the sentence examples). Students immediately mark "√" on the board if correct, and "×" if incorrect. Teacher then briefly explains the answer. Students who responded go to the end of their line, and the next students in line take next sentence, and so on. Teacher tallies the correct answers and declares the winning team.

Sample sentences:

1. 请打开窗，房间里一点儿热。(Incorrect; should be 请打开窗，房间里有(一)点儿热。)

2. 今天的清蒸鱼有(一)点儿不新鲜。(Correct)

3. 我喜欢吃有(一)点儿辣的豆腐。(Incorrect; should be 我喜欢吃辣(一)点儿的豆腐。)

4. 我要买一件便宜(一)点儿的运动服。(Correct)

5. 今天小弟弟比昨天一点儿安静。(Incorrect; should be 今天小弟弟比昨天安静(一)点儿。)

6. 做菜时盐少放有(一)点儿。(Incorrect; should be 做菜时盐少放(一)点儿 or 做菜时少放(一)点儿盐。)

Students then go online to the class Moodle page and download the following worksheet to the note-taking app on their tablet device and select the correct answers by circling either ① or ② .

Teacher projects their answers for a formative assessment.

Please circle ① for 有(一)点儿 adj. or ② for adj. 一点儿 .

1. 今天比昨天 ①冷② ，可以去滑雪。

2. 今天 ①冷② ，得穿两件毛衣。

3. 汤 ①咸② ，不太好喝。

4. 汤要 ①清淡② ，才好喝。

---

5. 宿舍①吵②，不能念书。

6. 这个饭馆的清蒸鱼①咸②，我们还是不点吧。

7. 他生病了，①不舒服②。

8. 糖醋鱼要①甜②，①酸②，才适合我的口味。

Answers [for teacher's reference]:

1.② 2.① 3.① 4.② 5.① 6.① 7.① 8.②,②

In-Activity 2: Practice grammar points "有 (一) 点儿 + adjective" and "adjective + (一) 点儿" which appear in ordering food

Group A and B students go back to their original pairs and make mild complaints about the taste from dish pictures, e.g., "麻婆豆腐味道怎么样?", to which the answer could be " 麻婆豆腐有一点儿太辣，有一点儿麻".

Activity 3 (For Objective 2, 30 minutes)

Purpose: To practice ordering dishes based on number of guests, such as 四个人点三菜一汤 , etc.

Pre-Activity

1. Introduce vocabulary of dietary restrictions: 对……过敏, 海鲜, 奶制品, 花生, 味精, 不吃 X 肉, 吃素 .

2. Go over the dialogue of Lesson 3 in *Integrated Chinese* Level Two to practice ordering dishes based on number of guests, different choices of meats, vegetables, staple foods, soups, and beverages.

3. Select groups of four from online number generator to role-play the dialogue from the textbook. Then rotate roles.

In-Activity 1: A mini-skit for ordering dishes

Students form groups of four. Distribute a dietary restriction card to each group, such as vegetarian, lactose intolerance, etc., as listed below.

对花生过敏	对海鲜过敏	对奶制品过敏	不吃 X 肉	吃素

Students are instructed to do a mini-skit about ordering food in a Chinese restaurant. They are encouraged to incorporate learned vocabulary to complete the tasks. Tasks include ordering dishes based on the number of guests and guests' dietary restrictions. Ask students to start by commenting on the dishes in the restaurant and make suggestions like "这家饭馆的牛肉做得挺地道的，特别是芥蓝牛肉，又香又嫩，点一个，怎么样？" or "这家饭馆儿的宫保鸡丁做得又香又辣，非吃不可". The student with the dietary restriction card stating 对花生过敏 needs to inform the host of their dietary restriction by saying "不好意思，我对花生过敏". Students rehearse until they are comfortable recording their skits with tablet devices. Each group saves its recording in their Dropbox for formative assessment. A sample for this skit is shown below.

Host: 这家饭馆儿的海鲜又鲜又嫩，特别是清蒸鱼，点一个，怎么样？

Guest A: 啊！我对海鲜过敏，真不好意思。

Host: 那我们点一盘雪花丸子。我觉得其他饭馆的雪花丸子都不如这儿的好吃。

Guest B: 叫半只烤鸭，怎么样？不过，烤鸭有（一）点儿油，也有（一）点儿咸，你们不在乎吧？

Guest C: 偶尔吃一次没有关系。再来一盘炒芥蓝，就够了。

Host: 还不够，再加一碗青菜豆腐汤，三菜一汤，每人一碗米饭，这样够了。想喝什么茶？

Guest A: 这就要看他们有什么茶了，最好有乌龙。

Host: 他们有乌龙。服务员，请给我们来一盘雪花丸子，半只烤鸭，一盘炒芥蓝，一碗青菜豆腐汤，四碗米饭和四杯乌龙茶。

Post-Activity

Students follow up with a handwritten list of their own choices from the skit, for example, "我们四个人点了三菜一汤：一盘清蒸鱼，一个红烧牛肉，一盘炒芥蓝，一碗酸辣汤，还点了四碗米饭和乌龙茶". Teacher collects the lists for participation grade.

Activity 4 (For Objective 3, 28 minutes)

Purposes:

1. To compare Chinese food culture to students' food culture;

2. To practice beyond the sentence level, on progression of ideas including personal experiences.

Pre-Activity

Students receive a formal Chinese banquet menu (see Appendix 2) and view a PPT for dish pictures. Teacher asks students to pay attention to 先上什么菜，再上什么，最后上什么？有哪几种肉？有什么青菜？有什么做法？是蒸的，炸的，还是炒的？ As part of food culture, students also watch a clip " 十大抢付账理由 " from YouTube, at https://www.youtube.com/watch?v=xQJ-c06E7gM about the art of paying the bill.

In-Activity: Peer learning

Pair a strong student with a less-engaged student in discussing the following six guiding questions.

---

1. 在餐馆里吃西餐只点自己要吃的菜，吃中餐也是这样吗？

2. 中餐上菜的顺序 (shùnxù) 跟西餐一样吗？

3. 中餐的主食跟西餐有什么不同？

4. 吃西餐用刀叉，吃中餐也用刀叉吗？

5. 中餐最常见的做法是蒸、炒、煮，西餐呢？

6. 吃中餐跟吃西餐还有什么不同？

The focus is on similarities and differences between Chinese and Western dining customs and the encouragement of peer teaching and learning. Based on their consensus from discussions, students move on to record their replies to the six questions online. The tasks are to address six prompts without delay and support them with three cohesive sentences and correct cultural registers. Fluency, accuracy in pronunciation, application of higher-level vocabulary, and complex sentence structures are in the rubrics for this formative assessment. The response time to each question is limited to 20 seconds to align with AP Conversation requirements. The answers could vary. See the Holistic Conversation Rubric in Appendix 3.

Post-Activity: Writing assignment on comparisons of Western dining and Chinese dining

Students collaborate and compose a paragraph based on their discussions of and responses to the six questions raised previously. They are instructed to use that paragraph as the core of their written assignment and add a beginning, a middle, and an end. Students need to pay attention to the cohesiveness of writing and application of vocabulary and grammatical structures (See Appendix 4 for Holistic Writing Rubric). Students might not have enough time to finish their draft before the class ends, but time should be allocated for them to ask questions and seek guidance if needed. Students know that turning to Google Translate for quick answers takes away the opportunity to process learning. Teacher asks students to finish the writing as a homework assignment and upload it to Google Drive and share it with teacher. The following writing is based on the responses from the six questions asked and is a student sample of this assignment.

我学中文学了四年多了，对中国文化很有兴趣，特别是饮食文化。去年我到中国旅行了十天，吃了各种不同的中国菜，我觉得吃中餐跟吃西餐很不一样。要是在西餐馆点菜，只要点自己要吃的菜就行了，所以每个人只吃一种主菜。但是在中餐馆点的菜是大家一起吃的，因此可以吃到不同的菜。吃西餐一般来说先上开胃菜，再上面包和汤，然后上主菜，最后上甜点和咖啡。中餐呢，先上茶，再上冷盘，然后上不同的主菜，吃完主菜，才吃主食。中餐的主食要么是米饭，要么是面食。汤和水果最后才上。吃西餐和中餐的餐具也不同，西餐用不同的刀、叉和汤匙，吃中餐只要用一双筷子和汤匙，比吃西餐简单得多。不过，做中餐一点儿也不简单，做法除了蒸、炒、煮以外，还有煎、炸、烤等。西餐大半是烤的和煮的，做法没有中餐那么五花八门。我在中国旅行的时候，觉得中国人吃饭时很轻松，很开心，没有吃西餐那么安静。这让我觉得学习中国饮食文化对认识中国文化很有好处。

Activity 5 (To end the class, 2 minutes)

Before the class ends, teacher shows students a one-minute song "送你葱" from YouTube at https://www.youtube.com/watch?v=6_uP6vrEHXk (1:05-2:10). The lyrics contains a total of seventeen meats and vegetables: 鸡腿, 鸡翅膀, 鸭腿, 鸭翅膀, 胡萝卜, 番茄, 大葱, 荠菜, 香菜, 芹菜, 大白菜, 辣椒, 西兰花, 黄瓜, 四季豆, 刀豆, 青橄榄. After watching the clip, teacher reads out the items in the lyrics, and students are to fold a finger whenever they recognize an item. Teacher goes over the list again with translation. Teacher quickly moves to the classroom door and hands out 利市糖 saying "送你糖" to bid students 再见 until next class.

Appendix 1: 四大菜系

Note: this reading piece can be used as a reading exercise, an assessment tool, and/or a review to summarize the unit content.

中国的四大菜系

中国由于地理、气候、农产品、习俗的不同，产生了不同的饮食习惯。长江以北多产小麦，人们以面食为主食；长江以南产稻米，人们以米饭为主食。一般来说，北方菜比较咸，南方菜比较甜。

中国地方饭菜各有特色，形成了不同的菜系。鲁菜、川菜、粤菜、苏菜被称为中国的四大菜系。鲁菜又叫山东菜，是宫廷菜的代表，讲究鲜嫩，以汤、海鲜出名，比如雪花丸子。川菜的特色在酸、甜、麻、辣，代表菜是麻婆豆腐。粤菜就是广东菜，粤菜的材料多到几千种，做法有煲、炸、蒸等，有名的菜有蚝油牛肉。苏菜又叫淮阳菜，注重刀工和颜色，口味咸中带甜，有名的菜有盐水鸭。

中国饭菜色、香、味俱全，吃中国饭菜是一大享受！

Appendix 2: Content and PPT for Chinese Dining

菜单

凉菜:	糯米藕	盐水鸭	凉拌凉瓜	
点心:	小豆凉糕			
热菜:	全家福	宫保虾球	红烧猪蹄	辣子鸡丁

	清蒸鱼	百合龙豆	肉末烧饼	
面点和水果：	宫廷面点	水果拼盘		

凉菜

全家福

宫保虾球

红烧猪蹄

辣子鸡丁

清蒸鱼

百合龙豆

肉末烧饼

宫廷面点

水果拼盘

Appendix 3: Holistic Conversation Rubric

Rating	Ability of Interaction	Delivery	Application of Vocabulary	Application of Grammar
10-8 Demonstrates High Proficiency	Demonstrates high ability of interaction with thorough answers	Speaks in articulate, flowing manner with minimal accent	Rich vocabulary and idioms with minimal errors	Wide range of grammatical structures with minimal errors
7-6 Clearly Demonstrates Proficiency	Demonstrates interaction with appropriate response and sufficient details	Speaks in acceptable pronunciation with some hesitation	Shows control of vocabulary with some errors in expression	General usage of grammatical structures with some errors
5-4 Demonstrates Progression Towards Proficiency	Demonstrates limited ability in interaction with insufficient details	Speaking with errors in pronunciation and unnatural hesitation	Simple vocabulary with limited control	Limited control of grammatical structures

| 3-2 Demonstrates Need for Major Intervention | Demonstrates little ability in interaction | Errors in pronunciation inhibit communication; excessive hesitation | Shows little control of vocabulary | Shows basic errors in grammar |
| 1-0 Unacceptable | Demonstrates no ability to interact | | | |

Appendix 4: Holistic Writing Rubric

Rating	Response to Prompts	Cohesiveness and Register	Application of Vocabulary	Application of Grammar
10-8 Demonstrates High Proficiency	Thorough response to prompts with elaboration	Ideas presented logically with cohesive devices; correct register	Rich vocabulary and idioms with minimum errors	Wide range of grammatical structures with minimum errors
7-6 Clearly Demonstrates Proficiency	Thorough response to prompts	Ideas presented loosely organized; sporadic register problems	General usage of vocabulary with some errors	General usage of grammatical structures with some errors
5-4 Demonstrates Progression Towards Proficiency	Partial response to prompts	Some attempts at organization, but sequencing very loose; major register problems	Problems with vocabulary usage	Limited grammatical structures
3-2 Demonstrates Need for Major Intervention	Insufficient response to prompts	Lack of organization; uses phrases or single words; lack of proper register	Significant vocabulary errors	Significant grammatical errors
1-0 Unacceptable	Clearly did not respond to prompts			

Jeannine Fan Subisak (范良琦) founded the Chinese program at Columbus Academy, Ohio in 1997. She teaches middle school and high school. She received her Ph.D. from Pennsylvania State University. Her professional credentials include teaching at the heritage Columbus Chinese Academy. She has been an Ohio State University Chinese CAAP Testing committee member, a State of Ohio Foreign Language Content Standards Revision Advisory member, an AP Chinese test scoring Table Leader and Question Leader to the annual ACTFL and OFLA conventions. She has served on CLASS and OFLA boards and as the president of OATC.

Dining in a Chinese Restaurant

Yan Zhao (赵燕)
Pershing Middle School, Houston, Texas

Language Proficiency Level: Intermediate Low

Age Range: 13-14 (8th Grade)

Class Size: 16 students

Time Frame: 90 minutes per lesson, 5 lessons in total

Essential Questions:

- How does food shape, as well as reflect, a culture?

- What special significance does Chinese food carry in Chinese culture?

- How do we explore and describe Chinese food culture without stereotyping it?

Unit Goals:

After learning this unit, students will be able to use culturally and linguistically appropriate language to order food and talk about different flavors of food. The optimal goal is to improve students' language proficiency skills by developing their ability to interact effectively in cultural contexts. Consequently, students participate actively in multicultural communities and become lifelong learners.

Standards: Based on National Standards for Foreign Language Learning

- **Communication:**

  -Interpersonal (1.1): Students engage in conversations related to Chinese food and exchange information about dining in a Chinese restaurant.

  -Interpretive (1.2): Students understand and interpret written and spoken language related to the unit topic by watching video clips and reading authentic language material (menus, grocery store weekly ads).

  -Presentational (1.3): Students are asked to present both orally and in writing about the unit topic.

- **Culture:** Students demonstrate understanding of Chinese food and dining culture by sharing their personal experience with Chinese food.

- **Connection:** Students gain perspective on Chinese food culture in terms of geographic locations of different regions.

- **Comparison:** Students observe, reflect on, and compare similarities and differences between restaurant dining in Chinese culture and American culture.

- **Community:** Students are encouraged to participate, e.g., dining in Chinese restaurants and going to Chinese cultural events in the local multicultural/ multilingual community. Students are also taught how to use community resources to benefit their learning, e.g., visiting the Asia Society Texas Center, exploring Chinese culture websites and the Internet, and reading books on related topics from the school and public libraries.

Unit Questions:

- Can students talk about Chinese food they like and ask about someone else's preferences?

- Can students order food in a Chinese restaurant using linguistically and culturally appropriate language?

- Can students ask for a check after a meal and pay for it?

- Can students ask and describe how food tastes?

- Can students apply courteous expressions when ordering food in a Chinese restaurant?

Lesson Outlines:

Day 1: Talking about if one likes Chinese food 我喜欢吃中国饭

Day 2: Excuse me, do you have...? 请问，你们有酸辣汤吗?

Day 3: How much in total? 一共多少钱?

Day 4: Commenting on tastes of various dishes 包子真好吃!

Day 5: Presentation: A glimpse of Chinese food culture 中国菜知多少

Learning Objectives:

Students will be able to:

Day 1

- Identify major categories of Chinese food (staple foods, dishes, and soups) (interpretive);

- Talk about their food preferences using 喜欢吃 / 喜欢喝 and 你喜欢吃 / 喜欢喝……吗? (interpersonal);

- Ask and respond to questions about availability of certain food and dishes (interpersonal).

Day 2

- Inquire about and order food by applying correct measure words to different staple foods, dishes, soups, and drinks (interpersonal);

- Read authentic menus with help of visuals (interpretive);

- Present some food items and dishes on the menu of a Chinese restaurant (presentational).

Day 3

- Understand conversion system of US$ and Chinese RMB (interpretive);

- Order food and drinks using linguistically and culturally appropriate language in the restaurant setting (interpersonal);

- Create an illustrated menu of an imaginary Chinese restaurant (presentational) (see Closure for detailed instructions for this assignment).

Day 4

- Describe how different food tastes (presentational);

- Discuss prices and quantities (interpersonal);

- Role-play an ordering food scenario with a partner (interpersonal);

- Understand and interpret authentic restaurant scenarios by watching video clips (interpretive).

Day 5

- Inquire about the menu, order food, ask prices, and pay bills (interpersonal);

- Give an oral presentation of their project on Chinese food (presentational).

Day 1 (Sample Day)

Learning Objectives:

Students will be able to:

- Identify major categories of Chinese food (staple foods, dishes, and soups) (interpretive);

- Talk about their food preferences using 喜欢吃 / 喜欢喝 and 你喜欢吃 / 喜欢喝……吗？ (interpersonal);

- Ask and respond to questions about availability of certain food and dishes (interpersonal).

Teaching Focus:

Grammar:

- Affirmative-Negative (A-not-A) questions

- Question with the end-of-sentence particle 吗 ?

- 请问 used before a question

Vocabulary:

- Common names of frequently consumed Chinese food/dishes

Phonetics:

- Initials "c" and "ch" as in 醋 , 春卷 , and 茶

Learning Difficulties:

- Forming a question is usually more difficult than answering a question. Students may miss the question mark 吗 when using 你们有……吗?

- It may be difficult to form the question 你们有没有……?

Teaching Materials and Resources:

- PPT showing different images of dishes and food

- Video clips about Chinese food culture in English and scenarios of ordering food in a Chinese restaurant in simple Chinese

- Pictures of Chinese food

- Pictures of common American food and beverages

- Authentic bilingual menu from local Chinese restaurants

- Bamboo clappers (竹板)

- *Kuaile Hanyu* (《快乐汉语》(Vol. 1)) by 人民教育出版社 (People's Education Press, Beijing, PRC)

- *Far East Everyday Chinese* (《远东天天中文》(Vols. 1 & 2)) by The Far East Book Co., Ltd.

Instructional Strategies:

Warm-up: Do It Now (5 minutes)

Rationale: A short activity that teacher has written on the board or at students' desks puts students to work when they enter the room. Students are held accountable since there should be a written product from it.

Students write five sentences using the given structures: 喜欢吃，喜欢喝，不喜欢吃，不喜欢喝，……喜欢吃……吗？The words for food, fruits, and drinks, with pictures, are displayed in the pocket chart. This short activity connects new learning to prior knowledge (students have learned how to use the above mentioned expressions and words) and sets a purpose for the lesson.

Teacher doesn't check answers with students, but may respond to questions. Class will revisit the above sentence patterns in Tasks 2 and 3.

Task 1: Can you use chopsticks? (10 minutes)

Purpose:

To help students gain understanding of Chinese food culture, and identify major categories of Chinese food (staple foods, dishes, and soups).

The Hook:

Show students pictures of Chinese meals served in the restaurant, Chinese food ingredients, Chinese cooking utensils, and chopsticks in PPT; also display pages from the English juvenile book *The Food of China*. This short introductory moment aims to build curiosity about the new topic, which in turn yields deeper engagement.

Rationale:

This task gives teacher a chance to assess whether students have grasped the information presented before moving on to next phase of instruction. Teacher gets immediate feedback. It also provides opportunity for discussion.

Pre-Task

Use PPT to briefly introduce Chinese food culture and its regional differences; explain the key cultural elements.

1. Different types and styles of Chinese food, e.g., 炒饭, 炒面, 包子, 饺子 vs. 炒菜, 糖醋鱼, 宫保鸡丁, 烤鸭.

2. Different kinds of chopsticks and how to use them, modeling the verb 夹.

3. Chinese cooking and its commonly used utensils.

In-Task

1. Students read aloud the Chinese food vocabulary and expressions presented in visuals: 炒饭, 包子, 饺子, 炒面, 北京烤鸭, 蛋花汤, 春卷, 夹.

2. Teacher then points to each picture of the above expressions by asking 这是什么？ Students answer the teacher's questions as a group using the 这是 N structure, such as 这是炒饭.

3. Teacher passes chopsticks to students and shows students how to use them by using the verb 夹 and the food names practiced in steps 1 and 2.

4. Students practice using chopsticks while saying: 夹炒面, 夹包子, 夹饺子, 夹鱼, 夹鸡丁, 夹炒菜, 夹春卷, 夹烤鸭 based on the pictures from the PPT that teacher is presenting.

Task 2: Chanting allegro 快板 : 你们喜欢吃什么？ (14 minutes)

Purpose:

Students will be able to identify major categories of Chinese food (staple foods, dishes, and soups).

Practice:

- New vocabulary and expressions used in sentences
- Questions with 喜欢 and 喜欢不喜欢

Rationale:

This task enhances interpersonal communicative skills through rhythms using simple Chinese structures. It also helps students internalize new vocabulary in meaningful contexts through meaningful activities.

Input (5 minutes): Introduce and review Chinese food names with visual aids and PPT:

主食 (面食, 米饭), 菜 , 汤

Staple foods and dishes: 饺子 , 包子 , 米饭 , 蛋炒饭 , 炒面 , 春卷 , 糖醋鱼 , 宫保鸡丁 , 北京烤鸭

Soups: 酸辣汤 ， 蛋花汤

Drinks: 冰水 , 可乐 , 茶

Pre-Task

Briefly review the structures 你喜欢吃什么？/ 你喜欢喝什么？and 我喜欢吃……/ 我喜欢喝……, e.g., 我喜欢吃蛋炒饭。我喜欢喝酸辣汤。

1. Do a model Q&A with a couple of students.

2. Pair students up and have each pair conduct their own Q&A. The teacher circulates around the room and gives feedback.

In-Task

1. Teacher leads the class in reading the lines of the chant, which is on the board or in PPT.

2. Teacher models the dialogue with a couple of students.

3. Class divides into Group A and Group B.

4. Each group has its own designated food/drinks. 我 / 你 change into 我们 / 你们 in this group dialogue.

Group A	Group B
你们喜欢吃什么？	我们喜欢吃饺子。
你们喜欢喝什么？	我们喜欢喝奶茶。
你们喜欢吃什么？	我们喜欢吃烤鸭。
你们喜欢喝什么？	我们喜欢喝可乐。
你们喜欢吃什么？	我们喜欢吃炒面。
你们喜欢喝什么？	我们喜欢喝酸辣汤。

5. Reverse group roles twice so that students have ample time to practice and internalize the structure.

   Note: My students have been familiar with the basic rhythms of 快板 since 7th grade.

Post-Task

Check students' learning by drawing a few names from the **Go-Around Cup**. The classroom Go-Around Cup is a cup of Popsicle sticks which each have a student's name on them. It gives the teacher the option of either randomly or intentionally picking students to answer questions. The teacher can identify the learning level and learning style of each student to determine who is chosen.

Task 3: Inside-Outside Circle (18 minutes)

Purpose:

To have students talk about their food preferences.

Practice:

喜欢吃 / 喜欢喝 and 你喜欢吃 / 喜欢喝……吗?

Rationale:

The activity encourages interaction and holds every student accountable for active participation.

Teacher can use this activity as a formative assessment by standing in the center of the circle and listening to students' dialogues.

Pre-Task

Use visuals to review structures students have learned.

1. Demonstrate the sample sentence.

2. Students practice with a partner.

Student: 您喜欢吃什么?	Teacher modeling: 我喜欢吃……。
Student: 你喜欢喝什么?	Student: 我喜欢喝……。
Student: 你喜欢喝可乐吗?	Student: 我不喜欢喝可乐。
Student: 你喜欢喝冰水吗?	Student: 我不喜欢喝冰水。我喜欢喝茶.

In-Task

1. Form two concentric circles containing the same number of students. Students

standing in the inside circle face their partners in the outside circle. Students from the inside circle ask their partners two questions:

a. 你喜欢吃什么？你喜欢喝什么？

Students from the outside circle answer the questions in complete sentences:

b. 我喜欢吃……。我喜欢喝……。

2. Students reverse roles. Students from the outside circle ask the same questions.

3. Teacher asks the inside circle to rotate (clockwise) and students turn to face their new partner.

4. Repeat steps 2 and 3, but with two different questions: 你喜欢吃……吗？你喜欢喝……吗？ If students answer in the negative, they then need to give an affirmative statement about their preference to make the answer complete.

Note: Teacher serves as a facilitator, coaching and scaffolding, while students are interacting with their peers. The advantage of this activity is that it engages all students simultaneously. This activity can also serve as an assessment tool.

Post-Task

Teacher will call two or three pairs of students to perform the dialogue before the group as formative assessment.

Task 4: Simultaneous Round Table (20 minutes)

Purpose:

Students ask and respond to questions to create a simple menu and inquire about availability of certain food or dishes in a Chinese restaurant. (Interpersonal)

Practice:

- Form a question with 吗
- Form a question with 有没有
- Use 请问 in meaningful context when making an inquiry

Rationale:

Simultaneous Round Table encourages students to work with each other in cooperative learning groups as they learn from and support each other.

Pre-Task

1. Briefly review the sentence pattern 你有……吗？/ 你有……没有？ by using items on students' desks or in the classroom.

   Example: 你有巧克力吗？

   有巧克力。/ 我没有巧克力。

   老师有英文书吗？老师没有英文书，老师有中文书。

2. Explain briefly that 请问 is a polite way to get people's attention before asking a question. Then demonstrate how to use it in meaningful contexts using PPT pictures.

   Example: 请问，你们有没有冰茶？

   请问，你们有饺子吗？

3. Students practice starting a question with 请问 in pairs, using PPT pictures as cue.

   Example: 请问，你们有没有北京烤鸭？

   请问，你们有筷子吗？

In-Task

1. Divide class into groups of four. Each student in the group is given a piece of paper. The papers are labeled with a team number rather than students' own names because the paper will be passed around the group.

2. Teacher poses four requests in Chinese: 请写一个中国菜的名字。请写一个主食的名字。请写一个汤的名字。请写一个饮料的名字。Each student writes four names on the given paper, then passes it to each group member four times. Each time the paper is passed to the next student, they must read aloud what is already on the list. This allows students to review the noun phrases individually, yet with support from peers. An example from a student-generated list could read: 烤鸭, 炒饭, 冰茶, 蛋花汤.

3. Students in each group then categorize what they have generated in writing into menu form and prepare to orally introduce their menu in simple but clear Chinese. The presentation should have a beginning (greeting), use the 有 structure, and have at least four staple food items, four dishes, and four soups/drinks. Each student needs to write their group's menu down as well (for Task 5).

4. One student from each group presents their menu to the class. All students take notes on note sheets.

Post-Task

Teacher applies ***Cold Call*** technique to assess students' learning. To cold call is to call on students regardless of whether they have raised their hands.

Task 5: Role-Play (Dialogues between customer and waiter/waitress, 20 minutes)

Purposes:

1. To have students talk about and explain their food preferences using 喜欢吃 / 喜欢喝 and 你喜欢吃 / 喜欢喝……吗？ (Interpersonal)

2. To have students ask and respond to questions about availability of certain food and dishes. (Interpersonal)

Practice:

● Start a question with 请问

● Ask questions using 有

Rationale:

● This task enhances the skills of politely making a request or asking a question.

● Students practice the negation form of 有 as 没有 .

● It also prepares students for more comprehensive tasks such as ordering food, describing how foods/dishes taste, and paying bills.

In-Task

1. Teacher explains and models the task with a student first, and then with the whole class twice.

2. Teacher explains the rubrics (see Appendix) for this task.

3. Students are divided into four groups. Students in Group 1 and Group 3 find partners in Group 2 and Group 4 to practice dialogues between customer and waiter/waitress based on the information they have on their menu.

The dialogue needs to have at least four questions, proper use of 请问，and all the answers be in complete sentences.

Example dialogue:

> Waiter: 您好！这是菜单。
>
> Customer: 你好！请问，有包子吗？（主食）
>
> Waiter: 我们没有包子，我们有饺子。
>
> Customer: 你们有没有糖醋鱼？（菜）
>
> Waiter: 我们有糖醋鱼。
>
> Customer: 请问，你们有蛋花汤吗？（汤）
>
> Waiter: 我们没有蛋花汤，我们有酸辣汤。
>
> Customer: 请问，有可乐吗？（饮料）
>
> Waiter: 我们没有可乐。我们有冰水和茶。

4. Teacher asks pairs to present their dialogue in the front of the classroom. Teacher listens, takes notes, and scores each pair using the rubrics (see the Appendix).

Assessment:

Assessment is ongoing and embedded into the 90-minute instruction period. The teacher can constantly evaluate students' learning and make instructional adjustments.

All tasks serve as formative assessments to provide students with immediate feedback. They can also be used by the teacher to monitor his/her teaching. Please see Appendix for Rubrics for Tasks 2-5.

Closure (5 minutes):

Assignments:

1. Students are encouraged to visit local Chinese restaurants with parents and bring names of their favorite Chinese dishes to share with classmates.

2. Students will create an illustrated menu of an imaginary Chinese restaurant. The restaurant should have a name. The menu will look neat and appealing and needs to have at least four items in each category (staple foods, dishes, and

soups/drinks). Four illustrations are required for the menu. Each student will present the menu to class the third time they meet.

Exit Ticket:

Each student will answer two questions using 你喜欢吃什么？你喜欢喝什么？ posed by the teacher before exiting classroom.

Instructional Reflections:

What went well? What didn't go as expected?

What changes or adjustments should teacher make for next lesson?

Appendix: Rubric for Assessing Oral Performance

	4	3	2	1
Task Completion	Fully completed	80% completed	50% completed	Less than 50% completed
Comprehensibility	Fully comprehensible to the audience	80% comprehensible to the audience	50% comprehensible to the audience	The audience barely understands what the speaker wants to say
Fluency	Near-native speech flow	Fluent, but with some hesitation	Understandable with frequent pauses	Halting speech with long pauses/ incomplete sentences that interfere with comprehension
Vocabulary	Accurate use of vocabulary, 1 or no errors	Adequate use of vocabulary, 2 to 3 errors	Somewhat adequate use of vocabulary, 4 to 5 errors	Poor use of vocabulary, 5 or more errors
Grammar	No errors	1 to 2 errors	3 errors	4 or more errors

Yan Zhao（赵燕）teaches Chinese at Pershing Middle School in Houston Independent School District. She served as an instructor for the 2012 and 2013 Rice University STARTALK Chinese Student Program and participated in the STARTALK Texas Teacher Program at the University of Houston. She also has extensive experience in teaching English as a second language in Texas public schools. As a faculty member, she taught for seven years in the Department of English at Shandong University, where she received both her B.A. degrees and M.A. in English Language and Literature.

Critique

Chinese Food Culture – Jeannine Fan Subisak
Dining in a Chinese Restaurant – Yan Zhao

"Dining" is a popular theme in any language curriculum. Using the same theme, Jeannine Fan Subisak and Yan Zhao put different focuses in their curriculum selection and instruction implementation. Subisak targets students at a relatively higher language proficiency level. She offers a rich curriculum that encompasses regional food, distinctive features of dishes, cooking methods and ingredients, healthy food choices, and food allergy concerns. The curriculum is summarized neatly into four categories (Activity 1) which help students understand the content easily and learn the vocabulary rapidly. Zhao cleverly narrows down the topic to "dining in a Chinese restaurant" which allows the advantage of greater focus. In a restaurant, people cannot escape being exposed to 5Cs: what kind of ethnic food (Culture and Comparison), budgeting (Connection), reading the menu and ordering (interpretive and interpersonal Communication), and using the language among friends and with waitstaff (Community).

In designing the curriculum, Subisak carefully combines language form and function and integrates food culture. The language forms, for example, include various basic structures, but pose challenges for acquisition: 有（一）点儿 + adjective versus adjective +（一）点儿；A 对 B 过敏；这就要看……

了；先 verb, 再 verb, 最后 verb; and comparative sentences such as A + 不 如 + B (+ adjective). The instruction directs students' attention not only to the form but also to the function. For example, Subisak pinpoints that "有 (一) 点儿 + adjective" has the tone of a complaint, such as 有 (一) 点儿 甜 indicating something a bit too sweet, whereas "adjective + (一) 点儿" indicates comparison, such as 甜 (一) 点儿 meaning relatively sweeter. She creates context for students, starting with identification tasks in reading. Gradually the exercises become more challenging; students must interact to complain about flavors of dishes in communication, as illustrated in Activity 2.

Both designs offer various well-structured activities. Zhao starts her lesson with a warm-up activity which not only checks students' homework for preparation, but also connects new learning to prior knowledge. She continues with an interesting question: "Can you use chopsticks?" The continued activity categorizes food, such as 主食, 菜, 汤, and 饮料, which helps learners understand that 主食 is an important concept in Chinese food culture. Zhao pays attention to language function and designs activities for students to make appropriate requests by using "请问, ……?" Subisak assigns students to watch a video clip in which the teacher touches upon topics such as main ingredients and nutrition values. Her warm-up activity immediately arouses students' interest in Chinese food culture in a daily setting. Her class activities are based on real-world tasks, including discussions of ordering food, diet preferences, food allergies, and different dietary restrictions, as well as language functions such as persuasion and making apologies and suggestions.

Language is acquired through experience and reflecting on experience to develop an accurate understanding. Subisak's design provides activities in which students use the language at the vocabulary level (Activity 1), sentence level (Activity 2), and discourse level (Activities 3 and 4). The requirements for language experience via interaction become more and more challenging, and include diet balance, investigating dining habits across cultures, and reporting one's discoveries to the class. The six questions provided in Activity 4 summarize the cultural differences in the areas of food content, cuisine, table manners, and the eating sequence. With such step-by-step instructional scaffolding, it is not a surprise that students successfully accomplished their projects, as demonstrated in Activity 4. Zhao's design also gives students many opportunities for language use: for example, 快板歌 is a lively tool for students to practice a dialogue in a group and use role-play to simulate a restaurant situation. Having students create a restaurant menu imparts a sense of responsibility for their task completion. Students practice the language repeatedly but with enthusiasm, because the methods are interesting and the content is useful. Both designs offer multiple instructional strategies. Regardless of what the strategies may be (e.g., Do Now, the Hook, Around-Cup, Simultaneous Round Table, or Cold Call, as they appear in the designs), rationales are provided, and readers may find the instructional strategies and tips useful.

Two major students' performances, the group skits in Activity 3 and students' discussion answering questions on cross-cultural dining in Activity 4, are both recorded in Subisak's design. It is easy to see the advantage of recording the performances. Class time is saved and the AP Conversation test is assimilated, but it is equally important for students to share their experience in class so that they learn from each other, especially when the activity is a skit performance. In Subisak's design, Teaching Focus may need further alignments with learning contents and activities. For example, frequently used expressions such as 非 V. 不可 and A 对 B 过敏 could have been listed under Teaching Focus. The interactions in Zhao's design are many but sometimes seem to be less communicative, given their focus on vocabulary. For example, the dialogue in Task 1 "- 这是什么？ - 这是炒饭" does not seem to be meaningful in the context. Perhaps different sentence patterns could be included to make learning more progressive in terms of difficulty and length of communicative exchanges.

Theme 4

Travel

Getting Around: Directions and Transportation

Xiaoyun Matthewson (张晓云)
Lakeside School, Seattle, Washington

Language Proficiency Level: Intermediate Low

Age Range: 14-18 (9th to 12th grade)

Class Size: 15-20 students

Time Frame:

45 minutes for Days 1-2 and Days 4-5, 75 minutes for Day 3; 5 lessons in total

Essential Questions:

- Does how we travel/get around reflect who we are as a culture?

- How does modern transportation shrink the world?

Unit Goals:

To help students ask for and give directions, to discuss distance and modes of transportation, to compare travel options in terms of convenience, speed, and cost, and to discuss relative positions of places.

Standards: Based on the National Standards for Foreign Language Learning

- **Communication:** -Interpersonal (1.1) -Interpretive (1.2) -Presentational (1.3)

- **Connection:** Knowledge of travel from other disciplines such as social studies; map reading skills (3.1).

- **Comparison:** Popular modes of transportation in the US and China (4.2).

- **Culture:** Getting around in China; the changing face of modern China through the lens of transportation: from bicycle-to-bicycle to bumper-to-bumper, and from bus to high speed railway (2.1).

Unit Questions:

- Can students ask, follow, and give directions?

- Can students use correct phrases to describe relative positions of places and locations?

- Can students discuss and compare different modes of transportation?

- Can students discuss the distance between two places?

- Can students compare different means of transportation in regard to cost, speed, and convenience?

- Can students discuss how long it takes to get to a place using a specific means of transportation?

- Can students plan or recommend travel options based on cost, speed, and convenience?

Lesson Outlines:

Day 1: Asking for and giving directions 问路和指路

Day 2: More on giving and following directions 从这儿往前走（指路和找方向）

Day 3: Compare modes of transportation 比较交通工具

Day 4: Taking the bus is the best 坐公交车最好

Day 5: How long does it take to get there? 到那儿要多长时间？

Learning Objectives:

Students will be able to:

Day 1

- Use different ways to ask for directions (interpersonal);

- Explain a general sense of distances (interpersonal);

- Understand and name positional terms and key vocabulary for giving directions (interpretive);

- Follow and give simple directional commands (interpretive and interpersonal).

Day 2

- Give directions from point A to point B using traffic lights and streets as reference points (interpersonal);

- Identify the destination relative to the traveler when the destination is reached (interpersonal);

- Follow directions on the map and ask for clarification when needed (interpretive and interpersonal).

Day 3

- Name and understand modes of transportation and related verbs (interpretive);

- Discuss speed and cost of different modes of transportation (interpersonal and presentational);

- Discuss travel/commuting habits (interpersonal and presentational);

- Present favorite mode of transportation for school commute, and the reasons for it (presentational).

Day 4

- Discuss specific modes of transportation using frequency words – 每天, 常常, 很少, 从来不, etc. (interpersonal);

- Use more advanced comparative structures to make more sophisticated comparisons of different modes of transportation (interpretive and interpersonal);

- Articulate preferences for a given mode of transportation over others, using extended discourse markers such as 不但……而且……, 还有, etc. (presentational).

Day 5

- Ask about distances between any two given locations (interpersonal);

- Discuss distance in terms of travel time using different modes of transportation (interpersonal);

- Make travel plans or give recommendations based on cost, travel time, etc. (presentational).

Day 3 (Sample Day)

Learning Objectives:

Students will be able to:

- Name and understand modes of transportation and related verbs (interpretive);

- Discuss speed and cost of different modes of transportation (interpersonal and presentational);

- Discuss travel/commuting habits (interpersonal and presentational);

- Present favorite modes of transportation for school commute, and the reasons for it (presentational).

Teaching Focus:

Grammar:

- Comparative structures:

  A 比 B + adjective

  B 没有 A (那么) + adjective

Vocabulary:

- Modes of transportation: 汽车, 公共汽车, 校车, 飞机, 火车, 地铁, 出租汽车, 马 , 自行车

- Different verbs for the word "riding":

  坐 + 飞机 / 火车 / 汽车 / 公共汽车 / 船 / 地铁

  坐出租汽车 = 打的

  骑 + 自行车 / 马 (and other large animals)

Phonetics:

- Homograph 的 in "打的"

- "chu" vs. "qu"

Learning Difficulties:

- It can be confusing to students that there are several different Chinese verbs for the English word "ride".

- Chinese has several different terms for taxi which reflect geographical origin and preference.

- In comparative structures, the items being compared have to be symmetric, i.e., both have to be nouns, noun phrases, or verb nouns (gerund). For example, 飞机比火车快 and 坐飞机比坐火车快 are both acceptable, but one cannot say 汽车比走路快 .

- The degree adverb 很 cannot appear before an adjective in comparison sentences. It is incorrect to say 飞机比火车很快 .

- When making a negative comparison the structure A 没有 B······ (那么) adjective is used rather than using 比 with the negation of the adjective, e.g., it's not correct to say 我的中文比他的不好 .

Teaching Materials and Resources:

- Images of different modes of transportation on PPT/Smartboard

- Names of different modes of transportation on PPT/Smartboard

- Grammatical structures on PPT/Smartboard

- *Encounters* Chinese Book I

- Video clips of city street scenes of a Chinese city that show different modes of transportation (optional)

- Still shots of street/airport scenes with various modes of transportation

- Sets of word/picture cards of modes of transportation for pair work

Instructional Strategies:

Warm-up (5 minutes)

The students have previewed the vocabulary of transportation modes the day before as homework. Watch a short clip on how people in China get around. Then show a few still shots of street/airport scenes. Ask students to identify as many modes of transportation as they see.

1. 你看到什么交通工具?

   It's OK if students give some of the names in English, but repeat back the names in Chinese.

2. 照片上的人在做什么?

   Point to the pedestrians, bicyclists and bus riders and model for students to say 他在走路，这个女孩子在骑自行车 etc., even though at this point most of them do not know the appropriate verb for different modes of transportation.

Activity 1 (For Objective 1, 20 minutes)

Purpose: To practice new vocabulary and expressions in context.

1. Use PowerPoint or Smartboard to introduce the names of modes of transportation. Make sure the students know the tones and help them pronounce the words correctly.

2. Introduce verbs expressing the meaning of "ride", 坐 and 骑, with 打的 as a special case imported from Cantonese dialect. Point to the images of modes of transportation and ask the class to give the verb phrase such as 坐公共汽车, 骑自行车. Encourage students to act out 坐 or 骑 as they give the answer.

3. Learning characters: Selectively explain the meaning of individual characters creatively. For example, think about a bicycle as a self-propelled vehicle, an airplane as a flying machine, and the subway as metal underground. Direct

students to recognize common radicals such as "water", "foot", "hand" and "metal" from the characters 汽, 路, 打, and 铁. Break up more complex characters into simple components to tell stories that can be related to the meaning of the character and/or to encourage students to think if they have learned other characters with the same component. For example, break up 骑 into 马 and 奇. Explain that 马 gives the meaning and 奇 gives the sound, and encourage students to come up with characters such as 妈 and 吗 they have already known and review the word 奇怪.

4. Formative assessment: Ask a few students to come to the front of the class to act out both modes of transportation and verb phrases, and have the rest of the class describe what they are trying to do. The volunteers are given cues by the teacher, either by whispering or showing word cards, for acting out. The same phrases can be repeated several times until all have been covered and all the students have the opportunity to speak. This activity can also be done in small groups where members take turns acting out and naming the terms. Alternatively, distribute to the class a worksheet with a variety of modes of transportation listed in English. Have the class listen to an audio narrative depicting how someone uses various modes of transportation to reach a destination, then mark numbers on the worksheet corresponding to the order in which the modes occurred, based on what they heard from the audio. Replay the audio as necessary. The narrative can also be read aloud by the teacher in class.

Activity 2 (For Objective 2, 20 minutes)

Purpose: To practice comparative structures.

● A 比 B + adjective

● B 没有 A (那么) + adjective

1. Ask students to brainstorm what adjectives they could use for comparing modes of transportation: 我们用什么 adjective 来比较呢？Write down on the board the words students come up with. The list may be quite long, but for the purpose of this lesson, focus on the description of speed (快, 慢) and cost (贵, 便宜).

2. Introduce "A 比 B + adjective" and "B 没有 A + (那么) adjective" on the board/Smartboard.

1) Show sample sentences such as:

Comparisons of speed (快 / 慢)	Comparisons of cost (便宜 / 贵)
汽车比自行车快。	打的比坐公共汽车贵。
自行车没有汽车（那么）快。	坐公共汽车没有打的（那么）贵。
骑自行车比开车慢。	坐公共汽车比打的便宜。
走路没有骑自行车（那么）快。	打的没有坐公共汽车（那么）便宜。

2) Point out to students that a) one can use different ways to express the same idea; b) two items compared need to be symmetric in the sentence pattern, i.e., they have to both be nouns or verb phrases; and c) it is not correct to say 自行车比汽车不快 or 出租汽车比公共汽车不便宜. Use the 没有……（那么）structure instead.

3) Show pictures of two modes of transportation and have the whole class brainstorm to produce as many comparative statements as they can.

3. Pair work: Pair students up to practice using comparative structures. Distribute picture cards to pairs. Display sample dialogue below. Have a confident student interact with the teacher to model the dialogue first, then have two students model the dialogue again in class. Student A asks a question, and Student B answers using a comparative structure. Reinforce the idea by using a different structure or by flipping the two items and using an antonym (see samples below). Return to pair work and have students switch roles for questioning and answering. Remind students that both comparative structures and comparison of both nouns and verb phrases should be practiced.

Examples:

1）A: 走路和骑自行车，哪个快？

B: 走路比骑自行车慢；骑自行车比走路快。

2）B: 开车和坐飞机，哪个便宜？

A: 开车比坐飞机便宜；开车没有坐飞机（那么）贵。

The teacher circulates to answer questions, offer guidance, and give feedback.

4. Survey and presentation: Have students choose any two modes of transportation and write them down on a sheet of paper. Then have them walk around the

classroom and poll at least five classmates, asking about if they feel it's more convenient/expensive to take transportation mode A than mode B. Wrap up the practice by asking a few students to report their findings to the class using a string of sentences.

Activity 3 (For Objective 3, 10 minutes)

Purpose: To review frequency words and new vocabulary on modes of transportation.

Students work in pairs to check what applies to them in the chart below.

1. Ask a confident student to interact with the teacher about their commuting habits.

   Example:

   > A: 你每天都坐公共汽车吗？
   >
   > B: 不，我有时候坐公共汽车。
   >
   > A: 你常常坐地铁吗？
   >
   > B: 对，我常常坐地铁。

2. Ask students to find out with their partner how often they use a specific mode of transportation by using the information in the chart below. (Interpersonal)

	每天都 verb	常常 verb	有时候 verb	从来不 verb
坐公共汽车				
开车				
走路				
骑自行车				
打的				
坐地铁				
坐火车				
坐飞机				
骑马				

3. Ask a confident student to summarize what they have found out from the conversation with their partner, e.g., John 每天都走路，他有时候骑自行车，可是他从来不骑马。(Presentational)

4. Ask a few students to report on the content of their conversations. (Presentational)

Activity 4 (For Objective 4, 15 minutes)

Purpose: To apply and assess use of vocabulary and structures in situational contexts.

Pre-Activity

Ask the class the questions: 你每天怎么来上学？你常常 / 有时候 / 从来不（坐车 / 自己开车）来上学吗？

In-Activity

Pair work: Have the students discuss commuting habits and the reasons why one mode of transportation is preferred over another. The teacher circulates through the room to answer questions and offer guidance. (Interpersonal)

Post-Activity

Ask two pairs (or more, if time allows) to recap their conversation's content with the class. (Presentational)

Closing (5 minutes):

Assignments: Review materials practiced today:

● Complete character writing worksheet with correct stroke order and write down the English meaning for the words and phrases.

● Write a short paragraph about the students' commuting habits and the reason why they prefer one mode of transportation over another. This writing assignment is based on the oral work done in class (Activity 4).

Exit Ticket: Each student answers the teacher's question "你今天放学以后怎么回家？" before the class is dismissed.

Rubric for Assessing Speaking (Activity 3)

	Excellent	Good	Unacceptable
Task Completion	Fully complete	Almost complete	Incomplete
Comprehensibility	Fully comprehensible to the audience	Comprehensible to the audience	Incomprehensible to the audience
Linguistic Accuracy (Grammar & Vocabulary)	1 or no errors	2-3 errors	Numerous errors
Fluency	Very fluent, with little or no hesitation	Fluent, with slight hesitation	Halting speech with frequent and long pauses
Pronunciation	Few or no errors	A few errors	Numerous errors

Rubric for Assessing Writing (Homework)

	Excellent	Good	Unacceptable
Task Completion	Fully complete	Almost complete	Incomplete
Functional Language Use	Uses two or more frequency words Correct use of both patterns of comparative structures; the structures are used multiple times No other grammatical errors	Uses one or two frequency words Correct use of both patterns of comparative structures; the structures are used at least once Few other grammatical errors	No frequency words used Structural mistakes with the comparative structures; only one pattern is used Numerous other grammatical errors
Appropriate Use of Vocabulary	Excellent use of vocabulary in correct context	Good use of vocabulary, almost all in correct context	Many words used incorrectly, impeding understanding
Accuracy of Characters	All characters are written correctly	A few errors	Numerous errors

Day 1: Asking for Directions

Teaching Focus:

Grammar:

- 从 place…… 到 place……
- 请问，从 A 到 B 怎么走？ 2) 请问，B 在哪儿？
- 往 / 向 + directional / positional word + verb

Vocabulary:

- 往/向, 拐/转, 红绿灯, 离 (离这儿两条街, 离这很近/很远/不太远), 一条街, 过 (过两条街 , 过一个红绿灯 / 十字路口), 远 / 近, 十字路口, 里 / 公里

Day 2: Giving and Following Directions

Teaching Focus:

Grammar:

- A 在 B 的 + position/direction
- 先……, 再……, 然后……
- 走到 / 到了…… A 就在你的前面 / 左边 / 右边

Vocabulary:

- 上 (面 *), 下 (面 *), 前 (面 *), 后 (面 *), 左 (边), 右 (边), 东 , 西 , 南 , 北 , [东南 , 东北 , 西南 , 西北]

* If introducing 面 adds another layer of complexity that is too much for the students to manage at this point, it can be substituted with 边 .

Learning Difficulties:

- Students may have difficulty distinguishing between 左 and 右 , and the four main compass directions, 东西南北 . Teach the mnemonic rhyme 上北下南 , 左西右东 to help students figure out directions.

- It is at the instructor's discretion whether the "diagonal directions" should be introduced. It will take students a while to get used to saying "diagonal direction" the Chinese way, where 东 and 西 precede 南 and 北 .

Day 4: Bus Is the Best

Teaching Focus:

Grammar:

- Word Order: "Frequency" words + verb
- Connectors: 而且 / 不但…… 而且……

Learning Difficulties:

- 而且 is used to introduce additional information that *complements, rather than contradicts*, what has been said before. For example, we say 坐公共汽车不但很便宜 , 而且很方便 . It's not appropriate to say 坐公共汽车不但很便宜 , 而且很慢 .

Day 5: How Long Does It Take to Get There?

Teaching Focus:

Grammar:

- A 离 B 有多远?
- 开车 * 从 A 到 B 要多长时间?

- 开车 * 从 A 到 B 要 + time duration

* By a specific means of transportation

Learning Difficulties:

- "开车" can be placed in two other places in the sentence structure: 1) 从 A 开车到 B 要多长时间？ 2) 从 A 到 B 开车要多长时间？However, for the purpose of simplicity and manageability, choose one form to teach and use.

Culminating Project for the Unit*:

Short oral presentation on travel. The presentation should include the following:

1. Choose two cities/locations to make a travel plan. Identify relative positions of two locations and the distance between them.

2. Present three workable travel options between two places. Also discuss another option that would not work and give the reason, e.g., 走路太远 or 没有飞机.

3. Compare the three workable travel options you come up with based on cost, travel time and convenience.

4. Recommend the best option and the reasons for it.

Note: Both comparative structures have to be used. The connectors "不但……而且……" or "而且" should be used.

Useful Phrases:

- A 在 B 的……（东边, etc.)

- 从 A 到 B 有……英里

- 从 A 到 B 你可以……（走路 / 开车 / 坐飞机）

- 从 A 到 B 不能……因为……

- Travel Option A 比 Option B……（贵 / 便宜 / 慢 / 快）

- Option B 没有 Option A 那么……

- Option A 不但……而且……

- 虽然 Option A……，可是……

- 我觉得……最好，因为……

---

* This project can be done in class as group/pair work or can be assigned as homework as an individual project.

Xiaoyun Matthewson (张晓云) is a Chinese instructor at Lakeside School in Seattle, Washington, where she teaches beginning to advanced level Chinese. She has presented at both the ACTFL and National Chinese Language Conferences on teaching advanced level Chinese in high school and on building a high-functioning secondary school Chinese program. She studied international business and economics in both China and the US, and also took part in the STARTALK/Pacific Lutheran University World Language Certification Program. She has served on the CLTA-Washington Board of Directors since 2012.

Travel

Jiayao Pang (庞嘉瑶)
Awty International School, Houston, Texas

Language Proficiency Level: Intermediate Low

Age Range: High School, 14-18 (9th to 12th grade)

Class Size: 10-20 students

Time Frame: 150 minutes per week, with 5 weeks in total

Essential Questions:

- What are the differences and similarities between traveling in China and the US?

- Why do these cultural/social differences and similarities exist?

- What challenges might environmental, social, and cultural issues pose to tourists?

Unit Goals:

To help students develop the four language skills, especially listening and speaking, on the topics of travel and transportation.

Standards: Based on the National Standards for Foreign Language Learning

- **Communication:**

  -Interpersonal (1.1)

  -Interpretive (1.2)

  -Presentational (1.3) Students create and perform short skits.

- **Connection:** Students relate what they learn in class to subjects such as geography.

- **Comparison:** Students compare differences between China and the US in terms of transportation systems.

- **Culture:** Students learn Chinese idiomatic expressions, such as 一路平安, and idioms pertaining to transportation, such as 车水马龙.

- **Community:** Students are encouraged to apply their Chinese knowledge in Chinese communities (e.g., Houston's Chinatown) and learn the language beyond the classroom. For example, call a Chinese travel agency for travel information, or make travel plans.

Unit Questions:

- Can students use transportation terms in a conversation?

- Can students make a suggestion or give a command?

- Can students talk about their past travel experience?

- Can students talk about where they want to travel and what they want to do?

- Can students explain a travel plan?

- Can students respond appropriately to invitations?

- Can students say the appropriate expression when they depart for a trip?

- Can students understand simple announcements encountered during travel?

Lesson Outlines:

Week 1: You forgot your passport 您忘了您的护照

Week 2: Wish you a pleasant trip 祝你旅途愉快

Week 3: I want to see the Great Wall 我想去看长城

Week 4: Travel plans 旅行计划

Week 5: (Final project) 以后的故事

Learning Objectives:

Students will be able to:

Week 1

- State their travel goals and a simple itinerary (presentational);

- Order tickets (interpersonal);

- State their desire to take up some activities when traveling (presentational).

Week 2

- Understand public announcements about a trip, such as announcements during a flight (interpretive);

- Respond to compliments and apologies in a culturally appropriate manner (interpersonal);

- Express concerns during a trip, such as "Am I late for the flight?" (interpersonal).

Week 3

- Give commands or instructions during a trip, such as "Please buckle your seat belt" (interpersonal);

- Give a self-introduction when meeting others for the first time (presentational);

- Ask for help during a trip, such as "Could you help me order a drink in English?" (interpersonal).

Week 4

- Make travel plans (presentational);

- Comprehend a video about a story from the text (interpretive);

- Bid farewell when seeing someone off (interpersonal).

Week 5

- Introduce oneself when meeting for the first time during travel (presentational);

- Become acquainted with people when traveling (interpersonal);

- Set up plans for an outing with people (interpersonal).

Teaching Focus:

Week 1: You forgot your passport 您忘了您的护照

- Understand difficult words in public announcements about travel, such as 航班号, 转机

- Describe distance between two locations by using the correct word order:

  Location A + 离 + Location B + 很远 / 近

- Describe a past experience that still has impact on today:

  verb + 过：
  你去过北京吗?
  Negation:
  没（有）+ verb
  我没（有）去过，打算今年去。

- Describe two actions, one taking place right after the other:

  一 + action 1 + 就 + action 2
  我一下飞机就去看长城和故宫!

Week 2: Wish you a pleasant trip 祝你旅途愉快

- Respond to a compliment with "哪里，哪里!" and an apology with "没关系。"

- Express concerns by using the question "没超重吧？"

- Describe something that is about to happen:

  （就）要 + action verb + 了
  Example: 中国民航飞往洛杉矶的飞机（就）要起飞了。

- Make descriptive compliments correctly:

  verb + 得 + adverb
  Example：您说得对。

Week 3: I want to see the Great Wall 我想去看长城

- Give commands or instructions:

请您系好安全带；关上手机；请不要吸烟

- Introduce oneself:

  很高兴认识你们。/ 您贵姓？

- Ask for help:

  你能帮我们点饮料吗？

- Conditional clauses:

  要是你找到一个中国女朋友，你会在中国玩儿久一点儿吗？

Week 4: Travel plans 旅行计划

- Make travel plans:

  Pattern of sequence: 先 + action 1, 然后 + action 2, 最后 + action 3

  Useful vocabulary: 打算，计划，可能，想

- Word order of the time duration:

  The time duration can be placed at the end of a sentence, while the point in time is placed either before or after the subject.

- Comparison:

  A + 和 + B + 一样 + adjective

  坐出租车和坐地铁一样快。

- Conditional clauses with 如果

  如果不堵车，坐出租车和坐地铁一样快。

  Compare 如果 with 要是 from previous session

- How to say goodbye:

  再见！/ 再会！/ 路上小心！/ 保重！

  Students will learn what to say in situations of farewell.

- Express gratefulness:

  Differences between 谢谢，多谢，感谢，非常感谢

Week 5: (Final project) 后来的故事

Teacher should encourage students to use the target language to create a continuation of the story by using the same main characters. Teacher can divide the class into a few groups for this project. The final production can be a skit, a video clip, or a series of photo slides. Teacher should help students coordinate the work for the final production.

Project requirements:

- Use vocabulary and grammatical patterns from this unit to write a play script with a few characters.
- Show skills of getting acquainted with people in the target language.
- Set up plans for an outing with friends or family.

Showcase day is the day when all groups demonstrate their productions. Teacher will give comments and grades to each group.

Week 4 (Sample Week)

Learning Objectives:

Students will be able to:

- Make travel plans (presentational);
- Comprehend a video about a story from the text (interpretive);
- Bid farewell when seeing someone off (interpersonal).

Teaching Focus:

Grammar:

- Comparison of the same degree:

  A + 和 + B + 一样 + adjective

  坐出租车和坐地铁一样快。

- Conditional clauses with 如果

  如果不堵车，坐出租车和坐地铁一样快。

- The word order of a sentence with time duration:

  Subject + verb + object + repeating the same verb + time duration

  哥哥每天玩儿电脑玩儿一个小时。

Expression:

- Seeing someone off:

  再见！／再会！／路上小心！／保重！

- Expressing gratefulness:

  Differences between 谢谢，多谢，感谢，非常感谢

Vocabulary:

旅行，有意思，打算，多久，可能，到达，服务，海关，出口，堵车，出租车，地铁，保重，接

Phonetics:

- "lǚ" in "lǚxíng 旅行"

- chūzūchē 出租车

- bǎozhòng 保重 vs. Chóngqìng 重庆

Learning Difficulties:

- Students may become confused between "time-when" expressions and "time-duration" expressions. "Time-when" should be placed before or right after the subject, whereas "time-duration" is placed after the verb.

- Students should learn how to appropriately express farewell and gratefulness, as well as respond to apologies in a culturally appropriate manner, while using a register appropriate to the situation.

Teaching Materials and Resources:

- Vocabulary flashcards with characters on one side and *pinyin*/English on the other

- Authentic pictures of popular places and means of transportation in China

- Worksheets

- PowerPoint slides

- Short movie/DVDs about travel in China

- Text created by the author of this chapter

  The vocabulary and grammar are compatible with those in the textbook series *Huanying*, Volume 2, Unit 1: Transportation.

  The story in the text unfolds with David, a young American traveling to China for the first time. On the flight to Beijing, he meets a Chinese couple named Mrs. and Mr. Wang, and becomes their friend. When David sees their daughter, who came to the Beijing Airport to pick up her parents, he is stunned....

- Entrance tickets of parks and museums in China

Sample tickets/receipts:

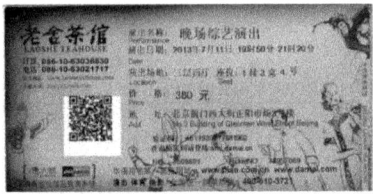

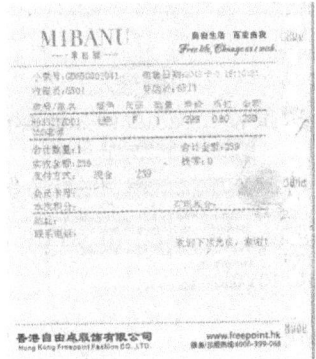

Instructional Strategies:

Part I (50 minutes)

Warm-up (10 minutes)

Relate and stimulate students' interest: Let the class watch a movie clip about famous scenery and transportation in China, and then ask students the following questions:

1. 你去过中国吗？你最喜欢什么地方？为什么？

2. 你是怎么去的？

3. 你最希望去中国的什么地方？

4. 旅游的时候你喜欢去看什么？自然风景？古迹名胜？博物馆？公园？

Useful links:

长城　http://video.nationalgeographic.com/video/exploreorg/china-great-wall-eorg

故宫　http://english.cntv.cn/program/newshour/20100721/101606.shtml

杭州　http://english.cntv.cn/program/newshour/20100913/102039.shtml

桂林　http://english.cntv.cn/program/newshour/20101101/103773.shtml

交通　http://www.youtube.com/watch?v=nZUcEShTqsw

Activity 1: Game: Charades 说来听听 (15 minutes)

Purpose:

To introduce new vocabulary and expressions in the text.

Objective:

This game can be used to study and review vocabulary from beginner to intermediate levels.

Preparation:

Teacher prepares word cards in both English and Chinese: 旅行，做梦，开玩笑，走，照顾，堵车，出租车，地铁．

Instructional steps:

1) The whole class is divided into teams A and B.

2) A volunteer student actor (from either team) comes to the front, facing the students.

3) The teacher stays behind the students in the back of the classroom, and shows one word card to the actor.

4) The actor looks at the word card that the teacher is holding, then acts out the meaning of the card repeatedly. At the same time, the teacher should repeatedly say the word aloud in Chinese so that all students can hear the Chinese pronunciation of the word and connect the pronunciation with the meaning of the word being acted out.

5) Neither team may turn around to see the card the teacher is showing. By watching the student's acting, the two teams of students try to guess the meaning of the word in English. Whichever team first guesses the meaning correctly will get one point.

6) The next volunteer student comes up to be the actor, and the game process repeats until all the cards are demonstrated.

7) The final winner is the team who gets the most points.

Activity 2: The Glove Game 手套游戏 (15 minutes)

Purpose:

To review vocabulary and practice listening and word recognition skills.

Preparation:

Teacher prepares one baking glove and word cards with learned vocabulary in English or in Chinese: 生活, 有意思, 打算, 多久, 可能, 到达, 气温, 服务, 拿, 过, 海关, 出口, 一定, 保重, 接, 招手.

Instructional steps:

1) The whole class reviews the vocabulary written on the word cards.

2) Students stand in a circle while one volunteer, wearing the baking glove, stands in the middle. He/She is the glove person.

3) Each student holds a vocabulary card facing the middle of the circle, with the other hand stretched out.

4) The teacher says a word in Chinese or English, and the glove person should search for the student who has the matching word on their card, then hit that student's hand with the glove. To avoid being hit by the glove, the card holder should say a word on any of the other cards before being hit. The glove person then has to search for the new card holder's hand again.

5) If a student gets hit before they say another word, they have to switch positions with the glove person.

6) After a few rounds, students should switch cards with their neighbors, so they will have a chance to become familiar with more vocabulary.

7) The key to winning this game is being familiar with the words' meanings in English, or being able to pronounce them in Chinese quickly and correctly.

8) The winner of the game is the one who becomes the glove person the least frequently.

Activity 3: Pattern Drill (10 minutes)

Purpose:

To practice the structure of comparison A + 和 + B + 一样 + adjective.

Preparation:

Teacher prepares picture cards of adjectives. For example:

| shòu | pàng | gāoxìng | shāng xīn | róngyì | nán |
| 瘦 | 胖 | 高兴 | 伤心 | 容易 | 难 |

nánkàn	piàoliang	niánqīng	lǎo	hǎo	huài
难看	漂亮	年轻	老	好	坏

Pre-Activity

1) Teacher presents the structure of comparison with the same degree using visual aids for comprehensible input: A＋和＋B＋一样＋adjective.

2) Students read aloud the sample sentence 坐出租车和坐地铁一样快 until they have memorized it.

Instructional steps:

1) Each volunteer student gets one picture card of an adjective and shows it to the class.

2) This student then thinks of two comparable subjects and makes a sentence of comparison by using the adjective.

3) The student says the sentence to the class while showing the picture word card.

   * Sample sentences made by students:

   "我爸爸和乌龟一样慢。"

   "在上海坐地铁和坐出租车一样难。"

Homework:

Ask students to finish the sentences in the table by following the given pattern:

	A	and	B	same	adjectives
1		和		一样	慢。
2		和		一样	漂亮。
3		和		一样	有意思。
4	坐汽车	和	坐火车	一样	
5	骑马	和	骑自行车	一样	

6	写小说	和	写作业	一样	
7		和		一样	
8		和		一样	
9		和		一样	

Part II (50 minutes)

Activity 4: Graphic Storytelling (25 minutes)

Purpose:

To describe a series of activities by using 先 + action 1, 然后 + action 2, 最后 + action 3.

Objective:

Make travel plans.

Preparation:

Teacher or students prepare the following picture cards with multiple copies.

Picture Group A (Interesting places in Beijing)

Picture Group B (Famous tourist destinations in China)

Pre-Activity

Introduce 先 + action 1, 然后 + action 2, 最后 + action 3.

Emphasize that 先 should be placed before a verb.

Vocabulary: 打算 , 计划 , 可能 , 想

Instructional steps:

1) Have each student select three pictures either from Picture Group A or Picture Group B and make sentences based on the selected pictures using 打算 / 计划 / 可能 / 想 + 先 + action 1, 然后 + action 2, 最后 + action 3.

2) Ask students to present the pictures and tell their travel plans to the class.

Continuation of the Previous Activity: Game 你说得对不对

Purpose: Informative assessment to check how much the students understand what the presenter says, how much information they can recall, and how well they can repeat the information in the target language.

Instructional steps (this is a continuation of the pre-activity above):

1) Teacher takes notes on what each student says in their presentation, while the

class listens and memorizes silently.

2) After everyone presents their travel plans as described in the above pre-activity, students will recall in turn what the other students have said. Students are allowed to give information about only one presenter at a time.

Example:

Student 1: "小文说，她先去香港，再去上海。"

(小文 will have to confirm with " 对 " or " 不对 ". If it is " 对 ", then student #1 will stay in the game and wait for the next round.)

Now it is student 2's turn:

Student 2: "大山说，他先去北京，最后去杭州。"

(大山 will confirm with 对 or 不对 . If it is 不对 , then student 2 will be out of the game.)

3) If a student cannot recall any more information on their turn, they are out of the game.

4) No repetition is allowed. The one who repeats what another has already said will also be out of the game.

5) The student who stays in the game the longest is the winner.

Activity 5: Watch an animated slide show and practice grammatical structures (20 minutes)

Purpose: To learn the grammatical rule of expressing time duration.

Instructional steps:

1) Teacher shows an animated slide about time duration:

Subject + verb + object + repeating the same verb + time duration

162

2) Students will read aloud the sample sentence on the slide several times following the correct word order.

3) Individually, the first student will read the first component of the sentence, the second student will read the second component, and the third one will read the third component. When the sentence is finished, the next student will read the sentence again, starting from the beginning.

4) After students become familiar with the sample sentence on the slide, they will be asked to switch subject, predicate, object, time point, etc. to create new sentences. For example:

Teacher: Please switch the time point.

Students: 昨天我也和弟弟在北京玩儿游戏玩儿了一个小时。

Teacher: Please switch the subject.

Students: 今天我和朋友在北京玩儿游戏玩儿了一个小时。

Notes:

For teacher's reference only: Please note that time duration can also be structured as subject + verb + time duration + 的 + object:

哥哥每天玩儿一个小时的电脑。

Written Assignment:

As homework or classwork, ask students to answer the following questions by using learned vocabulary and expressions:

- 如果你去中国旅行，你打算先去哪儿，然后去哪儿，最后去哪儿？

- 你打算在这几个地方玩儿多长时间？

- 你希望在这些地方参观什么景点或者名胜？

Cultural Entertainment (5 minutes):

As a short break, play another online video clip about traveling in China. You can select interesting places such as 丽江 , 阳朔 , 九寨沟 , 新疆 or 西藏 .

Useful links:

丽江：

http://www.youtube.com/watch?v=DnXM4IYqBA4

http://www.youtube.com/watch?v=XDlESIzvsEI

阳朔：

http://www.youtube.com/watch?v=PtcOu-Ty3QQ&list=UUIo92-cjOVZyrfRAXkNCyzg

http://www.youtube.com/watch?v=QqAnVoC2BT0&list=UUIo92-cjOVZyrfRAXkNCyzg

九寨沟：

http://www.youtube.com/watch?v=nQlQGhi3Sco&list=PLCCFE5671BB8A2ECA

http://www.youtube.com/watch?v=jpTgrtMOfQc

新疆：

http://video.travelchinaguide.com/heavenly-lake-xinjiang-000928.htm

http://video.travelchinaguide.com/001043.htm

西藏：

http://www.youtube.com/watch?v=EJc7LI9Xbcg

http://www.tibetodysseytours.com/?gclid=CLuJ69jh8b0CFckWMgodHEIAug

Part III (50 minutes)

Activity 6: Watch a video (10 minutes)

Purpose: To familiarize students with the story from the text (see the Appendix) and to enhance students' listening comprehension. Teacher plays one or two video clips based on the story from the text.

Instructional steps:

1) Show the videos in class.

2) Ask students the following questions based on the content of the story to evaluate students' listening comprehension:

- 大卫为什么到中国去？

- 大卫打算在北京先做什么、再做什么、最后做什么？

- 大卫想在中国玩儿多久？

- 大卫在北京有没有朋友？

- 谁来机场接王先生和王太太？

- 大卫为什么看见了他们的小女儿后呆住了？

Activity 7: Write and perform a short skit based on the following topic (40 minutes)

Purpose: To practice how to say farewell by using learned vocabulary and patterns.

Preparation:

1) The class watches video clips made by other classes (usually classes from previous years). The stories in these video clips are about bidding farewell in different locations and scenarios.

2) The class reads aloud the following sample conversation from the text (see the Appendix for the text):

王先生	zhàogù 大卫，再见。谢谢你一路照顾我们。 祝你在中国玩儿得开心！
王太太	你怎么去你住的饭店？
王先生	dǔ chē chūzūchē dìtiě 如果不堵车，坐出租车和坐地铁一样快。 路上小心！
王太太	大卫，别忘了给我们打电话。
大卫	yídìng bǎozhòng 一定，一定。谢谢。你们保重！ yí jiē 咦，怎么没有人来接你们？
王先生、王太太	看，那不是我们的小女儿吗？！
大卫往前边一看，看见了一个女孩向他们招手。他呆住了……	

Instructional steps:

1) Students pair up with a partner.

2) Each pair creates a scenario and writes their own short conversation by using learned vocabulary and patterns such as "再见！/ 再会！" "你们保重" "路上小心！" "你一定要来我们家玩儿！" "到北京以后给我们打电话吧！"

3) Teacher checks the skits written by students in class.

4) Within a limited time, each pair practices orally the skit they just wrote and had checked by the teacher, and tries to memorize the conversation in the skit.

5) Each pair performs their own skit in front of the class.

6) Teacher videotapes each pair's skit.

7) The class discusses the students' skits. Teacher can use the following questions to stimulate the discussion:

What was your favorite part of all the performances?

Which was the most interesting story?

What have you learned from the other skits?

What do you think could be improved?

8) The whole class votes for "Best Skit" and "Best Actor/Actress". The winning pairs can be awarded with extra credit for a quiz or a small souvenir from the teacher, such as a bookmark.

Post-Activity

The class watches the video of the skits. Teacher can also invite other classes to come and share the fun.

Sample skit written by students:

> A: 我要走了。
>
> B: 去哪儿？为什么？
>
> A: 我明年要去北京工作。
>
> B: 可是我爱你，别去！

> A: 我也爱你，可是我更爱北京。
>
> B: 那算了，我回家吧！(from the lyrics of a song that the class has learned before: 对面的女孩看过来)
>
> A: 路上小心。
>
> B: 保重！

Teacher Self-assessment:

- What went well?

- What needs to be improved?

- Did the activities enhance students' learning motivation?

- Did the activities help students learn effectively?

- What could be done differently?

Rubric for Assessing Speaking in Activities 3, 4, and 7

Rating	Excellent 4	Good 3	Average 2	Below Average 1
Interactive and Receptive Skills	Consistently sustained	Mostly sustained	Partially sustained	Limited comprehension and interaction
Fluency	Fluent	Pauses occasionally	Pauses frequently	Pauses most of the time
Pronunciation	Rare errors	Sporadic errors	Several errors	Numerous errors
Accuracy (Grammar & Vocabulary)	Accurate and effective	Mostly accurate and effective	Partially accurate and effective	Barely or not accurate and effective
Volume	Clear and loud	Occasionally low volume	Low volume most of time	Barely audible

Rubric for Assessing Homework Exercises and Skit Writing

	Task Completion	Comprehen-sibility	Level of Discourse	Vocabulary	Grammar
1	Not complete at all	Incomprehensible	Inadequate development: lacks examples or details	Inadequate word choice: rambling, inappropriate, incorrect	Inadequate structure: numerous incomplete sentences
2	Minimal completion of the task	Barely comprehensible	Minimal development/ response: lacks examples or details	Minimal word choice: inadequate, incorrect	Minimal sentence structure: some incomplete sentences and errors
3	Less than partial completion of the task	Partially comprehensible	Limited development: some use of examples or details	Limited word choice: 6 errors	Limited sentence structure: 6 errors
4	Partial completion of the task	Mostly comprehensible	Adequate development: sufficient use of examples or details	Adequate word choice: 4 errors	Adequate sentence structure: 4 errors
5	Appropriate and adequate completion of the task	Easily comprehensible	Effective development: clear use of examples or details	Effective use: 2 errors	Effective use: 2 errors
6	Superior completion of the task: appropriate and with elaboration	Fully comprehensible	Exemplary development: strong use of examples or details	Exemplary word choice: vivid, specific, precise	Exemplary use: complete and correct with sentence variety

168

Appendix (Created by Jiayao Pang)

dì èr mù   zài fēijī shang
第二幕　在飞机上　　　　　　Scene 2　　　　In the Airplane

（大卫正在飞往北京的中国民航六六六班机上。他坐在一对中国夫妇（fūfù, couple）——王先生和王太太的旁边。）

Loudspeaker on board:	nǚshìmen xiānshengmen 女士们　先生们	Ladies and gentlemen,
	chéngzuò 您乘坐的是中国国航 飞往北京的班机。	The flight you are taking is Air China heading to Beijing.
	飞机就要起飞了。	The plane is about to take off.
	jìhǎo ānquándài 请您系好 安全带；	Please fasten (your) seat belt;
	guānshang 关上手机。	turn off (your) cell phone.
	xī yān 请不要吸烟……	Please do not smoke...
大 卫：	你们好!	Hello!
王先生：	你好! 哦，你会说中国话?	Hello! Oh, you can speak Chinese?
大 卫：	我会说一点儿。 guìxìng 我叫大卫。您贵姓?	I can speak a little bit. My name is David. What is your honorable surname?
王先生：	我姓王。这是我太太。	My last name is Wang. This is my wife.
大 卫：	很 高兴 认识 你们。	(I am) very glad to meet you.
王太太：	niánqīngrén jíle 年轻人，你的中文说得好极了。	Young man, your Chinese is extremely good.
大 卫：	nǎli 哪里，哪里。	You are flattering me.
	bì yè 三年前我大学毕业。	Three years ago I graduated from college.
	shíyóu gōngsī 现在我在一家石油公司工作。	Now I work for an oil company.
	gōngchéngshī 我是一个工程师。	I am an engineer.
王先生：	búcuò 不错，不错。	Not bad, not bad.
大 卫：	你们从哪儿来，王先生、王太太？	Where are you from, Mr. and Mrs. Wang?

王太太：	我们从北京来。	We come from Beijing.
	nǚ'ér 我们有两个女儿。	We have two daughters.
	上个月我们来美国看大女儿。	Last month we came to visit (our) elder daughter.
	Jiùjīnshān 她住在旧金山。	She lives in San Francisco.
	zuòjiā xiě xiǎoshuō 她是个作家，写 小说。	She is a writer, (she) writes novels.
	zhàopiàn 看，这是她的照片……	Look, this is her photo…
飞机乘务员：	What would you like to drink?	
王太太：	zāogāo dǒng 糟糕！ 我们不懂英文。	Oops! We don't understand English.
	diǎn yǐnliào 大卫，你能帮我们点 饮料吗？	David, could you help us order drinks?
	jiā bīng 我想要一杯可乐，不加冰。	I'd like to have a Coke; don't add ice.
大卫：	没问题！	No problem!
王太太：	xiōngdì jiěmèi 大卫，你有没有兄弟姐妹？	David, do you have brothers (and) sisters?
大卫：	我有。你们看！ （大卫打开他的手提电脑。）	I have (do). Look here! (David opens his laptop.)
王太太：	xìngfú 幸福的一家。	A happy family.
王先生：	大卫，你为什么到中国去？	David, why are you going to China?
大卫：	lǚxíng 我喜欢旅行。	I like traveling.
	zuò mèng 我小时候就做梦去中国。	When I was a child, I dreamed of going to China.
	xiān 在北京，我想先去长城， ránhòu bówùguǎn zuìhòu qí 然后看博物馆，最后 骑 yóu hútòng! 自行车 游胡同！	In Beijing, I want to first go up to the Great Wall, then visit the museum, and at last ride a bike to tour the Beijing alleys!

	cāi shēnghuó yǒu yìsi	
大卫：	我猜北京的生活会很有意思。	I guess life in Beijing must be fun.
	dǎsuàn duō jiǔ	
王先生：	你打算在中国玩儿多久？	How long do you plan to stay in China?
	kěnéng	
大卫：	可能四个星期。	Probably 4 weeks.
	yàoshì	
王太太：	要是你找到一个中国女朋友，你会玩儿久一点儿吗？	If you find a Chinese girlfriend, would you play (stay) a little longer?
	kāi wánxiào	
大卫：	王太太，您真会开玩笑。我在北京没有朋友。	Mrs. Wang, you know how to make fun of me. I don't have friends in Beijing.
王太太：	我们就是你的朋友了。你一定要来我们家玩儿！	We are your friends. You must come visit us!
王太太：	（王太太给大卫一张纸条。）这是我们的电话号码。到北京以后给我们打电话吧！	(Mrs. Wang gives David a note.) This is our phone number. Call us after you arrive in Beijing!
大卫：	王先生，王太太，你们太好了！	Mr. and Mrs. Wang, you are so nice!
	fēicháng gǎnxiè	
	非常 感谢！	Thank you very much!
王先生：	别客气，年轻人。我们已经是朋友了。	No need to be so polite, young man. We are already friends.
大卫：	你们是我的第一个中国朋友！	You are my first Chinese friends!
Captain:	女士们，先生们，	Ladies and gentlemen,
	dàodá	
	我们快要到达北京首都国际机场了。请系好安全带，关上手机。	We are about to arrive at Beijing Capital International Airport. Please fasten (your) seat belt, and turn off (your) cell phone.
	qìwēn dù	
	今天的气温是二十八度。	Today's temperature is 28 degrees.
	谢谢你们乘坐我们的航班。	Thank you for taking our flight.
	fúwù	
	希望以后再为你们服务。再见。	We hope to serve you again. Goodbye.

	（大卫和王先生，王太太一起拿了行李，过了 hǎiguān zǒu chūkǒu 海关，然后走到机场出口。） ná guò	(David, Mr. Wang and Mrs. Wang pick up their luggage, pass through customs, and then walk out of the airport exit together.)
王先生：	大卫，再见。谢谢你一路照顾 我们。 zhàogù 祝你在中国玩儿得开心。	David, thanks for taking care of us on the way. We wish you a great time in China.
王太太：	你怎么去你住的饭店？	How are you going to your hotel?
王先生：	如果不堵车，坐出租车和坐 dìtiě 地铁一样快。路上小心！ dǔ chē chūzūchē	If there is no traffic jam, taking a taxi is as fast as taking the subway. Be careful on your way!
王太太：	大卫，别忘了给我们打电话。	David, don't forget to call us.
大卫：	一定，一定。谢谢你们。你 bǎozhòng 们保重！ yídìng	For sure! Thank you. Take care!
	唉，怎么没有人来接你们？ yí jiē	Oh, how come no one came to pick you up?
王先生 王太太：	你看，那不是我们的小女儿 吗？	See, isn't that our little daughter?
	（大卫往前边一看，一个女孩正向他们招手。 dāi 他呆住了……） zhāo shǒu	(David looks over there. He sees a girl waving to them. He is stunned...)

Jiayao Pang（庞嘉瑶）has 21 years of teaching experience at various schools, such as the State Secondary School in Zurich, Switzerland and the University of Houston, Texas. Currently she is a teacher and coordinator of the Chinese program at the Awty International School, Houston. She has a Master's degree in Educational Psychology from the University of Zurich, Switzerland, and a Bachelor's degree in Chinese Language and Literature from South China Normal University. Ms. Pang has participated in several professional development programs such as ACTFL and the STARTALK projects. She is the President of the Chinese Language Teachers Association of Texas 2012-2014. Ms. Pang was awarded the "Excellent Achievement Award 2009" & recognized as "Outstanding Teacher for Chinese Bridge Competition 2010" by the Consulate-General of China in Houston.

Critique

Getting Around: Directions and Transportation – Xiaoyun Matthewson

Travel – Jiayao Pang

Under the theme of "Travel", Xiaoyun Matthewson and Jiayao Pang present two designs: *Getting Around: Directions and Transportation* and *Travel*. Matthewson's content is down to earth: getting around is a big part of life, and being able to ask directions and talk about transportation is essential even for beginning learners. Asking, following, and giving directions, and describing relative positions, are by no means easy tasks. Linguistically the word order in Chinese is quite different from students' first language; cognitively, the concept of space is abstract. The focus of the language form on the Sample Day, however, includes two comparative structures. Matthewson highlights the challenging points of the structures:

1. The degree adverb 很 may not appear in a Chinese comparative structure, although students frequently do use it: * 飞机比火车很快.

2. When making a negative comparison, the structure "A 没有 B 那么 adjective" is used rather than 比 and the negation of the adjective, e.g., 我的中文比他的不好.

Matthewson's instructional steps are internally structured and creatively designed. For example, she first leads students to determine the objects of comparison: the speed and cost of transportation. After adjectives are selected, instructional input is carefully provided based on Activity 1, in which vocabularies and idiomatic expressions have just been practiced. The instructional input controls vocabulary but offers language variations which are essential for comparisons in the context (see Activity 2). This is a clearly different method of teaching a second or foreign language, as opposed to teaching a first language; the challenging task for students is usually not vocabulary, but structures. Students practice the comparison structures in pairs based on picture cards. Before the pair work, modeling between the teacher and an advanced student, and then among two confident students, is conducted to show the class how the dialogue will be carried out. New vocabulary is abundant but the picture cards reduce the memory load and help with comprehension. Activity 2 ends with a walk-around survey and reports from students. Activity 3 follows a similar approach, and focuses on interpersonal communication by means of frequently used words and students' daily modes of transportation. Interaction is conducted via meaningful dialogues based on an innovatively designed survey table, and a summary of the activities and reports from students conclude Activity 3.

Pragmatics and socio-linguistic functions have been largely neglected in Chinese curriculum and instruction. Pang's design fosters students' ability to function as competent language users. This is demonstrated not only in accomplishing real-world tasks such as ordering airline tickets, stating travel goals and desired activities, and introducing oneself on the airplane, but also in speech acts such as making and responding to compliments and apologies in a culturally appropriate manner, making requests with varying degrees of politeness according to socio-cultural situations, and bidding someone farewell in different contexts. When the purpose is to help students use language for real communication, instruction provides students with more freedom, fun, and opportunities to apply their language skills to problem-solving. The sample day begins with two activities, both of which are vocabulary games. The games fit the students' age group, are easy to conduct in class, and include the practice of a good number of vocabulary words. Even the so-called "pattern drill" exercise looks fun because of vivid pictures and the way sentences are practiced. The activity is meaning-based and situations are true to life. Form and meaning are naturally connected when practicing 12 adjectives in comparative sentences, as is done in Activity 3.

Both designs show that visual aids play a significant role in helping students with comprehension when meaning is immediately clear, and with production when the memory load is reduced. One distinctive feature of Pang's design is the use of varied visuals, ranging from authentic props such as transportation and parking gate tickets to vivid cartoons and photographs produced by the author. What is even more important is the way Pang uses the visuals. For example, while laying out the photos of Beijing and Shanghai, the learning task is to describe a series of activities by using 先 + action 1, 然后 + action 2, 最后 + action 3. Visual aids make the task easier and fun.

The last activity in Matthewson's design seems to provide a level of difficulty equal to or perhaps easier than that of the previous activities. It may be necessary to extend the last activity a bit more, increasing the level of sophistication in form and meaning. In regard to Pang's design, although grammar is practiced in context via communicative modes throughout the design, the sentences "昨天我也和弟弟在北京玩儿游戏玩儿了一个小时" and "今天我和朋友在北京玩儿游戏玩儿了一个小时" do not sound authentic and natural. Even sentences constructed for the sake of grammar practice should be contextually functional.

Theme 5

Shopping

Shopping

Dai-Hau Ruth Tang (唐代豪)
Round Rock High School/Cedar Ridge High School, Round Rock, Texas

Language Proficiency Level: Novice High

Age Range: 15-17 (high school students)

Class Size: 12 students

Time Frame: 90 minutes for each lesson, with 5 lessons in all

Essential Question:

What can be learned about a person's purchasing habits based on his/her willingness to haggle?

Unit Goals:

To help students use the target language to make purchases and to recognize differences between Chinese and American shopping cultures.

Standards: Based on the National Standards for Foreign Language Learning

- **Communication:**

  -Interpersonal (1.1)

  -Interpretive (1.2)

  -Presentational (1.3)

- **Connection:** Social studies, math, technology. (3.1)

- **Comparison:** Compare similarities and differences between the ways of bargaining in China and the US.

- **Culture:** (2.1: Cultural Practice) Chinese customs when bargaining.

Unit Questions:

- Can students describe the color of an item of clothing?

- Can students negotiate a better price when making a purchase?

- Can students make comparisons in terms of price and size?

- Can students ask the payment methods that a store accepts?

- Can students know the currency, pay for a purchase, and get the right change back?

- Can students exchange merchandise if not satisfied?

Lesson Outlines:

Day 1: What's the color of your top/pants/skirt? 你的上衣／裤子／裙子是什么颜色的？

Day 2: It's too expensive. Can you lower the price? 太贵了，可以便宜一点儿吗？

Day 3: This red shirt is more expensive than that one. 这件红衬衫比那件贵。

Day 4: How much is it altogether? Do you accept credit cards? 一共多少钱？可以刷卡吗？

Can I exchange this shirt for another one? 我可以换另外一件衬衫吗？

Day 5: Performance Assessment: Shopping Role-Play

Learning Objectives:

Students will be able to:

Day 1

- Talk about their dream wardrobe with friends (interpersonal);

- Talk about colors, sizes, and quantities with proper measure words (presentational).

Day 2

- Ask and give the price of an item (interpersonal);

- Complain about an item being too expensive (interpersonal);

- Bargain for a lower price until a deal is made (interpersonal).

Day 3

- Ask the salesperson about two items' similarities or differences regarding size and color (interpersonal);

- Ask and compare prices to get a better deal (interpersonal).

Day 4

- Exchange an item for one of the right color and size (interpersonal);

- Recognize the currency exchange rates between US dollars and RMB and be able to compare prices when traveling in China (interpretive);

- Inquire about acceptable payment methods for a purchase and get the right change back if paying cash (interpersonal).

Day 5

- Purchase an ideal outfit, from hat to shoes, within a budget in order to attend a friend's birthday party (interpersonal, interpretive, and presentational).

Day 1 (Sample Day)

Learning Objectives:

Students will be able to:

- Talk about their dream wardrobe with friends (interpersonal);
- Talk about colors, sizes, and quantities with proper measure words (presentational).

Teaching Focus:

Grammar:

- Number + Measure Word + Noun 一件衣服 / 衬衫 / 上衣, 一条裤子 / 裙子 / 长裤, 一双鞋子 / 袜子
- 这件衬衫是黄的。

Vocabulary:

- 穿, 衣服, 衬衫, 上衣, 长裤, 裤子, 牛仔裤, 裙子, 鞋子, 袜子, 大号, 中号, 小号, 颜色
- Measure Words: 条, 件, 双

Phonetics:

- "j" as in 件
- "z" as in 仔
- "un" as in 裙
- "ie" as in 鞋
- Tone change for 一 and 不 : When followed by a 4th tone, 一 and 不 change to a 2nd tone.

Learning Difficulties:

- Different measure words for different apparel items.

Teaching Materials and Resources:

- A variety of apparel items (real objects preferred, but picture printouts would be okay)

- PowerPoint slides of different items of clothing

- A deck of 3 × 5 index clothing picture cards, cut in half

- Markers and paper

- Colored construction paper

- Chinese clothing catalogs

- *Integrated Chinese* textbook and other selected materials

Instructional Strategies:

- By the end of the Day 1 lesson, two friends will be able to find out what clothes they have.

- Sample Dialogue Input (written on whiteboard or shown on PowerPoint):

> A: 你有什么颜色的上衣 / 衬衫 / 长裤 / 裙子?
>
> B: 我有黄（颜）色的，红（颜）色的，还有蓝（颜）色的。你呢?
>
> A: 我有白（颜）色的和蓝（颜）色的。你有几件 / 条蓝（颜）色的?
>
> B: 我只有一件 / 条。你穿多大的（衬衫）? 大号的，中号的，还是小号的?
>
> A: 我穿中号的。

Warm-up 1 (Teacher-students, 5 minutes)

Purpose: To get students ready for the new unit.

1. Teacher shows a Chinese shopping video clip.

2. After students finish watching it, teacher asks students the following questions:

- 他们在哪里? 在学校还是在商店?

- 他们正在做什么? 看东西还是买东西?

Warm-up 2 (Color review, 3 minutes)

Purpose: To prepare students for the new lesson by reviewing color words they have learned before.

1. Teacher uses colored construction paper as visual cues to review different colors.

2. Teacher asks students: 你喜欢什么颜色？ or 你不喜欢什么颜色？
   Students: 我喜欢黄色、白色，还喜欢蓝色。 or 我不喜欢紫色，也不喜欢黑色。

3. Teacher asks the questions a couple of times.

4. Students ask each other questions in this format to practice saying different colors.

Pre-Activity: Teaching Measure Words (Teacher's demonstration, 5 minutes)

Teacher introduces clothing vocabulary and measure words with visual aids, such as real clothing items or PowerPoint slides.

Language form: number + measure word + noun

Activity 1: "Heart Attack" vocabulary and measure word games (10 minutes)

Purpose: To help students practice new vocabulary and measure words.

1. Teacher asks students to name the clothing items shown, one by one, in order to practice pronunciation.

2. With visual cues, have students practice "number + measure word + noun" (一件 ／两件上衣, 一条／两条裤子, 两双鞋子 ...).

3. Divide students into groups of four.

4. Place a deck of clothing picture cards face down in the center of each group. Moving clockwise, students take turns flipping over the top card. Whoever first names the noun in the picture correctly gets the card.

5. After students finish practicing naming the clothing on the cards, have them start the same deck of cards again, this time adding the proper measure words. The same cards have different clothing items and various quantities of the items for students to practice (e.g., 两件衬衫, 一条牛仔裤, 三双鞋子). Whoever

first uses the expression of "number + measure word + noun" correctly wins the card, and whoever wins the most cards wins the game.

Teacher walks around and assists students as needed.

Activity 2: Add "colors" to the expression (Interpersonal: teacher-student and student-student, 5 minutes)

Purpose: To continue practicing the expression "number + measure word + color + noun".

1. For this activity, teacher uses images of clothing in different colors or indicates something a student is wearing. For example, pointing to a student's black shoes, teacher says, with a stress on 黑色的, "我喜欢这双黑色的鞋子" or "我喜欢这双黑鞋子".

2. Teacher picks up a yellow shirt and a red shirt and asks a student:

   Teacher: 杰克，你喜欢什么颜色的衬衫？黄色的衬衫还是红色的衬衫？
   Student（杰克）: 我喜欢黄色的／红色的衬衫。

   Note: Since students practiced the vocabulary and measure words in the previous activities, they now can answer questions in complete sentences together.

3. Teacher walks around and asks what a couple of students are wearing, e.g.,
   Teacher: 艾莉，约翰的衬衫是什么颜色的？他的鞋是什么颜色的？
   Student（艾莉）: 约翰的衬衫是粉红色的。他的鞋是咖啡色的。

4. Pair students up and have them ask one another about the colors of their outfits. (interpersonal)

Activity 3: Think → Pair → Share (7 minutes)

Purpose: To talk about one's dream wardrobe.

A dialogue sample as instructional input:

> Q: 你有什么颜色的上衣／衬衫／长裤／裙子／鞋子／袜子？
> A: 我有（红色的）（鞋子）。（我有（红）（鞋子）。）
> Q: 你有几双红色的鞋子？（你有几双红鞋子？）
> A: 我有一双红色的鞋子。（我有一双红鞋子。）

1. **Think**: Each student gets a 3 × 5 card and markers to dream up their ideal wardrobe by drawing a set of clothing items in colors they like.

2. **Pair**: Have two students work together. Student 1 points at the clothes student 2 drew and asks student 2 questions such as "你有几件上衣／几条裤子／几双鞋？" and "你有几件 X 色的上衣／裤子／鞋？". Student 2 answers those questions. Teacher walks around to assist students as needed. (interpersonal)

3. **Share**: Group two pairs together and have each pair introduce their partner's wardrobe to the other pair. Example: Student 1 of pair 1:"玛丽有两条黑色的长裤。"Student 2 of pair 1: "汤姆有三条蓝色的牛仔裤。"

4. Randomly ask a couple of pairs to recap what they have learned about their fellow pairs' wardrobes.

Activity 4: Add "size" to the sentence pattern (Interpersonal, 5 minutes)

Purpose: To practice word order with measure words, colors, and size words in a longer sentence.

1. Teacher takes one large yellow shirt out and says, with a stress on "大号", "这是一件大号的黄衬衫。"Teacher models the sentence pattern a couple of times using different clothing items in different colors and sizes.

2. Teacher then walks around, pointing at students' clothing and asking questions such as the following:

Example 1:

> Teacher: 凯莉, 你这条蓝裤子是多大的? 大号的, 中号的, 还是小号的?
>
> Student (凯莉): 是中号的。
>
> Teacher: 你有几条中号的蓝裤子?
>
> Student (凯莉): 我有两条中号的蓝裤子。

Example 2:

> Teacher: 汤姆, 你这双黑鞋是几号的? 九号的还是十号的?
>
> Student (汤姆): 是十号的。
>
> Teacher: 你有几双十号的黑鞋?
>
> Student (汤姆): 我有两双十号的黑鞋。

3. Pair students up and have them ask each other about the size of their clothing.

Activity 5: Inside-Outside Circles (10 minutes)

Purpose: To have students interview each other to get information about the sizes and quantity of their clothing.

1. Form Inside-Outside Circles: All the students make a big circle. Ask them to count off, alternating between one and two. All #1 students step inward to form an inner circle, while #2 students remain where they are to form an outer circle; the circles face each other. The teacher gives each student an image of an item of clothing that includes the clothing's size and color.

2. Have inside circle students ask their outside counterparts about the colors and sizes of the outfit they see on the outside circle student's printout.

3. Reverse roles and have outside circle students ask the questions.

4. Rotate students by having outside circle students move clockwise and start another round of conversation; teacher may ask students to rotate several times. The teacher walks around to assist students as needed.

5. Randomly pick two or three students to recap the information they have gathered in front of the class. (presentational)

Ask the class to draw the clothing items that they have heard from the recaps in order to check everyone's listening comprehension. (interpretive; formative assessment)

Activity 6: Talk about your wardrobe 你有什么衣服？ (10 minutes)

Purpose: To have students practice inquiring about a person's wardrobe.

Instructional input, in the form of the sample dialogue below, is presented via PowerPoint. Teacher can first model it with a single student, a group of students, or the whole class.

Clothing interview dialogue sample:

> Q: 你有什么衣服?
>
> A: 我有衬衫和裤子。
>
> Q: 你有几件衬衫? 是多大的? 是什么颜色的?
>
> A: 我有三件中号的衬衫, 一件是黄色的, 两件是蓝色的。

1. Teacher first talks about their own wardrobe, (e.g., 我有五件衬衫, 两件黄色的, 一件黑色的, 两件蓝色的; 四件中号的, 一件大号的), and then randomly asks a student "你有几件衬衫?" "是什么颜色的?" "是多大的?".

2. Teacher does another round of modeling, this time focusing on pants and/or shoes.

3. Teacher distributes an interview sheet to students (see below) and has them walk around to interview three classmates about their wardrobes. (interpersonal)

4. Students jot down their classmates' answers on the sheet. Teacher walks around and assists students as needed.

5. After the interviews, ask a couple of students to report their findings to the class. "XXX 有两双小号的黑(色的)(袜子)。"

Clothing Interview Sheet

你有什么衣服?

姓名: _____ 日期: _____ 年级: _____ 第 _____ 节课

You are going to interview three classmates. Ask questions similar to the ones that you just practiced. Write down the answers in the table. You will report your findings to the class afterwards.

Name	Number + MW	Size	Color	Clothing
Yourself				
1.				
2.				
3.				

Activity 7: Talk about wearing Chinese clothing (7 minutes)

Pre-Activity:

Purpose: To have students describe what they are wearing by using the verb 穿 .

1. Teacher introduces 穿 by describing what him/herself and students are wearing.
   Teacher: "老师今天穿着一件红衬衫，一条黑裙子。安琪今天穿着一件黄上衣，一条牛仔裤。" Teacher will repeat it a couple of more times.

2. Teacher then asks the class 约翰今天穿着什么衣服？

3. Teacher continues to ask 玛丽今天穿着什么衣服？ and randomly picks students to answer.

In-Activity: Play the game "The Big Wind Blows" (大风吹) *(7-10 minutes)*

1. Ask the class to arrange chairs to form a circle.

2. Ask one student to stand in the center of the circle and conduct the first round of the game as 大风 . However, their chair has to be removed from the circle before the game begins. All the other students remain seated in the circle.

3. 大风 : 大风吹 ! (The big wind blows!)
   Students: 吹什么 ？(What does it blow?)
   大风 : 吹穿黑裤子的人 ! (It blows whoever wears black pants!)

4. Whoever is wearing black pants needs to stand up to switch chairs. 大风 takes advantage of the time when people are switching seats to find an empty chair for themselves. The student who cannot get a chair will become 大风 and start another round of the game. The game continues for a few rounds.

Homework (2 minutes):

1. Ask students to write down what they have in their wardrobes, counting how many shirts, pairs of pants, skirts, etc. and what colors/sizes they are.

2. They will then use Audacity to record themselves speaking what they have written and send the link to the teacher through Edmodo. (technology)

   Note: Audacity is a free audio editor and recorder that most school laptops already have installed on the desktop. Go to http://www.audacity.com for more information. Edmodo is a free educational platform, similar to Facebook, but with a more secure classroom use-only environment. More details can be found at http://www.edmodo.com.

Closure (Presentational, 3-5 minutes):

Exit ticket: Ask students to answer questions about the lesson before they leave the class.

1. Teacher shows items of clothing in different sizes, colors, and quantities on PPT.

2. Each student writes his/her name and answer to the question 老师的衣柜里有什么? on a sticky note.

3. Students answer teacher's question with a complete sentence and post it on the bulletin board.

4. Teacher checks their responses afterwards.

Teacher Self-assessment:

- What went well?

- What needs more review in the next class?

- Did the activities help students learn effectively?

- What should be done differently?

Day 2

Teaching Focus:

Grammar:

- 太贵了!

- 可以便宜一点儿吗? 可不可以便宜一点儿?

- 便宜十块钱, 怎么样?

Vocabulary:

- 买, 东西, 贵, 便宜, 多少, 钱, 块, 毛, 分, 百, 夹克

Phonetics:

- "x" as in 西

- "q" as in 钱

- "j" as in 夹

Day 3

Teaching Focus:

Grammar:

- A 比 B + adjective →A 比 B 贵。

- A 跟 B 一样 + adjective →A 跟 B 一样贵。

Vocabulary:

- 商店, 这家店, 比, 一样, 大小, 合适, 外套, 毛衣, 大衣, 西装, T 恤衫

Phonetics:

- "j" as in 家

- "sh" as in 适

- "xi" as in 西 and 小

- "zh" as in 这 and 装

- "ü" as in 恤

Performance Assessment:

Mini-Project: Write an editorial for your local newspaper stating and defending your opinion on the clothing prices of local shops.

- **Goal:**　　　To express and defend your opinion
- **Role:**　　　Reporter
- **Audience:**　Newspaper subscribers, editors, consumers
- **Setting:**　　Comparing clothing prices in different shops
- **Product:**　　A written editorial
- **Standards:**　1.1, 1.3, 2.1, 2.2, 3.1

Day 4

Teaching Focus:

Grammar:

Subject＋付＋（人）＋$（钱）：我付他十块（钱）

Subject＋找＋（人）＋$（钱）：他找我两块五毛（钱）

虽然……, 可是……

Vocabulary:

售货员, 换, 另外, 刷卡, 收, 信用卡, 现金, 一共, 付钱, 找钱, 美金, 人民币, 新台币

Phonetics:

"uo" as in 货

"ü" as in 员

"x" as in 信 and 现

"j" as in 金

"q" as in 钱

"r" as in 人

Day 5

Review and Performance-based Assessment

Objectives:

Students will be able to:

Purchase an ideal outfit, from hat to shoes, within a budget in order to attend a friend's birthday party (interpersonal, interpretive, and presentational).

Props needed:

Each student will bring 5-10 different clothing items, ranging from head to toe

Self-made price tags

A calculator

Handmade currency (fake money)

Teaching Focus:

Help students utilize the language forms and functions they have learned in this unit in a meaningful context.

Warm-up (8 minutes)

Review measure words; Number + Measure Word + Size + Color + Noun

A 比 B + adjective

A 跟 B 一样 + adjective

Subject + 付 + (人) + $ (钱)

Subject + 找 + (人) + $ (钱)

虽然……, 可是……

Activity 1: Performance-based Assessment (Presentational, 72 minutes)

Scenario: You are going to attend your friend's birthday party this weekend and need to put together an ideal outfit, from hat to shoes, within a set budget. You need to inquire about the size and color of each item before deciding upon and purchasing your ensemble. Bargain over the price and exchange merchandise if necessary to accomplish your task. Whoever gets the most items for the least amount of money in six minutes is the winner.

Speaking Formative Assessment Rubric

Category	5 Well Done	4 Good	3 Acceptable	2 Needs Improvement
Required Vocabulary	All used	Missing 1	Missing 2	Missing 3 or more
Grammar	No errors	Few errors	Some errors	Many errors
Pronunciation	Near native	Intelligible with some mistakes	Intelligible with many mistakes	Unintelligible
Fluency	Smooth	Occasional hesitation	Some unnatural pauses	Many unnatural pauses
Task Completion	All tasks completed	Missing 1 part	Missing 2 parts	Missing 3 parts

Performance Rubric (for Performance Activity)

Category	5	4	3	2
Comprehensibility	Fully comprehensible: no interpretation required on listener's part	Very comprehensible: minimal interpretation required on listener's part	Quite comprehensible: some interpretation required on listener's part	Incomprehensible: listener cannot understand speaker
Grammar	A couple of errors	Some errors	Many errors that do not obscure meaning	Numerous errors that obscure meaning
Fluency	Smooth	Occasional hesitation	Some unnatural pauses	Many unnatural pauses
Pronunciation	Near native	Intelligible with some mistakes	Intelligible with many mistakes	Unintelligible
Required Vocabulary	All used	Missing 1	Missing 2	Missing 3 or more

Writing Rubric

	Task Completion	Compre-hensibility	Level of Discourse	Vocabulary	Grammar
6	Superior completion of the task: appropriate and with elaboration	Fully compre-hensible	Exemplary development: strong use of examples or details	Exemplary word choice: vivid, specific, precise	Exemplary use: complete and correct with sentence variety
5	Appropriate and adequate completion of the task	Easily compre-hensible	Effective development: clear use of examples or details	Effective use: 2 errors	Effective use: 2 errors
4	Partial completion of the task	Mostly compre-hensible	Adequate development: sufficient use of examples or details	Adequate word choice: 4 errors	Adequate sentence structure: 4 errors
3	Less than partial completion of the task	Partially compre-hensible	Limited development: some use of examples or details	Limited word choice: 6 errors	Limited sentence structure: 6 errors
2	Minimal completion of the task	Barely compre-hensible	Minimal development: lacks examples or details	Minimal word choice: inadequate, incorrect	Minimal sentence structure: some incomplete sentences and errors
1	Not complete at all	Incompre-hensible	Inadequate development: lacks examples or details	Inadequate word choice: rambling, inappropriate, incorrect	Inadequate structure: numerous incomplete sentences

For Day 5: Holistic Rubric for Performance Assessment – Role-Play (Shopping)*

Holistic Scoring		
Exceeds Expectations 3	Meets Expectations 2	Does Not Meet Expectations 1
Effective communication Highly accurate vocabulary More self-correction	Comprehensible communication Appropriate vocabulary Occasional self-correction	Unable to communicate clearly Inappropriate vocabulary Repeats same content

* For the Day 5 grading rubric, teacher may choose either the Performance Rubric or the Holistic Rubric for Performance Assessment – Role-Play (Shopping).

Dai-Hau Ruth Tang (唐代豪) received her B.A. degree from Providence College with a major in Chinese Literature and a minor in Western Languages and Literature. She later obtained master's degrees in Marriage, Family and Child Counseling and in Religion in the United States. She started teaching Mandarin Chinese as a second language in 2004, and now teaches at Round Rock High School / Cedar Ridge High School in Round Rock, Texas. She teaches all levels of Chinese language courses, including Pre-AP and AP Chinese. She attended STARTALK Chinese language teachers' training at the University of Houston and the University of Nebraska in the past few years, and was an instructor for the 2013 Rice University STARTALK Student Program.

Shopping

Xiaoyun Matthewson (张晓云)
Lakeside School, Seattle, Washington

Language Proficiency Level: Intermediate Low

Age Range: 14 to 18 (9th to 12th grade)

Class Size: 15-20 students

Time Frame: 45 minutes for Days 1, 3, 4, and 5, 75 minutes for Day 2; 5 lessons in total

Essential Questions:

- Does how we shop reflect who we are as a culture?

- How do shopping habits reflect our values?

Unit Goals:

To help students handle basic shopping transactions and to discuss their shopping experiences.

Standards: Based on the National Standards for Foreign Language Learning

- **Communication:**

  -Interpersonal (1.1)

  -Interpretive (1.2)

  -Presentational (1.3)

- **Connection:** Names of major currencies such as US dollar, RMB, Euro, etc.; exchange rates (3.1).

- **Comparison:** How shopping experiences differ in China and the US, including how customers pay for goods and services (4.2).

- **Culture:** Haggling is an "art form" that reflects the value of seeking harmony, which is at the core of Chinese culture (2.2); how shopping reflects the changing face of China (2.1).

Unit Questions:

- Can students make simple statements indicating what they wish to buy?

- Can students inquire about the price of an item and bargain for it if appropriate?

- Can students inquire about the availability of an item based on color, size, and price?

- Can students make comparisons of merchandise based on color, size, and price?

- Can students ask for a discount in an appropriate setting?

- Can students discuss the pros and cons of different forms of payment?

- Can students understand key information on shopping-related signs and promotional materials?

- Can students read, write, and discuss simple statements about purchases made or planned?

- Can students discuss their preferences for certain stores and explain the reasons?

- Can students get around a department store by reading signs or asking for directions?

Lesson Outlines:

Day 1: Money and forms of payment

Day 2: Bargaining – shopping for clothing articles

Day 3: Colors and sizes

Day 4: Picking a store – Where is the best place to buy...?

Day 5: Sales

Learning Objectives:

Students will be able to:

Day 1

- Understand and name key and commonly known currencies and their denominations (interpretive and interpersonal);

- Ask the price of an item (interpersonal);

- Discuss the pros and cons of different forms of payment (interpersonal);

- Ask which forms of payment are accepted at a store (interpersonal).

Day 2

- Understand and name clothing articles and accessories and the appropriate measure words associated with them (interpretive);

- Understand the bargaining practices and culture of China (interpretive and culture);

- Inquire about prices and engage in bargaining (interpersonal);

- Make comparisons of merchandise based on cost and looks (interpersonal).

Day 3

- Understand different color palettes and sizes of clothing articles (interpretive);

- Ask about colors and sizes of clothing items at a store (interpersonal);

- Discuss clothing sizes and color preferences (interpersonal);

- Read and write a shopping list with specific information on color and size (interpretive).

Day 4

- Discuss favorite stores and explain reasons for the preference (interpersonal);

- Articulate features of stores, using the extended discourse marker 虽然……但是……, etc. (presentational).

Day 5

- Understand key information on ads and read sale signs in the store (interpretive);

- Find their way around a department store (interpretive and interpersonal);

- Inquire about discounts (interpersonal);

- Group work: start writing skits for culminating project of the unit.

Day 2 (Sample Day): Bargaining – Shopping for Clothing Articles

Learning Objectives:

Students will be able to:

- Understand and name clothing articles and accessories and the appropriate measure words associated with them (interpretive);

- Understand the bargaining practices and culture of China (interpretive and culture);

- Inquire about prices and engage in bargaining (interpersonal);

- Make comparisons of merchandise based on cost and looks (interpersonal).

Teaching Focus:

Grammar:

- Measure words for clothing articles: 件 , 条 , 双 , 只 , 顶

- Soliciting agreement: 怎么样?

- 太 + adjective + 了!

- Expressing plurality with 些

Vocabulary:

- Tops: 衣服 , 毛衣 , 大衣 , 衬衫 , T 恤衫 , 外套

- Bottoms: 裤子 , 长裤 , 短裤 , 内裤 , 牛仔裤 , 裙子

- Footwear: 鞋子 , 袜子

- Accessories: 帽子 , 围巾 , 领带 , 手套

- Measure words: 件 , 条 , 双 , 顶

- Verbs: 穿 , 戴

Culture:

Haggling is an "art form" in Chinese culture. While the goal is to get the best price, establishing a relationship between the buyer and the seller is also important. The process should be friendly and tempered with humor, rather than confrontational and adversarial. The price arrived at should be satisfactory to both parties, and the seller and the buyer should depart on friendly terms.

Learning Difficulties:

While the use of measure words (MW) is not unique to the Chinese language, they are much more prevalent in Chinese than in English. There are some general rules to follow, but for the purpose of this unit, we'll only focus on a few of them. Almost without exception, 件 is used for tops and 条 is used for bottoms. 条 is also used for items that are long and narrow, such as 围巾 (scarves) and 领带 (ties). 双 is used for things that come in pairs, such as shoes, socks, and gloves/ mittens.

Students often forget to use 戴 for wearing accessories and instead use 穿 for everything, which leads to comic effect in the eyes of native speakers.

Teaching Material and Resources:

- *Encounters: Chinese Language and Culture*, Book I, Units 9 and 10

- Picture of clothing articles and selected accessories on PPT/Smartboard and/or real clothing articles, if feasible

- Chinese names of clothing articles and selected accessories and related measure words on PPT/Smartboard

- Video clip (from *Encounters: Chinese Language and Culture* or other source) of a shopping scene that includes price inquiry and bargaining

- Worksheet to record price negotiation from the video clip

- Reading handout on price haggling, one copy per pair

- Handout of drawings/pictures of selected clothing articles/accessories in pairs, with different prices and designs for students to make comparison; one copy per pair (see Appendix I)

Instructional Strategies:

Warm-up: "Stand up if you are wearing... 穿……的人请站起来" (3 minutes)

The students have previewed the clothing articles/accessories vocabulary the day before as homework. The teacher models by naming one clothing item, such as 衬衫, then the students wearing a shirt have to stand up. After modeling a few times, ask a few students to take turns practicing in the same manner.

Activity 1: 学习生词 (For Objective 1, 25 minutes)

Purpose: To practice new words and expressions in context.

1. Use PPT or Smartboard to teach the names of clothing articles. Make corrections on tones as necessary and help the students pronounce them correctly. Chinese multi-syllabic nouns are often visual and self-explanatory. Point out to the students that adding a modifier to the main word creates new terms which are intuitive and easy to remember once the students know the main word, e.g., from the word 裤 we make the new words 长裤, 短裤, 牛仔裤.

2. Study characters: Instead of pointing out that 裤, 裙, 衬, 衫 all share the same radical 衣, let students make the discovery themselves by asking if they notice

anything these characters share in common.

3. Teach measure words: Before introducing the measure words used in this unit, do a quick review of the measure words the students already know, such as 个, 张 and 位. Make sure they name a few nouns used with these measure words, such as 一个苹果, 一张纸 and 一位老师. Point out 件 is used for all the tops and 条 for bottoms. Point out that 条 is also used for long and narrow things, such as 围巾, 领带, and snakes! It's always handy to have some real items to give students stronger visual cues to facilitate their understanding. The teacher can bring these items to class or point to the clothing articles on him/herself or on the students for instruction and practice.

4. Introduce verbs 穿 and 戴: Remind the students that for accessories, 戴 has to be used. Point to the pictures of clothing items and ask the students to give the verb phrase, such as 穿衬衫, 戴帽子, to reinforce the correct use of 穿 and 戴.

5. Make formative assessment: Work in groups of three, have two students ask each other about what the third person has on that day. The teacher models the description first: 玛丽今天穿了一件 T 恤衫、一件外套、一条牛仔裤和一双鞋子。她还戴了一顶帽子、一条围巾。Each student should describe the clothing of two classmates in the group. If any accessories are worn, they need to be included. Alternatively, the teacher can prepare picture cuttings from magazines or newspapers with people sporting an array of clothing articles and accessories for this activity. It's OK to use English for the accessories that the students haven't learned in Chinese as long as the correct verb and measure word are used.

6. Display the images of clothing articles on the Smartboard and have class sing a rhyme based on the tune of the English nursery rhyme *Michael Finnegan* (http://www.youtube.com/watch?v=_0mkLKBPJ6o) to further practice naming clothing articles along with the proper measure words. For example, the items can be listed from head to toe, or from accessories to clothes in groups of four: 一顶帽子，一条围巾，一条领带，一双手套；一件衬衫，一件 T 恤衫，一件毛衣，一件大衣；这些都是我的！一件外套，一条裤子，一条裙子，一条牛仔裤；一条短裤，一条内裤，一双鞋子，一双袜子；这些都是我的！Students sing out the item as the teacher points to the image on the board. Do this a couple of times with images, and then a couple more times with just words (in Chinese characters).

Activity 2: 砍价文化 * **(For Objective 2, interpretive and culture, 10 minutes)**

Purpose: To help students understand the prices being discussed, how bargaining is done, and provide a model for students for the next activity.

1. Distribute the worksheet below. Play a short video clip of shopping that includes several rounds of back-and-forth price negotiation. Replay the clip if necessary. Have students write down the prices they heard in the video clip. Check the answers with the class.

Seller's starting price:	Buyer:
Seller:	Buyer:
Seller:	Buyer:
Final price:	# of items purchased:

2. True/False statement on price haggling: The students read FYI on price haggling as part of the homework from the day before and each came up with two true/false statements. (See assignment instructions for Day 1.) Have different students share their statements with the class to test their understanding of the material.

Examples:

1) 如果东西太贵了，你应该让售货员／卖东西的人知道你很生气。—— 对不对？

（答案：不对，你不应该生气，你应该很客气。）

2) 你可以用买两件东西的钱买三件东西。—— 对还是错？

（答案：对。）

* The activity and material of this segment is adapted and modified from Cynthia Ning and John Montanaro, *Encounters: Chinese Language and Culture*, Book I, pp. 220~221.

Activity 3: "太贵了！便宜一点儿吧。" **(For Objective 3, interpersonal, 25 minutes)**

Purpose: To practice using expressions for shopping and bargaining.

1. Have students draw two simple clothing items or accessories they just learned

today in their notebook or on a piece of paper, then set a price for each of them. The price should be higher than what they are willing to sell the item for.

2. Lead the class to brainstorm expressions they could use for price haggling based on what they have watched. Start with price inquiry. Guide, correct, and trim what the class comes up with so you have a workable list that resembles the one below that students can use in their oral practice.

- 这个多少钱?/ 这个怎么卖？ Ask students to name the specific item with the appropriate measure word, such as 这件毛衣, 那条围巾, etc.

- 太贵了！/ 有点儿贵。

- 能不能便宜一点儿?

- 不贵, 不贵, 很便宜。

- 这件 / 那条很好看!

- X 块（钱），怎么样？

- 太少了！

- 还是太贵了！

- 好吧，好吧，X 块（钱）卖给你。

3. Students work in pairs to practice bargaining for the article they just drew in their notebooks. The seller tries to sell for as much as they can and the buyer tries to get it at the best price. As a review of the three forms of payment learned in the last lesson, ask students to add payment discussion to their dialogue. Switch roles after the transaction is done, and find a different partner to sell the second item.

4. Have one or two pairs present their skits to class.

Activity 4: 你喜欢哪一个 ? (For Objective 4, interpersonal, 10 minutes)

Purpose: To review new words, and to review comparative structures and the use of connective devices students learned previously (from the Direction and Transportation Unit).

1. Distribute handouts to class. On the handout are pictures of three or four of selected clothing articles and accessories. Each category has two items that are different in price and design. (Please see Appendix I.)

2. Have a confident student improvise a dialogue with the teacher to make a comparison of two items in the same category and discuss their preference, based on cost and looks. The dialogue can start by discussing prices and then incorporate connective devices such as 不仅……而且……，虽然……但是…… into the discussion to make the dialogue more sophisticated. The dialogue may look something like this:

> A: X 商店的围巾一条多少钱？
>
> B: 一条 $29.99。
>
> A: Y 商店的围巾呢？
>
> B: 一条 $16.50。
>
> A: 你喜欢 X 商店的围巾还是 Y 商店的？
>
> B: 我喜欢 Y 商店的那条。
>
> A: 为什么？
>
> B: 因为那条不仅好看，而且比 X 商店的那条便宜。你喜欢哪一条？
>
> A: 我喜欢 X 商店的那条。
>
> B: 为什么？那条围巾很贵啊！
>
> A: 对，可是我觉得比 Y 商店的那条好看。

3. After a couple of models done, pair students up and have them come up with their own conversation with the help of the graphics. The teacher circulates the classroom to offer guidance and give feedback.

Closing: (2 minutes)

Assignments:

Complete character writing worksheet for the clothing articles with correct stroke order and write down the English meaning of the words and phrases.

Write a note (2-4 sentences) about a recent clothing purchase. Include the price and reasons for buying it.

Preview vocabulary for colors and sizes to prepare for next class.

Day 1: Money and Forms of Payment

Teaching Focus:

Grammar:

- Review comparative structures:

  A 比 B + adjective

  B 没有 A (那么) + adjective

- A 还是 B？ (美元还是人民币？现金还是信用卡？)

Vocabulary:

- Currencies: 人民币，美元，欧元，英镑，加元／加拿大元，日元

- Measure words for denominations:

  Verbal: 块，毛，分

  Written: 元，角，分

- Forms of payment: 现金，信用卡，支票

- Verbs: 付钱，付 (现金)，带，刷卡，写 (支票)

- Other: 换 (一块美元可以换六块人民币)

Culture:

China is largely a cash-based society in daily consumer transactions, although debit cards and credit cards are becoming increasingly popular, with most department stores and other large stores accepting both. Personal checks are not used in China.

Learning Difficulties:

- It can be confusing to students that measure words for currency denominations are different in verbal and written form in Chinese. Point out the difference, but focus on the verbal forms of 块，毛 and 分 .

- In speech, when the last unit is 毛 or 分, it's often omitted, e.g., ¥3.20 is expressed as 三块二 , and ¥2.56 is expressed as 两块五毛六.

- 或者 vs. 还是

Homework Assignment:

To prepare for the Day 2 lesson, assign reading on price haggling as a homework assignment for Day 1. Based on the FYI below, each student should come up with 2 true/false statements to share their knowledge of the material with the class the next day. Students should try to write the statements in simple Chinese they have learned, but it's also fine to write them in "fun Chinglish", using Chinese structures with some English words or English structures with Chinese words they know. For example: Haggling 的时候不要生气，要很客气。

FYI

Haggling over Price*

An astute observer of Chinese culture has remarked that bargaining is an "art form much beloved by Chinese". However, it's not all about getting a lower price. Of course the price is important, but establishing a relationship between buyer and seller that is friendly, not adversarial, is also important. Neither side wants to take advantage of the other; rather, a solution that is pleasing to both is usually the goal for each side. This is entirely within the tradition of seeking harmony, something that lies at the core of Chinese culture.

Tips for bargaining:

- Keep the negotiation good-natured and friendly. Use expressions such as 怎么样? 可以吗? 行不行?
- Know when to bargain and when not to. Department stores are generally not the place to engage in bargaining. If you are in doubt, watch the local shoppers or ask a Chinese friend.
- Start by offering less than you are willing to pay and go up slowly.
- If the seller doesn't budge, consider walking away, feigning disinterest, and then return later.
- Offer to buy multiple items for a lower price, or getting a second item thrown in for free or at a significant discount.
- Keep in mind this handy line: " 能不能便宜一点儿 ?" (Can it be a little bit cheaper?)
- Tell the seller that you really like the item, but explain you are only a student and you don't have very much money. It is known that vendors sometimes have a soft spot for young scholars!

---

* This material is adapted from Cynthia Ning and John Montanaro, *Encounters: Chinese Language and Culture*, Book I, p. 221.

Day 3: Colors and Sizes

Teaching Focus:

Grammar:

Degree comparison – much more and a little bit more

A 比 B + adjective + 得多 / 一点儿

Vocabulary:

- Colors: 颜色, 红色, 黄色, 蓝色, 绿色, 黑色, 白色, 粉红色, 咖啡色
- Sizes: 号码, 大号, 中号, 小号
- Other: 深, 浅
- **Note:** Use 深 and 浅 to describe darker or lighter shades of a color.

Learning Difficulties:

- It's a common mistake that students place 很 / 一点儿 before the adjective to express the degree in comparison as in the English structure. For instance, it is incorrect to say 这条裤子比那条一点儿贵.

- Different ways of using the color as a noun modifier: 红色的毛衣 and 红毛衣 are both acceptable.

- There are several ways to describe the colors brown and orange. To keep it simple, choose one and stick to it. 咖啡色 and 橘色 for the two colors are used in this lesson.

Day 4: Picking a Store – Where Is the Best Place to Buy…?

Teaching Focus:

Grammar:

去哪儿买……最好？

Vocabulary:

- Stores: 商店 , 百货商场 , 超市

- Categories of goods: 日用品 , 蔬菜 , 水果 , 肉 , 海鲜

- Other (criteria for choosing a store): 服务 , 工作人员 , 友好 , 新鲜 , 离家很近 / 远

Note:

All the merchandise categories can be added in front of 店 for names of specialty stores, i.e., 书店 , 水果店 , etc.

Culture:

(The following can be a FYI handout for students to read as homework for cultural understanding.)

The shopping scene in China has undergone major changes in the last 10-15 years. China now boasts one of the largest luxury consumer goods markets in the world. In major cities, stores such as Prada, Louis Vuitton, Cartier, and home-grown high-end shops are commonly seen, doing brisk business at prices that are often much higher than in the West. However, for an overseas visitor, interesting places to shop would probably be local markets and shopping alleys where prices are generally lower and haggling is frequently expected.

Instructional Strategies:

As a speaking activity, have students compare a couple of similar stores based on price, quality of goods, service, and convenience, then make a recommendation based on those criteria.

210

Day 5: Sales

Teaching Focus:

Grammar:

Review grammatical structures covered in this unit.

Vocabulary.

层, 楼, 打折, 电梯

Learning Difficulties:

Discounts in Chinese are expressed in the opposite way of those in English. 20% off is 打八折 rather than 打二折. 15% off is 八五折, without mentioning the decimal point.

Culminating Project for the Unit:*

Group skit on shopping: Form groups of three or four students. Divide the group into shopper(s) and vendor(s). Encourage the students to come up with creative ways to assign the roles. The following are a couple of examples of possible scenarios: two friends going to a shop to buy a birthday present for another friend or a family member, or two neighboring vendors competing for the business of a buyer. The skit can also have a narrator. Each partner should have a minimum of 10 lines. The length of the skit will be 3-5 minutes, depending on the size of the group. The group may choose to include a couple of scenes in the skit. It should include at least five of the following:

- Make plans to go shopping.

- Discuss which store to go and give reasons.

- Ask about prices.

- Make comments on the merchandise.

- Inquire about the availability of other sizes and colors.

- Ask for or offer discounts.

- A few rounds of going back and forth on the prices between the seller and buyer. The exchange should be friendly, not adversarial.

- Discuss forms of payment and make payment.

Encourage the students to include a conflict and its resolution into the plot of the skit to make it more fun. For example, one of the buyers doesn't have any cash but the seller only accepts cash, or a particular color is not available and the seller tries to offer other alternatives.

Language use: 1) Incorporate at least two comparative structures; 2) Use connective devices 因为……所以……, 不仅……而且……and 虽然……但是…….

*The students will start writing the skit in class on Day 5, when they decide on the theme of their group skit, assign roles, and set up the framework of the skit. The rest of the work is assigned as homework. However, students may need to be given more time in class to work on writing and presentation preparation, where the teacher can give feedback on the spot, and therefore it may be necessary to add a sixth day to the unit. Alternatively, partial class time may be given for the preparation of this project while the class starts working on a different unit.

Rubric for Assessing Speaking (unit skit presentation)

	Excellent	Good	Unacceptable
Task Completion	Fully complete	Almost complete	Incomplete
Comprehensibility	Fully comprehensible to the audience	Comprehensible to the audience	Not comprehensible to the audience
Linguistic Accuracy (Grammar & Vocabulary)	1-2 errors	3-4 errors	Numerous errors
Fluency	Very fluent, with little or no hesitation	Fluent, with slight hesitation	Halting speech with frequent, long pauses
Pronunciation	Few or no errors	A few errors	Numerous errors

Rubric for Assessing Writing (script for skit)

	Excellent	Good	Unacceptable
Task Completion	Fully complete	Almost complete	Incomplete
Functional Language Use	Correct use of two or more comparative structures Uses all three connective devices multiple times No other grammatical errors	Uses at least two comparative structures Uses all three connective devices at least once Minor other grammatical errors	Only one or no comparative structure is used Doesn't use all three connective devices Numerous other grammatical errors
Appropriate Use of Vocabulary	Excellent use of vocabulary in right contexts	Good use of vocabulary in mostly correct contexts	Many words are used incorrectly, impeding understanding

Appendix I: Which one would you buy?

Shopping Unit – Which one would you buy? 你会买哪个？

X 商店 $29.99   Y 商店 $16.50   X 商店 $27.50   Y 商店 $27.50

X 商店 $159.90   Y 商店 $235.99   X 商店 $35.00   Y 商店 $85.99

Xiaoyun Matthewson (张晓云) is a Chinese instructor at Lakeside School in Seattle, Washington, where she teaches beginning to advanced level Chinese. She has presented at both the ACTFL and National Chinese Language Conferences on teaching advanced level Chinese in high school and on building a high-functioning secondary school Chinese program. She studied international business and economics in both China and the US, and also took part in the STARTALK/Pacific Lutheran University World Language Certification Program. She has served on the CLTA-Washington Board of Directors since 2012.

Critique

Shopping – Dai-Hau Ruth Tang
Shopping – Xiaoyun Matthewson

Shopping is a theme that can be used at all proficiency levels. Both Dai-Hau Ruth Tang and Xiaoyun Matthewson write about shopping, but their designs differ in the selection of textbooks, curriculum focus, and their students' proficiency levels. Tang's sample day design aims at building on clothing-related expressions and linguistic structures, which are concerned with the usages and comparisons of color, numbers, size, and price. She carefully limits the vocabulary input, yet has designed a series of activities for students to practice language structures and word order through a variety of group activities. Matthewson's sample day design imparts multifaceted areas to help students function as competent communicators and polite bargainers.

A distinctive feature shared by both Tang's and Matthewson's curriculums and instructional strategies is scaffolding. Tang designs instructional steps to assure students' learning success. Even vocabulary learning (Activity 1) is arranged in five steps with different interactive formats and review processes. The first three steps show how noun phrases are introduced and practiced in an interactive format between a teacher and students, and the last two steps are activities among students themselves. Activity 2 consolidates the learning from Activity 1 and expands the language form by adding color words. Activity 3 has students investigate each other's dream wardrobes to review the structure that appeared in Activity 2 and to practice new sentence patterns in conversations. The input dialogue and the Think → Pair → Share game clearly give students ideas on what their task is and how to accomplish it. Activity 4 completes the information on number, color, and size of clothing items naturally used in communication. The author knows that the word order of these clustered modifiers would be challenging. Therefore, Activities 4, 5, and 6 are designed to practice the language form in Communicative Language Teaching. Although the last activity is at a higher level of difficulty, students should be able to fulfill the task easily because they have practiced in various activities in addition to a visual aid, "Clothing Interview Sheet".

Xiaoyun Matthewson's design reflects the concept that "the classroom is a small world; the world is a large classroom". The author proposes that "Haggling is an 'art form' in Chinese culture. While the goal is to get the best price, establishing a relationship between the buyer and the seller is also important." Her sample day design helps students build bargaining skills first with listening comprehension (the warm-up activity) and then by practicing vocabulary that includes verb phrases with 穿 and 戴, and noun phrases with classifiers and clothing items. Similar to Tang's design, Matthewson's design demonstrates solid steps in conducting a series of small activities and guiding students to achieve learning objectives. Her Activity 1 consists of 6 steps, which make learning easier and more engaging. Before providing the bargaining activity, Matthewson makes sure that students understand the Chinese bargaining culture. Activity 2 is a fun learning activity based on the Chinese bargaining culture. With the culture understanding developed from Activity 2 and linguistic skills accumulated from Activity 1, students are now able to carry on the conversation of bargaining. Once again, facilitating input is provided via students' brainstorming for useful expressions and negotiation strategies. In the process, students are stimulated to not only practice grammatical forms, but also function as competent bargainers to forcefully persuade each other, make suggestions/requests, and accept or decline offers in a socio-culturally acceptable manner.

Clothing-related expressions and purchasing daily necessities, as basic as they are, pose difficulties for English-speaking learners. This is not only because the word order and sentence structures in Chinese are quite different from those in English, but also because shopping is a complex social activity that involves cultural differences and value systems. As demonstrated in both designs, students are very likely to succeed in acquiring the language through detailed instructional scaffolding and various group activities.

The activities in Tang's design are varied, which exemplifies her teaching efficiency. Fortunately her class size is small and her class period is 90 minutes. Although some activities indeed do not take a long time (e.g. warm-up activities 1 and 2), nine activities are many. Readers can make choices on the activities that are more appropriately and easily adapted into one's own instructional setting. The vocabulary seems to be a bit overwhelming in Matthewson's design, considering the low proficiency level and very basic grammar structures.

Theme 6

Time and Dates

Time and Dates

Wenya Lu (卢文雅)
Walter Payton College Preparatory High School, Chicago, Illinois

Language Proficiency Level: Novice High

Age Range: 14-17 (high school students)

Class Size: 13-21 students

Time Frame: 90 minutes for each lesson, with 4 lessons in total

Essential Question:

What can be learned from how a culture perceives the temporal sequence via the use of word order in its language?

Unit Goals:

Students will be able to: tell time, dates, and days of the week; make appointments involving future events; use adverbial time phrases and place them correctly in sentences following basic word order in Chinese; talk about school schedules; talk about the similarities and differences between Chinese culture and students' own cultures when celebrating birthdays.

Standards: Based on the National Standards for Foreign Language Learning

- **Communication:**

  -Interpersonal (1.1)

  -Interpretive (1.2)

  -Presentational (1.3)

- **Connection:** Number-reviewing activities stimulate students' mathematical faculties.

- **Comparison:** Traditional ways of celebrating selected "special" birthdays vs. modernized, Western ways of celebrating birthdays; Beijing time zone vs. America's different time zones.

- **Culture:** Some traditional birthday celebration etiquette, such as eating 长寿面, giving gifts in pairs to honor 好事成双, and never giving a clock as a birthday gift 生日不送钟 (终) are included in this unit.

- **Community:** Students are encouraged to learn and practice Chinese beyond the classroom walls. Go to Chinatown and take pictures of various shop signs that tell those shops' business hours (营业时间); interview a Chinese-speaking person about his/her daily routine.

Unit Questions:

- Can students tell and ask the days of the week, dates and clock time in Chinese? What are some patterns that are unique in Chinese? 点 , 分 , 半 and 刻 are essential in learning how to tell time. 分 is optional in spoken Chinese, but the word for zero 零 is necessary if the minutes are less than ten. 差 is common to tell remaining minutes when close to a new hour and 过 is also used right before the minute to indicate how many minutes have passed the hour.

- Can students identify some traditional ways of celebrating one's birthday in China? What parts of those traditions have been changing?

- Can students talk about school schedules, including time and dates?

- Can students make appointments involving future events?

Lesson Outlines:

>**Day 1:** My Birthday 我的生日
>
>**Day 2:** What Time Is It Now? 现在几点？
>
>**Day 3:** My Daily Routine 我的一天
>
>**Day 4:** My Classes 我的课

Learning Objectives:

Students will be able to:

Day 1

- Ask and tell the days of the week (interpersonal);

- Ask and talk about each other's birthday (interpersonal);

- Comprehend and use time words appropriately in contextual sentences (interpretive and presentational).

Day 2

- Ask and tell clock time (interpersonal);

- Comprehend various "business hours" signs (interpretive);

- Ask about and state pre-scheduled activities at different times (interpersonal).

Day 3

- Ask and tell each other about their daily routine at school (interpersonal);

- Communicate with a pen pal in writing about school routines (presentational).

Day 4

- Exchange information about class schedules (interpersonal);

- Share and comment on classmates' class schedules (presentational, interpersonal).

Day 1 (Sample Day)

Learning Objectives:

Students will be able to:

- Ask and tell the days of the week (interpersonal);

- Ask and talk about each other's birthday (interpersonal);

- Comprehend and use time words appropriately in contextual sentences (interpretive and presentational).

Teaching Focus:

Grammar:

- A time adverbial phrase precedes a verb or a verb phrase

- One verb after another, such as 去看电影 and 来上课

- Duplication of a verb to indicate an action done in a casual manner or lasting for a short time, such as 看看 in 看看电视 and 玩玩儿 in 玩玩儿电脑游戏

Vocabulary:

- Key words used in telling the days of the week and dates: 年, 月, 日 / 号, 星期 / 礼拜 / 周 (focus on 星期, but do let students know that there are variations in spoken and written styles of the language)

- Other words that are introduced in the sample text: 课, 看, 电影, adverb 只, 去, and 太好了

Phonetics:

- Compound finals: "ao", "uo" and "ou"

- Polyphonic character: 只 in the first tone as a measure word; 只 in the third tone as an adverb meaning "only"

Learning Difficulties:

- Basic word order in arranging year, month, and day in Chinese. Students may make the mistake of putting the month and day before year due to their habits in English.

- Students may also put an adverbial time phrase at the end of a sentence instead of before a verb.

- Verb duplication: Students may be confused with the following three patterns involving verbs:

  1) AA format, i.e., the verb is a monosyllable and repeats itself twice, e.g. 看看, 说说, 听听, 试试, 等等;

  2) A 一 A format, i.e., inserting 一 in between the monosyllabic verb, e.g. 看一看, 说一说, 听一听, 试一试, 等一等;

  3) ABAB format, i.e., the verb consists of two syllables and each repeats once in order, e.g. 学习学习, 练习练习, 考虑考虑. Teachers don't have to teach all the three patterns at one time or right away. Such verb patterns occur frequently in spoken Chinese, as illustrated in various dialogues in the *Huan Ying* textbook. Instead of drilling students in all the three formats, just having them model off the sample dialogues would probably be a more realistic approach at this level.

Teaching Materials and Resources:

- Chinese calendars
- Stacks of colored paper cards and markers
- A timer or clock (an online timer also works), small white boards, and dry erase markers
- PowerPoint slides of key vocabulary with visual images
- *Huan Ying* Vol.1 textbook and workbook

Instructional Strategies:

Warm-up (5 minutes)

Number game: a review of basic addition and subtraction as a connection to students' math class. Divide the class into two teams: Team A and Team B.

Game 1: Make 10: Randomly select one student from Team A and one student from Team B. Ask the student from Team A to call out a number between 0 and 10 randomly. The student from Team B has to say a number within five seconds to make the two numbers add up to 10.

Game 2: Make 30: Student A says a randomly chosen number between 0 and 30, and student B has to say a number within eight seconds to make the two numbers add up to 30.

Call on 8-10 pairs of students for either game.

Activity 1 (35 minutes)

For Objectives 1 and 2

Purpose: To practice new words and expressions in meaningful contexts.

1. Use PowerPoint slides and calendar pages to introduce the first set of new time words: 一月～十二月；星期一～星期天 / 星期日. Have students summarize the patterns of saying 12 months in Chinese and the seven days of the week. Have class come to an agreement in asking questions to get days of the week and calendar date, 今天几月几号？今天星期几？ Emphasize that 星期天 or 星期日 is used for Sunday, rather than a number to indicate "day seven". (The question word 几 was already introduced previously in the context of telling and asking about one's age, i.e., 你几岁？ is used to ask someone whose age appears to be under 10.)

2. Game: 猜猜是哪一天？ Teacher says a day of the week or any month, and has students say either the day before, after, two days ago, or two days after in Chinese. You set the pattern first and have one or two practice rounds. For example, 老师说"星期一"，同学们说"星期三，对吗？"Then choose a couple of students to demonstrate, giving verbal compliments such as 很好，太好了 and 非常好 when the answers are correct, as always. Then have the whole class participate. To make the game more challenging and fun, you can secretly choose a day of the week or a month and then have the class guess your choice by asking 是不是星期一？or 是不是九月？No need to worry about explaining the 是不是 pattern, as students will naturally understand it's a way of asking for "Yes" or "No" confirmation. Do give a clear verbal response whether they guess correctly or incorrectly by saying 是，是星期一 or 不是，不是九月. Decide before the guessing game starts the number of guesses the

students can have. Allow some flexibility when playing games, for example, students usually like this type of game and want to be the secret day/month selector. If that's the case, allow some volunteers to act as the teacher. Below is a demo round in Chinese:

老师：我说一月，同学们说三月。我说三月，同学们说五月。我说五月，同学们说 (pause here, and wait for class to say the answer. Yes, they get the pattern by now.) 七月！对，很好！非常好！现在我们开始玩儿游戏。(If you have been playing these kinds of 游戏 often, your class will show excitement when they hear the term 游戏 for sure.）

> 老师：四月。
>
> 学生 A：六月！
>
> 老师：对！很好！十二月。
>
> 学生 B：一月？
>
> 老师：不对。你再看看，十二月，然后，一月，然后，二月！

3. Show on PowerPoint slides the key word 生日，along with birthday candles and cakes. Then ask the question: 你的生日（是）几月几号？ Followed by teacher-student (T-S) and student-student (S-S) interactions:

   1) Have students write their birthday information in Chinese (only the birth date, not the birth year) on a prepared stack of cards. Then collect the cards from students and place them into a pile. A student volunteer picks a card from the stack and reads aloud what's written on the card. Then the person whose birthday was just called out has to respond by saying 我的生日（是）X 月 X 号 . If the student volunteer happens to pick their own card, then after reading aloud the date, they will say 我的生日（是)X 月 X 号. (If students ask how to include year information in their birthday, then also introduce by asking 你是哪年 / 哪一年生的？ and responding by saying 我是 XXXX 年生的.) Then, pair students up and have them practice asking one another their birthday.

   2) Before proceeding to the next game, use a current monthly calendar. Point at the date of the class and model by saying 今天 X 月 X 号 . Repeat a couple of times. Point at the day of the week of the date and model by saying 今天星期 X. Repeat it a couple of times. Then ask students questions such as 今天几月几号？ and 今天星期几？ Now start the game.

Speed "dating": Students form two lines facing each other. Teacher decides the time duration for each round of "dating time", for example, 40 seconds. Only students in one of the two lines take turns switching to one end of their line after the designated 40 seconds have expired to ask a new "partner" (whom they are facing after the switch) the following questions. Encourage students to keep playing, as "speed" is key to this game. As the target questions are repeatedly practiced, students will be able to catch up and have the language items integrated into these questions and responses practiced.

A: 今天几月几号？

B: 今天 X 月 X 号。

A: 今天星期几？

B: 今天星期……

A: 今天是你的生日吗？

B: 不是。我的生日是 X 月 Y 日。

Again, encourage students to be flexible about applying the sample dialogue. For example, they can replace 今天 with 明天，or 昨天．They can also add tag questions like 你呢？if applicable, and before you call time.

3) Formative Assessment (interpersonal): Mixed activity. Form groups of five. In each group, students ask each other 你的生日是几月几号？ Based on the answers, form a straight line in front of the classroom, with the student whose birthday is the earliest in the year at the head of the line and the student whose birthday is the latest in the year at the end. Language assessed: expression of months and dates in a meaningful context, use of correct tones.

Activity 2 (20 minutes)

For Objective 3: Comprehend and apply an adverbial time phrase in a sentence. (Interpersonal and presentational)

Pre-Activity

1. Demonstrate where adverbial time phrases go in a sentence.

Write these words/phrases on the board and have the class rearrange them in the possible correct word orders:

没有课　　我们　　星期五 → 星期五我们没有课 or 我们星期五没有课。

我们　去　看电影　星期六 → 星期六我们去看电影 or 我们星期六去看电影。

2. Summarize the basic word order of a Chinese sentence:

Somebody (S)　Adverbial Phrases (time, place, etc.)　Do (V)　Something (O)

Distribute small whiteboards along with dry erase markers to the class, one board and one marker per two students. Have students write down their "plan(s)" on their board, applying the above pattern after hearing a situation prompt in English from you or seeing a situation prompt prepared by you, e.g., "The weekend is coming and you would like to make plans with your friends. Jot down your plans and show them to the class." Allow them to use their books and notes for reference. After you call time, have each pair show the class their board and report to the class their plans. (presentational)

Main Activity: Sentence Formation Race (Interpersonal and presentational)

1. Divide the class into two teams. One team is to write up as many time phrases as possible, for example, 星期一～星期天 / 日, x 月 x 号, 今天, 明天, 昨天, 我的生日, 老师的生日, 现在, etc. The other team is to contribute activity phrases: 上学, 回家, 做功课, 去看电影, 吃饭, 上课, 下课, 打开书, etc. (Some of the phrases may seem new here, but as common classroom terms/expressions are usually put up in the classroom, students will use those resources as well.) Allow both teams to use up to three or four words in *pinyin* format, in case they find some Chinese characters challenging. The phrases can be written on boards in your classroom, if there are two boards or if your board is big enough, or have two teams choose two different colors from the card stack.

2. After the two teams have finished creating their word banks, announce the start of the activity. First, call one representative from each team, student A and student B, then point to one time phrase and one activity phrase, or have someone hold up the two cards. The two representatives have to compete to say a correct sentence in Chinese using the two chosen phrases. Watch the word order!

3. To make the activity a little bit more challenging, have student A ask a grammatically correct question, including words on the two chosen cards, to which student B has to offer a grammatically correct response. Below is a demo round for this activity:

The teacher holds up two cards: 晚上 , 看书 .

Student A may then ask 你晚上看书吗 or 晚上你看书吗 .

Student B may then say 对 , 我晚上看书 or 晚上我看书 .

If either one of them happens to say 晚上 after they say 看书 , then the teacher simply restates the question or response in the correct form until the representative naturally repeats it after them correctly.

Have the class vote on the funniest and/or the most creative sentences. (A good way of developing students' habit of voting in Chinese would be having students write 很好 , 非常好 and 最好 on strips of paper and then hold up the appropriate strip for sentences they think are well done, extremely well done, and the best.)

Post-Activity

Ask students to do a short survey by going around the classroom and asking three classmates if their nightly routine includes reading, watching TV, etc.: 你晚上看书吗? 你晚上看电视吗? After time is up, call on a couple of students to report their findings to the class: Lisa, Juan 晚上看书; Aisha, David 晚上看电视 , etc. (Interpersonal and presentational)

Activity 3: Listening (20 minutes)

For Objectives 1, 2, and 3

Pre-Activity: 课文理解 *(Interpretive)*

Go over the textbook lessons (*Huan Ying, Vol.1,* pp.110-113) and let students read the texts as they listen to the accompanying audio recordings online. After students hear the text recording 2-3 times, have them respond to the following questions from the textbook by writing down the answers in English or Chinese (as some students will insist) in their notebook:

1. 玛丽娅的生日是几月几日? (Students have become familiar with 几月几号 by now, but you should have explained in the beginning when 生日 was introduced that 几月几日 is more commonly used when written, although people still pronounce it as 几月几号 .)

2. 她的生日是星期几?

3. 星期六玛丽娅和凯丽有课吗?

4. 凯丽星期六请玛丽娅做什么?

5. 汤姆知道奶奶的生日吗?

6. 谁知道爷爷的生日是几月几号?

Main Activity: Summative Listening Assessment for This Lesson (Interpretive)

Students are to complete the listening practice in their *Huan Ying, Vol.1* Workbook, pp.153-154. There are four tracks in total. Track 1 assesses students' understanding of the new time words, some in month and day format, some combined with days of the week, and some combined with the year. During a set amount of pause time between each question, e.g., five seconds, students write down answers in their workbook in numerals. Track 2 is a set of comprehension questions of the second sample dialogue in the textbook. Questions are in true/ false format. Confirm answers with class at the end of this track and encourage students to explain why they chose what they did. Track 3 is a conversation between two friends talking about days of the week, based on a calendar page. Students need to decide true or false after they listen to the conversation. Track 4 is five pre-recorded questions for students to respond to in English based on their personal experience.

Post-Activity

Ask students to prepare verbally for an "improvised" five-question interview with each other at the beginning of the next class, using the last five questions from the listening practice.

> Question 1: 今天星期几?
>
> Question 2: 你的生日是几月几号?
>
> Question 3: 你好朋友的生日是几月几号?
>
> Question 4: 星期六你去上课吗?
>
> Question 5: 星期天你看电影吗?

Homework Assignments (including a Q & A session for the day) (10 minutes):

1. Chinese character practice for the lesson. Follow stroke orders highlighted in the workbook.

2. Write 5-8 sentences using new words from the lesson, in both *pinyin* and Chinese characters.

   Always allow students to ask questions about the lesson, key vocabulary, or anything that are confusing them before dismissing the class.

Day 2

Teaching Focus:

Grammar:

- Word order in telling clock time by using 点 , 分 , 半 , and 刻 , 差

- Location of time words in a sentence

Vocabulary:

- 现在 , 几点 , 回 , 宿舍 , 电脑房 , 打 , 网球 , 作业

Learning Difficulties:

两点 : Use 两 instead of 二 when saying "two o'clock", etc.; say 零 before the number of minutes if the minutes are less than 10, for example 两点零二分 , 四点零七分 ; 一刻 , 三刻 ; 半 replaces 三十分 , and no 分 comes after 半 .

Day 3

Teaching Focus:

Grammar:

Use of 以后：三点以后，下课以后

Use of 以前：三点以前，上课以前

Vocabulary:

每天，国际学校，起床，吃午饭，看电视，睡觉，电影院，早上，上午，中午，晚上，祝，见

Phonetics:

Compound finals such as "iao", "iu" and "ie"

Day 4

Teaching Focus:

Grammar:

- The measure word 门 for counting school courses

- The interrogative pronoun 哪，for example, 你喜欢哪门课？我们去哪个电影院？我们看哪个电影？

Vocabulary:

第，节，数学，历史，化学，英语，体育，物理，法语，西班牙语，经济学，课程表，所以，学期，然后

Phonetics:

Compound final "un" as in "jun", "qun", "xun" and "ian"

Sample Formative and Summative Assessments for Days 2, 3, and 4:

- **Summative assessments:** On Days 2 and 4, students will take vocabulary and key sentence structure tests. New words from the previous lesson will be shown in Chinese characters and students are to write down their definition in English. If they also provide *pinyin* along with tone marks for the words, they earn extra points. For an average vocabulary test in this format, they get about 20-30 new words in total. Key structure tests are usually given in half Chinese-to-English format and half English-to-Chinese, along with a word bank for the second half. Students will be completing translations for both sections in class. The main purpose of this kind of regular summative assessment is to help students master new concepts in each lesson and form good habits of reviewing regularly.

- **Formative assessments:** They are given throughout each class. Some can be graded, others don't have to be. For vocabulary, you can try keyword bingo, "around the classroom" translation, and Chinese character races on the board. For sentence structures, you can try crossword puzzles (preferably in Chinese characters), speed matching, and sentence charades. At the end of each unit, students are usually assigned a project. In the "Time and Dates" unit on Day 3, students see a sample text in letter/email format from a Chinese pen pal. As homework, they will draft a response to the pen pal, answering questions he/she asked in his/her letter/email and asking him/her similar questions. On Day 4, as one of the activities, students will be peer editing their letter/email responses. You will need to supervise to see if everyone's school schedule is clearly communicated in the response. Make sure each student applies adverbial time phrases correctly in their responses, and make sure they talk about their weekend routine as well. Finally, tell the class that the final version of the letter/email response will be their end-of-unit project. You will need to let them know the due date for the project once it's assigned. A rubric will be attached below for your reference.

- Here is a copy of the sample letter that students will be reading in class on Day 3. Depending on your teaching pace, a word bank could be included for some essential new words, or you can have student representatives "act out" meanings of the new words. If the latter, prepare a definition list or cards for the new words for you to show the student representatives on the side:

> 小明：
>
> 　　你好！
>
> 　　我叫玛丽娅。我是美国人，现在在上海国际学校学习。我们学校的学生每天都有很多课。我每天早上六点半起床，七点半去学校，上午八点一刻开

始上课。中午十二点在学校吃午饭。下午两点四十五下课。下课以后，我有时候做作业，有时候和朋友去运动，我很喜欢运动。晚上我学习，有时候也看看电视，玩儿玩儿电脑。我十点睡觉。

你在学校的一天是怎么过的？也很忙吗？你喜欢运动吗？

祝好！

你的朋友玛丽娅

2014 年 11 月 15 日

Rubric for Assessing Speaking

Rating	Excellent 4	Good 3	Average 2	Below Average 1
Task Completion	Fully complete	Almost complete	Mostly complete	Barely or not complete
Comprehensibility	Fully comprehensible	Comprehensible	Mostly comprehensible	Barely or not comprehensible
Fluency	Very fluent with nice flow	Occasional pauses	Lots of pauses	Pauses most of the time
Pronunciation	All correct	Sporadic errors	Several errors	Numerous errors
Accuracy (Grammar & Vocabulary)	All sentence structures correct	Sporadic errors	Several errors	Numerous errors
Volume	Clear and loud	Occasionally low volume	Low volume most of the time	Barely audible

Rubric for Assessing Writing

	Task Completion	Comprehen-sibility	Level of Discourse	Vocabulary	Grammar
1	Not complete at all	Not comprehensible	Inadequate development: lacks examples or details	Inadequate word choice: rambling, inappropriate, incorrect	Inadequate structure: numerous incomplete sentences
2	Minimal completion of the task	Barely comprehensible	Minimal development/ response: lacks examples or details	Minimal word choice: inadequate, incorrect	Minimal sentence structure: some incomplete sentences and errors

3	Less than partial completion of the task	Partially comprehensible	Limited development: some use of examples or details	Limited word choice: 6 errors	Limited sentence structure: 6 errors
4	Partial completion of the task	Mostly comprehensible	Adequate development: sufficient use of examples or details	Adequate word choice: 4 errors	Adequate sentence structure: 4 errors
5	Appropriate and adequate completion of the task	Easily comprehensible	Effective development: clear use of examples or details	Effective use: 2 errors	Effective use: 2 errors
6	Superior completion of the task: appropriate and with elaboration	Fully comprehensible	Exemplary development: strong use of examples or details	Exemplary word choice: vivid, specific, precise	Exemplary use: complete and correct with sentence variety

Wenya Lu (卢文雅), born and raised in China, attended Peking University for both her B.A. and M.A. degrees in Japanese Language and Culture. Having taught both Chinese and Japanese at Walter Payton College Preparatory High School since 2000, Lu has worked with many brilliant young minds in classes, clubs, and on exchange trips to her school's sister schools in Japan and China. Lu feels it is most rewarding to see students strive for excellence in applying their language skills. She also participates in Chinese language teacher training workshops both locally and nationally.

Time and Dates

Zhiqun Song (宋智群)
San Jacinto College, Houston, Texas

Language Proficiency Level: Intermediate Low

Age Range: 18-30 (college students)

Class Size: 15-20 students

Time Frame: 90 minutes per lesson, 5 lessons in total

Essential Questions:

- How does culture influence people's perception of age?

- How does culture influence people's celebration of birthdays?

Unit Goals:

Develop students' abilities to talk about time, dates, and the dates of some important festivals, set up invitations, and make appointments.

Standards: Based on the National Standards for Foreign Language Learning

- **Communication:** -Interpersonal (1.1) -Interpretive (1.2) -Presentational (1.3)

- **Comparison:** Compare customs of birthday celebration and age counting between America and China, as well as important Chinese and American festival dates.

- **Culture:** Chinese animal zodiac signs are taught along with birthday and age.

Unit Questions:

- Can students say and write dates and times?

- Can students ask someone's age and birthday?

- Can students give their age and birthday?

- Can students name their favorite cuisines?

- Can students ask about someone's availability and set up a dinner appointment?

Lesson Outlines:

Day 1: Happy birthday to you! 祝你生日快乐!

Day 2: May I take you out for your birthday tomorrow? 明天是你的生日,我请你吃饭,怎么样?

Day 3: I am very busy, when shall we eat? 我很忙,我们几点吃饭?

Day 4: Can you tell the time difference between New York and Beijing? 现在北京几点? 纽约几点?

Day 5: Review and Summative Assessment 复习总结测试

Learning Objectives:

Students will be able to:

Day 1

- Understand, ask, and give the time and date (interpersonal);

- Ask and answer someone's birthday and age, as well as their zodiac animal sign (interpersonal);

- Wish someone a happy birthday (interpersonal).

Day 2

- Understand, ask, and give the time (interpretive and interpersonal);

- Make an invitation to treat a friend for their birthday (interpersonal);

- Talk about one's food preferences (interpersonal);

- Set up a time for dinner invitation (interpersonal).

Day 3

- Arrange and negotiate a dinner date or time (interpersonal);

- Describe a typical weekly schedule (presentational).

Day 4

- Ask and give the time in New York and Beijing (interpretive);

- Associate dates with corresponding festivals in China and the US (interpretive and presentational);

- Design a holiday greeting card, such as a New Year greeting card, in Chinese (presentational).

Day 5

- Make a self-introduction (presentational);

- Converse about eating out with friends (interpersonal).

Day 1 (Sample Day): Happy
Birthday to You! 祝你生日快乐！

Learning Objectives:

Students will be able to:

1. Understand, ask, and give the time and date (interpersonal);

2. Ask and answer someone's birthday and age, as well as their zodiac animal sign (interpersonal);

3. Wish someone a happy birthday (interpersonal).

Teaching Focus:

Grammar:

- The usage of the particle 的 in 我的生日

- Question formation: the word order between forming a question and giving a statement to answer the question asked: 你的生日（是）几月几号？ 我的生日（是）五月七号。今天星期几？今天星期六。

- Word order for dates: X 年 X 月 X 号 / 日 , 星期 X

Vocabulary:

- Transitional conjunction: 可是

- Time words: 年 , 今年 , 月 , 星期 , 天 , 日 , 号 , 点

- Verbs: 属 , 喜欢 , 谢谢 , 吃

- Question words for number and age: 多大 , 几岁 , 几号 , 几月 , 几点

- Animal names appearing as Chinese zodiac signs: 鼠 , 牛 , 虎 , 兔 , 龙 , 蛇 , 马 , 羊 , 猴 , 鸡 , 狗 , 猪

Phonetics:

- Neutral tone for the second syllable in "rènshi" 认识 , "wǎnshang" 晚上 , "xièxie" 谢谢 , "xǐhuan" 喜欢

Learning Difficulties:

- The basic word order in Chinese involving a time word: the position of a point of time expression in a sentence;

- The position of a question word in an interrogative sentence.

Teaching Materials and Resources:

- A big authentic Chinese monthly calendar

- Pictures or photos of celebrities and 12 animal zodiac signs with magnets on back

- Flashcards of 12 animal zodiac characters with magnets on back

- Small loose monthly calendar cards with certain dates circled

- Colored paper card stacks, markers, and worksheets

- Two puppets

- PowerPoint slides for language structures

- Short movie clips about birthday celebrations and traditions in both English and Chinese

- *Integrated Chinese* textbook and other selected materials

Instructional Strategies:

Warm-up review and practice: Numbers (15 minutes)

1. Exchange phone numbers:

   1) Pair students up and have them exchange phone numbers.

   2) Randomly select students and have them write their partner's phone number on the board.

   3) Have a student read any random phone number on the board. The student whose number was called must respond by saying " 我的电话是……". The phone number called then will be erased. The activity continues until all the numbers are erased.

2. Present the starting time for the 2008 Beijing Olympic Games: 二零零八年八月八日八点八分, and ask students why that time was chosen. Introduce lucky (八) and unlucky (四) numbers in Chinese.

3. Students individually say numbers in the sequence 1-20. Those who have a lucky or unlucky number must stand up to say the number.

Activity 1 (For Objective 1, 15 minutes)

Purpose: To practice new words and expressions in sentences.

1. Use realia and pictures to introduce dates and time-related vocabulary: 点 , 天 , 日 , 月 , 年 , 星期 , 号 , 半 , 刻 , 晚上 , 见 , 再见 , 生日 , 多大 , 太 , 了 , 哪年 .

2. Have students find out the radicals in common for several groups of words, such as 日 in 明, 昨, and 星.

3. Flip pages of a monthly calendar and introduce 12 months at the same time, then select one month from the calendar and practice naming dates and days of a week of that month.

4. Divide the class into three groups by having students count from 1-3 and grouping students by the same number. Each group gets the same set of small calendar cards with a certain date circled on each card. When they hear the teacher calling dates and day of the week, such as "十一月五号" and "星期五", students compete to pull out the right calendar card from the piles on the table.

Activity 2 (For Objective 1, 20 minutes)

Practice 今天是几月几号？星期几？

Pre-Activity

Have two puppets model the conversation by showing different calendar dates on PowerPoint slides.

> A: 这个月是几月？
> B: 这个月是十一月。
> A: 今天（昨天/明天）是几号？
> B: 今天是十八号。
> A: 今天是几月几号？
> B: 今天是十一月十八号。

Do the same thing with week expressions.

> A: 今天是星期几？
> B: 今天是星期三。
> A: 十一月十八号是星期几？
> B: 十一月十八号是星期三。

Main Activity: Information Gap (Interpersonal)

Have students fill in highlighted blanks on their worksheet by asking appropriate questions. Students work in pairs. Student A and student B have different worksheets with matching questions and answers. Cells marked with NA ("Not Available") should be ignored. Tell students to add 是 between subjects (such as 这个月) and questions (几月) .

Example: A. 这个月是几月？   B. 这个月是十一月。

Student A:

	几月？	几号？	几月几号？	星期几？
这个月	11	NA	NA	NA
上个月		NA	NA	NA
下个月	12	NA	NA	NA
今天	NA		11/5	
昨天	NA	4th		1
明天	NA		11/6	
后天	NA	7th		4

Student B:

	几月？	几号？	几月几号？	星期几？
这个月		NA	NA	NA
上个月	10	NA	NA	NA
下个月		NA	NA	NA
今天	NA	5th		2
昨天	NA		11/4	
明天	NA	6th		3
后天	NA		11/7	

Post-Activity

Randomly ask a few pairs to present the work they have just done to the class. Teacher also checks if they can ask and answer questions based on the calendar dates.

Summarize the word order for dates, and have students fill in the blanks for the sentence:

今天是_____年_____月_____号 / 日，星期_____。

Activity 3 (For Objective 2, 10 minutes)

Practice 你今年多大？我今年二十岁。

Pre-Activity

Show a photo of a celebrity and tell students: X 今年五十二岁 . Show a few more photos of other celebrities and give their ages, then use those same photos to ask students: X 今年多大 ? Also ask students: 你今年多大 ?

Main Activity (Interpersonal)

Divide students into two standing groups, A and B. Group A forms an inside circle and Group B forms an outside circle. Both circles face each other. Students ask and answer 你今年多大 ？ 我今年 X. After 15 seconds, have the outside circle move one step left to meet a new partner and find out each other's age.

Post-Activity

Choose a few students to report one of their classmates' ages, such as 他今年 Y 岁.

Activity 4 (For Objective 2, 20 minutes)

Practice the Chinese Zodiac 例如：你属什么？我属兔。

Pre-Activity

1. Before class, have students research the story of the origin and order of the 12-animal cycle of the Chinese zodiac. Go over the Chinese characters and images of the

12 zodiac animals. Teach the zodiac song (《生肖歌》) with the melody of "London Bridge" to reinforce the order of the animals in the cycle. At this stage, students are required to remember their own and one of their friends' zodiac signs. To practice the lyrics, show the zodiac song online as well: https://www.youtube.com/watch?v=mWkrNQAdMXM

2.. Distribute a picture of a zodiac sign to each student. Students raise their hands if their animal is called.

3. Character recognition: Randomly paste the 12 character cards on the board. Have students come up to the board to match the character cards with animal zodiac pictures.

4. Hold a card with the "马" image up to students, and say "我今年四十八岁，我属马". Apply the structure to some popular celebrities: "Y今年二十四岁，他属猪".

5. Have students go online to research what the Chinese character of their own sign looks like and the correct stroke order used to write it, then use a marker to write the characters on flashcards. Finally have students ask their neighbor: 你属马吗？（我不属马。）你属什么？（我属牛。）

Main Activity (Interpersonal)

Ask all the students to stand up and interview three classmates: 你的生日是几月几号？你今年多大？你属什么？ Record the information gathered on to the chart below in either English or *pinyin*.

	Name (English or *pinyin*)	Birth Date (numerals)	Age (numerals)	Zodiac Sign (*pinyin*)
1				
2				
3				

Post-Activity (Presentational)

Ask a few students to report the information gathered from their interviews. For example: 李中十八岁，他的生日是十二月六号。李中属狗。

Activity 5 (For Objective 3, 15 minutes)

Practice 你的生日是几月几号？祝你生日快乐！

Pre-Activity

1. Briefly ask students the differences between birthday celebration traditions in China and America. Teach students to sing the birthday song: 祝你生日快乐！

2. Ask 今天是几月几号？ Then have students use the same pattern to inquire their classmates' birthday: 你的生日是几月几号？ 我的生日是三月九号。

Main Activity (Interpersonal)

Have students stand up to ask each other 你的生日是几月几号, then have them form a line, like a dragon, based on their birthdays. Students whose birthdays are earlier in the year will line up in front of people whose birthdays are later.

Post-Activity

1. Teacher checks to see if everyone is at the right place in the dragon line, asking the first student 你的生日是几月几号？ The first student answers and asks the second student the same question, the second student answers and asks the third, and so on, until the end of the line is reached. In the meantime, ask each student to remember his neighbor's birthday and tell the class: 王云的生日（是）六月七号。

2. End the activity by singing 祝你生日快乐！

Homework:

Written assignment: Tell students to write the sentences for the following prompt and submit them through Course Blackboard. Have students prepare to orally present what they write next class.

Prompt:

Who is your idol? Your idol could be one of your family members or someone famous. If your idol is someone famous, go online to find out his/her age, birthday, zodiac sign, family members, etc. Write a few sentences on your idol in Chinese. For example:

Celebrity A 今年 X 岁，他属 X，他的生日是 X 月 X 号。他家有 X 口人，他没有哥哥，也没有姐姐，他有一个弟弟和妹妹。

Day 2: May I Take You Out for Your Birthday Tomorrow?
明天是你的生日。我请你吃饭，怎么样？

Teaching Focus:

Grammar:

- Alternative questions:（是）___A___，还是___B___
- Pivotal construction: 我请你吃饭
- Tag question word: ……，怎么样？

Vocabulary:

- Transition conjunction 可是
- Time words: 星期，天，日，月，号，年，今年，点
- Verbs: 喜欢，谢谢，吃，请客，上课，下课
- Question words for age and number: 多大，几岁，几号，几月，几点

Phonetics:

- Compound final "ian" as in "nian" 年，"jian" 见，"xian" 现

Teaching Materials and Resources:

- "Will return" clocks (either handmade or purchased from a store)

- Colored paper card stacks, pins, markers, and worksheets

- Pictures or photos of some celebrities

- Two puppets

- PowerPoint slides for language structures and lesson summary

- DVD (Cheng & Tsui Chinese Language Series): lessons and cultural minutes

- *Integrated Chinese* textbook and other selected materials

Instructional Strategies:

Activity 1 (Formative assessment of previous class, 20 minutes)

Check students' oral presentations of their idol homework assignment from last class. Rubric for speaking is provided (see Appendix).

Activity 2 (For Objective 1, 10 minutes)

May I take you out for your birthday tomorrow? 明天是你的生日，我请你吃饭，怎么样？

Pre-Activity: 现在几点?

Hold a "will return" clock, ask 现在几点? and answer 现在十点五分！ Change the hour and minute hands to quarter 刻 and half 半 positions specifically to practice.

Main Activity

1. Teacher says a certain time, such as (现在) 十一点 and students write out the time that they hear in a digital clock format, for purposes of listening comprehension.

2. Expand this activity by adding 早上 , 晚上 , 中午 , 下午 before the specific time, such as 十一点 . The previous example then becomes (现在) 早上十一点 .

3. Holding the "will return" clock and moving the clock hands, teacher asks students (现在) 几点? Students provide solutions by answering the questions orally. After a few rounds, have students come to the front to do this. Before

wrapping up this part of the practice, ask students to look at the classroom clock or their watches, and ask and answer (现在) 几点?

Activity 3 (For Objectives 1 and 4, 10 minutes)

Practice 几点见?

Pre-Activity

Show construction of the following sentences, emphasize the position for 几点.

我们几点见? (Subject + Time + Verb)

我们<u>晚上十一点</u>见。

Main Activity (Interpersonal)

1. Show PowerPoint slides with the following times: 3:00, 4:15, 10:30, 12:50 pm, 8:10 am, 9:30 am Sunday, and 5:20 pm Friday. Teacher asks 我们几点见? and students answer using the time shown on PowerPoint: 我们三点见.

2. Tell students that 我们 is often omitted, as the subject is mutually understood by both parties. Have students practice again without 我们 as in 几点见? and 三点见.

3. Ask students if they can think of any scenarios using 几点? and instruct them to replace verb 见 with provided verbs, such as 下课, 上课, 吃饭, 工作 and 做饭. Show a few examples of dialogues such as: 他们几点吃饭? 他们八点吃饭。你们几点下课? 我们九点下课。Then ask students to interview each other to find out when they get up, eat lunch, or go to work.

Activity 4 (For Objective 2, 15 minutes)

Practice pivotal sentence A 请 B 吃饭

Pre-Activity

Show PowerPoint slides with pictures of someone having Chinese and American food, telling students 王朋请 John 吃中国饭; in return, John 请王朋吃美国饭.

Main Activity (Interpersonal)

1. Instructional input: Provide students a scenario, such as A and B are good friends. A would like to know details after B tells A that B has made a lunch appointment with a friend. The conversation is as follows (PowerPoint can be used for this sample dialogue):

> A: 你请谁吃饭?
>
> B: 我请玛丽吃饭。
>
> A: 你请玛丽吃什么饭?
>
> B: 玛丽喜欢吃中国饭。
>
> A: 你星期几请玛丽吃饭?
>
> B: 我星期六请她吃饭。
>
> A: 你们星期六几点见?
>
> B: 十二点见。

2. Guided dialogue: Have students follow the scenario and role-play the dialogue in pairs. They need to replace the underlined words to make the dialogue fit into their situation.

3. Create a dialogue. Teacher gives instruction: 感恩节快到了，你想谢谢你的一位新朋友，请他吃饭。你知道你的同学已经请了他的朋友，你想问问他请了谁，客人喜欢吃什么饭，他们什么时候几点见。你们说完要汇报。 You will report the information gathered from the conversation to class.

Post-Activity

Ask several students to report their conversation results by using the following sentence patterns: 李明请 X 吃饭。X 喜欢吃中国菜。他星期六请 X 吃晚饭。他们星期六晚上七点见。

Activity 5 (For Objective 3, 15 minutes)

Practice 还是

Pre-Activity: Input for 还是

Use separate pictures of celebrities, a dinner table, a clock, and so on, to direct students to answer the questions: 他们是中国人还是美国人？他们六点吃饭还是七点吃饭？他请她吃饭还是她请他吃饭？他喜欢吃中国饭还是美国饭？她喜欢吃中国菜还是美国菜？他是老师还是律师？今天是星期四还是星期五？

Main Activity (Interpersonal)

As a class, do the previous Thanksgiving activity (Activity 4) again by encouraging students to incorporate alternative questions:

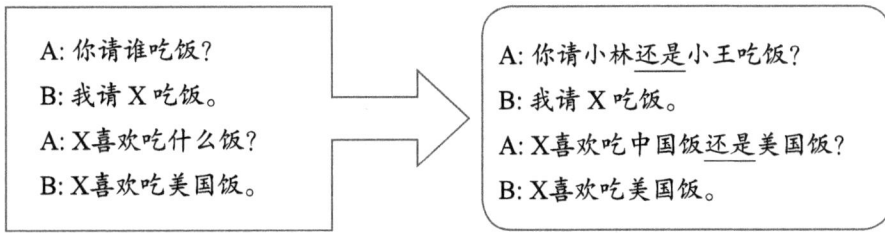

A: 你请谁吃饭？
B: 我请 X 吃饭。
A: X喜欢吃什么饭？
B: X喜欢吃美国饭。

A: 你请小林还是小王吃饭？
B: 我请 X 吃饭。
A: X喜欢吃中国饭还是美国饭？
B: X喜欢吃美国饭。

Then have students continue their conversation by asking one another questions to determine a date, day of the week, and time for the dinner date.

A: 你们星期三还是星期四吃饭？

B: 我们星期三吃饭。

A: 你们七点还是八点见？

B: 我们八点见。

Activity 6 (For Objectives 1, 2, 3, and 4, overall practice, 20 minutes)

Pre-Activity 课文理解 (Interpretive)

1. Watch the accompanying DVD for both lesson and cultural minutes.

2. Provide an audio recording of another sample dialogue as a listening comprehension exercise. After playing the audio a couple of times, provide a list of times and cuisines and have students check the one they heard from the audio recording.

Main Activity

Have students role-play in pairs to make a dinner invitation by replacing the underlined words with their own choices.

> A: 我请你吃<u>晚饭</u>，怎么样？
>
> B: <u>太好了</u>，谢谢，谢谢。
>
> A: 你喜欢吃<u>美国饭</u>还是<u>中国饭</u>？
>
> B: 我是<u>中国人</u>，可是我喜欢吃<u>美国饭</u>。
>
> A: 好，我们吃<u>美国饭</u>。
>
> B: 请问，我们<u>星期六</u>还是<u>星期天</u>吃饭？
>
> A: <u>星期天</u>，怎么样？
>
> B: 好！几点？
>
> A: <u>晚上七点半</u>，好吗？
>
> B: 好，我们<u>星期天晚上七点半</u>见。

Post-Activity

1. Ask a few pairs to present their dialogues in front of the classroom.

2. Teacher chooses individual students to answer questions while they exit the classroom. For instance: 现在几点？明天星期几？我们明天八点见还是九点见？你的生日是几月几号？你喜欢吃中国饭还是美国饭？

Day 3: I Am Very Busy, When Shall
We Eat? 我很忙，我们几点吃饭？

Teaching Focus:

Grammar:

- Affirmative + Negative (A not A) questions 忙不忙，认识不认识

- Adverb 还 ＋ Verb
- Adjectives or stative verbs as the 忙 in 我很忙

Vocabulary:

- Cause and effect: 为什么，因为
- Time words: 现在，刻，晚饭，明天
- Verb: 认识
- Nouns: 同学，朋友，事儿

Phonetics:

- "er" phenomenon for Beijing dialect 儿化音：事儿

Day 4: **Can You Tell the Time Difference between New York and Beijing?** 现在北京几点？纽约几点？

Teaching Focus:

Vocabulary:

- Festival names: 圣诞节，感恩节，春节，中秋节，龙舟节，情人节
- Verb: 打算

Day 5: Review and Summative Assessment 复习总结测试

Teaching Materials and Resources:

- Worksheets

- Computers

Teaching Focus:

Whole unit review

Activity 1: Personal Profile (Presentational, 45 minutes)

Please introduce yourself to your class, including your birthdate, age, things you like to do, food you like to eat, a typical day's schedule in school, etc.

1. Brainstorm in pairs what could be included in a self-introduction.

2. Rearrange the things that you come up with in an order suitable for a presentation.

3. Do a practice round in pairs based on the two-step prep work.

Write the things about yourself down in complete sentences as the draft of a speech, first for practice and rehearsal, and then do an oral presentation without looking at the draft. For example:

我姓……，我叫……，今年……岁，属……，我的生日是 5 月 8 号。我是学生。因为我喜欢中国文化，所以我学中文。我也喜欢吃中国饭。我星期一和星期三很忙，可是周末不忙。周末我们去吃中国饭，好吗？

Call on one or two students to do their presentations as the wrap-up.

Activity 2: Eating out with friends (Interpersonal, 45 minutes)

Have students find a partner and make a conversation for the following situation:

To celebrate Spring Festival, you are inviting your friend out to dinner.

1. Pick a day that works for both of you.

2. Decide on the time of day when you would like to meet.

3. Find the right restaurant at which to eat, based on your friend's preference.

Rubric for Assessing Speaking

Rating	Excellent 4	Good 3	Average 2	Below Average 1
Task Completion	Complete	Almost complete	Mostly complete	Barely or not complete
Comprehensibility	Fully comprehensible	Comprehensible	Mostly comprehensible	Barely or not comprehensible
Fluency	Fluent	Occasional pauses	Lots of pauses	Pauses most of the time
Pronunciation	Few errors	Sporadic errors	Several errors	Numerous errors
Accuracy (Grammar & Vocabulary)	Few errors	Sporadic errors	Several errors	Numerous errors
Volume	Clear and loud	Occasionally low volume	Low volume most of the time	Barely audible

Rubric for Assessing Writing

	Task Completion	Comprehensibility	Level of Discourse	Vocabulary	Grammar
1	Not complete at all	Not comprehensible	Inadequate development: lacks examples or details	Inadequate word choice: rambling, inappropriate, incorrect	Inadequate structure: numerous incomplete sentences
2	Minimal completion of the task	Barely comprehensible	Minimal development: lacks examples, evidence, or supporting details	Minimal word choice: inadequate, incorrect	Minimal sentence structure: some incomplete sentences and errors

3	Less than partial completion of the task	Partially comprehensible	Limited development: some use of examples or details	Limited word choice: 6 errors	Limited sentence structure: 6 erros
4	Partial completion of the task	Mostly comprehensible	Adequate development: sufficient use of examples or details	Adequate word choice: 4 errors	Adequate sentence structure: 4 errors
5	Appropriate and adequate completion	Easily comprehensible	Effective development: clear use of examples or details	Effective use: 2 errors	Effective use: 2 errors
6	Superior completion: appropriate and with elaboration	Fully comprehensible	Exemplary development: strong use of examples or details	Exemplary word choice: vivid, specific, precise	Exemplary use: complete and correct with sentence variety

Zhiqun Song（宋智群）is an adjunct professor of Chinese at San Jacinto College, Houston, Texas. She received her Bachelor's degree in English Language and Literature from Hunan Normal University, and her Master's degree in Library and Information Science from the University of Iowa, Iowa City. She also received postgraduate training for Teaching English as a Second Language (ESL). She has worked as a librarian and an ESL teacher in the US. As an active STARTALK participant and a popular instructor with her students, Zhiqun Song has gained a wealth of insights about student-centered Chinese language instruction, and developed new skills that improve her teaching effectiveness.

Critique

Time and Dates – Wenya Lu
Time and Dates – Zhiqun Song

"Time and Dates" is a theme indispensable to the curriculum of a second language program. The usage of temporal expressions poses difficulties to English-speaking Chinese language learners. Linguistically, the word order of temporal expressions, either within a phrase or in a sentence, is different from English; cognitively, the concept of time is abstract. Wenya Lu and Zhiqun Song write on the same theme, but their designs vary to a large extent. The differences are testimony to the learner-centered nature of their respective designs. Lu and Song target learners of different ages and in different educational settings.

Numbers are the fundamental components of time expressions. Both authors start their Sample Day teaching with warm-up games about numbers. They continue to use games in activities: the games are cleverly designed and interesting, involving all students' participation, and furthermore are all very easy to conduct in class. Such games indeed warm students up cognitively, linguistically, and emotionally; as Lu comments, "your class will show excitement when they hear the term 游戏".

In helping students use time expressions in sentences and in discourse, Lu carefully designs a series of activities that starts with instructional input immediately followed by students' practice, and ends with a survey in which students converse with each other at the discourse level. For example, the pre-activities in Activity 2 help students clearly understand the word order in a sentence. The main activity, *Sentence Formation Race*, is conducted in a few instructional steps to facilitate students' success in their presentations, the last step of the activity.

It should be noted that Lu's design presents a good balance in the amount of input regarding certain language variations. Language variations occur among words and other elements, e.g., the expression of week 星期, 礼拜, 周 and the verb duplications 看看, 说说, 听听, 试试, 等等 versus the form 看一看, 说一说, 听一听, 试一试, 等一等. Although the teacher should be aware of the variations, it is important to teach one form with one meaning at one time.

Song's design provides rich curriculum content wherein students learn not only how to ask about time, describe their daily schedules, and make an appointment or invitation, but also understand cultural knowledge and practice related to significant events such as birthdays and cultural festivals. Song pays special attention to a distinctive feature of the Chinese language when she points out that Chinese pronouns can be dropped. The author facilitates learning in the process of practicing the change from " 我们几点见？我们三点见 " to " 几点见？三点见 ".

Both designs provide a variety of innovative instructional strategies. Readers easily see how the activities are organized step by step, and how learners' needs are accommodated via scaffolding procedures. Each of Song's learning objectives is fulfilled through a few different but internally connected activities. These activities vary in instructional techniques (games, Information Gap, step-wise tasks, songs, a birthday dragon line, making invitations and appointments, self-information presentations, etc.), duration, interactive format, group scale, and teaching resources/aids (cards, puppets, photos, pictures, etc.). The activities engage students in various meaningful communications in daily situations. Different contents and communicative modes all aim at acquiring the language forms and functions in context. One can clearly see and reflect on the authors' instructional tips on planning exercises, including drills in communicative contexts, monitoring teacher-student interaction, carrying out open-ended tasks, and including authentic materials in activities. In addition, since Song's students are at the college level, acquiring a considerable vocabulary is a requirement. Both designs show various methods of using activities at different stages to help students review, expand, and retain vocabulary items.

Lu's design shows a highly interactive class in which students communicate ideas and solve problems. The summative tests, an important integral part of the curriculum, however, could be modified to better assess the objectives or students' ability to use language in context. The tests would better suit the design's purpose if their content went beyond vocabulary recognition and key-sentence structure translation. One of Song's activities (Activity 4) requires students to interview their classmates to find out their ages and report back to the class. Given the wide age range of her students, it is likely that some of them may feel uncomfortable providing that information if it is to be shared with the class.

Theme 7

Hobbies

Hobbies

Zhiqun Song (宋智群)
San Jacinto College, Houston, Texas

Language Proficiency Level: Intermediate Low

Age Range: 18-30 (college students)

Class Size: 15-20 students

Time Frame: 90 minutes per lesson, 5 lessons in total

Essential Questions:

- What is the relationship between pastimes and healthy lifestyles?

- How do one's pastimes develop over time?

Unit Goals:

Help students develop their abilities to talk about hobbies, plan an outing with friends, and extend and decline an invitation with proper cultural etiquette.

Standards: Based on the National Standards for Foreign Language Learning

- **Communication:**

  -Interpersonal (1.1)

  -Interpretive (1.2)

  -Presentational (1.3)

- **Connection:** Pastime sports with students' PE class performances.

- **Comparison:** Different hobbies, pastimes, and weekend activities in China and the US.

- **Culture:** Popular traditional Chinese pastimes and hobbies such as 太极拳，功夫，象棋，围棋 and 乒乓球 are introduced.

- **Community:** Students are encouraged to apply their Chinese knowledge in Chinese communities and learn Chinese beyond the classroom. Example: Take 功夫，太极拳，or 少林拳 lessons.

Unit Questions:

- Can students talk about their favorite pastimes and ask about someone else's?

- Can students invite someone to a weekend activity?

- Can students comment on how well they do with their pastimes or hobbies?

- Can students accept or decline an invitation to a weekend activity?

- Can students find someone else to do activities with?

Lesson Outlines:

- **Day 1:** Talk about hobbies 谈爱好

- **Day 2:** Would you like to play ball? 你想打球吗？

- **Day 3:** I only want to relax and have a good sleep. 我只想休息一下，好好睡一觉。

- **Day 4:** He runs fast! 他跑得真快！

- **Day 5:** Look for a language partner. 找语言学习伙伴

Learning Objectives:

Students will be able to:

Day 1

- Ask about someone's hobbies and name their own hobbies (interpersonal);
- Make a date with a friend to do an activity, such as seeing a movie (interpersonal);
- Suggest an alternative activity if the proposed one doesn't work (interpersonal).

Day 2

- State their desire to take up a hobby or do an activity (presentational);
- Set up future plans and invite someone to do some weekend activities (interpersonal);
- Ask and state if one likes or dislikes doing certain activities and if those activities are fun (interpersonal).

Day 3

- Accept or decline an invitation to an activity (interpersonal);
- Find someone else to do activities with (interpersonal);
- Describe the sport/activity that someone is able to do, or can do well (presentational).

Day 4

- Describe how well someone can do with regard to their hobbies (presentational);
- Comment on how well someone can do a certain sport/activity (interpersonal).

Day 5

- Find a language partner who shares the same interests or hobbies/activities (interpretive and interpersonal);
- Describe others' hobbies or favorite pastimes (presentational);
- Make plans for an outing with friends (interpersonal).

Day 1 (Sample Day)

Learning Objectives:

Students will be able to:

- Ask about someone's hobbies and name their own hobbies (interpersonal);

- Make a date with a friend to do an activity, such as seeing a movie (interpersonal);

- Suggest an alternative activity if the first proposed one doesn't work (interpersonal).

Teaching Focus:

Grammar:

- Word Order: Subject + Adverbial (time, place, manner, etc.) + Verb + Object

- Affirmative + Negative (A not A) questions

- Conjunction 那 (么) combining with 怎么样?

- 去 + V: go (to a place) to do something

Vocabulary:

- Popular hobbies: 打球 , 唱歌 , 跳舞 , 听音乐 , 看书 , 看电影 , 看电视 , 运动

- Tag question words: 对吗 and 对不对

- Question and conjunction words: 为什么 , 因为

Phonetics:

- "iu" is pronounced as "iou" in "qiú" 的 球

- Polyphonic characters：

  好 as in 爱好 "àihào" and 好看 "hǎokàn"

  乐 as in 音乐 "yīnyuè"and 快乐 "kuàilè"

Learning Difficulties:

Students may make the mistakes of placing the "time-when" expression and other adverbs at the end of sentences due to possible interference from their native language. They may also be confused by the order of time and place.

Teaching Materials and Resources:

- Hobby/activity vocabulary flashcards with *pinyin* and English translation
- Authentic pictures or photos of some popular activities
- Colored paper card stacks, markers, and worksheets
- Two puppets
- PowerPoint for language structures
- Short movie clips about typical Chinese hobbies and pastimes
- DVD (Cheng & Tsui Chinese Language Series): lessons and cultural minutes
- *Integrated Chinese* textbook and other selected materials

Instructional Strategies:

Warm-up: Relate and Get Ready (T-S interpersonal, 5 minutes)

Watch a movie clip about how Chinese people spend their weekends and leisure time, then ask students the following questions:

1. 中国人喜欢做什么？打球还是打太极拳？

2. 中国人周末常常做什么？

Activity 1 (For Objectives 1 and 2, 20 minutes)

Purpose: To practice new words and expressions in context.

1. Use PPT and pictures to introduce hobby-related vocabulary.

   1) Direct students to recognize common radicals from characters on PPT such as 打, 唱, 看, 跳.

   2) Introduce the "V+O" structure of 打球, 唱歌, 跳舞, 听音乐, 看书, 看电影, 看电视 through PPT.

3) Show students pictures of certain sports such as 水球, 马球, 乒乓球, 网球, 篮球, and help them practice vocabulary expansion using 球.

2. Use the "老师说" game to practice construction: 去＋VO (interpretive)

Choose a hobby or activity and play "Simon says" using 老师说 instead. For instance, teacher gives a command to students: "老师说, 我们听音乐（打篮球……）", and students need to act out that action. Play a few rounds, mentioning different actions each time.

3. Teacher does the motion, and students say the hobby or activity in Chinese such as 打篮球, 听音乐, etc. Correct students' pronunciation whenever possible. Then have a student volunteer come to the front to redo "老师说".

4. Use two puppets to model the following dialogue after giving a context, such as A and B meet at the gymnasium and would like to play ball together. The dialogue can be presented on PPT. A starts the conversation.

> A: 你喜欢做什么?
>
> B: 我喜欢打球。
>
> A: 你喜欢打什么球?
>
> B: 我喜欢打篮球。
>
> A: 我也喜欢打篮球。
>
> B: 你喜欢唱歌吗?
>
> A: 我不喜欢唱歌。

Then give each student a hobby/activity character flashcard, and have them stand up and form two circles facing each other, one inside the other. The inside circle students ask the outside students whether they like the hobby on their card, and the outside circle students ask the inside circle students the same question. If the answer is negative, a follow-up question is asked about what game or activity is preferred. After finishing one set of Q&A, the inside circle moves one position clockwise until everyone has talked with three students.

5. Formative Assessment (interpersonal): Form the class into several groups. Each group is given a stack of flashcards containing sport/pastime vocabulary. Each student picks up a card from the stack and asks another student to guess what he/she likes to do based on the card information. A model conversation is provided. Call on a few students to perform in front of class.

> A: 你知道我喜欢做什么吗?
>
> B: 你喜欢打篮球, 对不对?
>
> A: 对, 我喜欢打篮球。／ 不对, 我不喜欢打篮球。
>
> B: 你知道我喜欢做什么吗?
>
> A: 你（也）喜欢打篮球。

Activity 2 (For Objective 1, 10 minutes)

Purpose: To practice the following language structures.

- "A not A" structure
- Basic Chinese word order involving point of time and location

Pre-Activity

1. Review previously learned "A not A" pattern: 吃不吃 , 玩儿不玩儿 , 看不看 , 好不好 , 有没有 , 是不是 , 请不请 , 吃（饭）不吃饭 . Pair up students to ask a series of questions incorporating the "A not A" question format. For instance: 你吃不吃中国饭? 你有没有弟弟? 你是不是纽约人? 你今天忙不忙? 你请不请我吃饭? Then ask students how to express whether they like something or not（喜欢不喜欢）.

2. Introduce the following sentence patterns:

   A: 你喜欢不喜欢＋VO? B: 喜欢, 我周末常常＋VO。

   Have students substitute the subjects with other nouns or pronouns such as 你 , 他 , 姚明 and 王朋 .

3. Have students summarize the basic word order of Chinese sentences, while instructor makes comments about them.

Somebody (S) 高大伟	Adverbial (time, place, etc.) 星期六下午常常在学校	Do (V) 打	Something (O) 篮球

In-Activity: An Information Gap Activity

Pair students up and distribute Sheet A to one student and Sheet B to the other. Have each pair complete their charts by asking each other questions without looking at the other's sheet. For example, B asks: "高大伟喜欢不喜欢打球？" A looks at their sheet and responds by saying: "高大伟不喜欢打球。" From A's response, B then can fill in a "No" on his chart under 高大伟.

Student A: Student B:

Sheet A: Sheet B:

	高大伟	王丽莎
打球	No	
唱歌		Yes
跳舞	No	
听音乐		No
看书	Yes	
睡觉		Yes
看电影	No	
看电视		Yes

	高大伟	王丽莎
打球		No
唱歌	Yes	
跳舞		No
听音乐	Yes	
看书		Yes
睡觉	Yes	
看电影		No
看电视	No	

Post-Activity

Follow up by asking: 王丽莎不喜欢做什么？ and so on for formative assessment.

Activity 3 (For Objective 1, 20 minutes)

Purpose: To practice the following:

1. Word order reinforcement

2. Conditions that prevent the formation of an "A not A" question

Pre-Activity

Help students review the basic word order involving time-when expressions and other adverbial phrases. Show a set of graphics depicting activities, locations, and time. Then ask students to complete the paragraph by filling in the blanks. The following is the answer key after all the blanks have been filled in.

这个星期小高<u>天天晚上</u>都很忙。今天星期一，<u>晚上八点</u>小高请朋友跳舞，<u>明天晚上六点半</u>请同学吃饭，<u>星期三晚上九点一刻</u>请女朋友看电影，<u>星期四晚上</u>打球，<u>星期五晚上</u>唱歌。那<u>周末</u>他做什么呢？看书吗？不对！小高不喜欢看书，<u>周末那两天上午</u>他和朋友<u>去健身房</u>运动，晚上<u>在宿舍</u>看电视。

In-Activity: Cooperative Learning: Think, Pair and Share

Each student gets three pieces of colored paper card (red, blue, and green). Have students brainstorm and make a sentence by writing with markers a subject (nouns or pronouns) on red paper, time-when expression on blue paper, and a VO on green paper. Then divide students into groups of three. Have them scramble their cards to get the best sentence for presentation in class.

爸爸	星期一晚上	去图书馆看书。
我	星期五晚上常常	跳舞。
我们	周末常常	看电影。

Post-Activity: What Do You Like to Do on Weekends?

Have students interview at least three classmates about their weekend activities and report to the class.

A: 你周末常常做什么？   B: 我周末常常……

Teacher may jump in by asking:

琳达周末常常做什么？ 小白呢？ 约翰周末看书吗？

Cultural Entertainment (5 minutes)

As a short break, play another short online video clip about Chinese people's favorite hobbies and pastimes such as 太极拳 and 象棋 . Briefly show students how to do 太极拳 by performing and chanting the verse "我有一个大西瓜，一半给你，一半给他，你们都不要，我来抱着它。"

Activity 4 (For Objectives 2 and 3, 10 minutes)

Purpose: To practice combining the conjunction 那（么）with 怎么样？／好吗？

Pre-Activity: Input for 那 and 请客

Have two groups (A and B) of students read out the following dialogues, then ask them how to end the dialogue by filling in the blank. The answers are open-ended. The purpose is to help students see how 那 works in a conversation and feel its transitional function.

今天吃中国菜还是美国菜？

A: 你喜欢不喜欢吃美国菜？

B: 不喜欢。

A: 那我们吃中国菜，怎么样？

B: 我也不喜欢。

A: ＿＿＿＿＿＿＿＿ （One possibility: 那你喜欢吃什么菜？）

A: 今天晚上我有空。

B: 那我们去看电影，好吗？

A: 好，我请客。

B: 是吗？太好了！谢谢，谢谢。

A: ＿＿＿＿＿＿＿＿ （不客气。）

In-Activity: Role-play Making a Proposal

Instruct students to discuss what to do right after class. Propose at least three activities until both parties agree on one. Ask them to incorporate 那……, 好吗？怎么样？into their discussion. For example, A and B meet on the way to their dorm, and would like to plan activities for the coming weekend.

A: 我们去唱歌，好吗？

B: 对不起，我不喜欢唱歌。

A: 那我们去打球，怎么样？

> B: 我也不喜欢打球。
>
> A: 那你喜欢做什么？
>
> B: 我喜欢看电影。
>
> A: 那你请客。

Post-Activity

Call on a couple of pairs to perform. The rest of the class may vote on who acts the best.

Activity 5 (For Objectives 1, 2, and 3, overall practice, 20 minutes)

Pre-Activity: Textbook Comprehension

1. Let students watch the accompanying *Integrated Chinese* DVD and have them answer the following questions:

   1. 白英爱周末喜欢做什么？

   2. 她有的时候还喜欢做什么？

   3. 高文中周末喜欢做什么？

   4. 高文中为什么请白英爱看电影？

   5. 高文中请不请王朋、李友？

2. Besides the lesson, provide an audio recording of another sample dialogue as a listening comprehension exercise. For example:

   A and B are friends planning a weekend activity together.

   > A: 小明，你周末喜欢做什么？
   >
   > B: 我周末喜欢去看电影、打球。
   >
   > A: 那我们今天去看一个外国电影，怎么样？
   >
   > B: 好。今天我请客。
   >
   > A: 为什么你请客？
   >
   > B: 因为你昨天请我吃饭，所以今天我请你看电影。

3. Have students unscramble the text: Distribute scrambled pieces of text to students in groups of three and have each group work together to put the pieces back in order. The fastest group wins.

In-Activity: Role-play, Summative Assessment

Two people meet for the first time at a party. They greet each other, and then:

● Find out what each other likes to do on weekends;

● Suggest doing something together this coming weekend;

● If the first suggestion doesn't work, give an alternative suggestion;

● Agree on a time, identify whose treat it is, and explain why.

Post-Activity: Assignment

In the next class, ask students to act out the dialogue that they have developed and practiced.

Homework Assignments:

1. Continue to practice the role-play and ask them to perform in the next class.

2. Continue to work on their "All About Me" project by adding their hobbies or pastimes, such as 我喜欢_____，_____，有的时候也喜欢_____，可是我不喜欢_____。我周末_____忙，常常_____。Expand it by adding more of what they have learned.

3. Leave a short note to a classmate asking them to hang out the coming weekend.

Day 2

Focus:

Practice speaking about one's hobbies and make future plans to invite someone for weekend activities.

Grammar:

想，只，觉得

Vocabulary:

所以，好久不见，不错，觉得，有意思，只，睡觉，算了，找，别人

Day 3

Focus:

Accept or decline an invitation, and find someone else to do activities with.

Grammar:

会，想，最

Vocabulary (Supplementary):

画画儿，下棋，上网聊天儿，玩儿游戏机，逛街，乒乓球

Phonetics:

Polyphonic character: 觉 as in 睡觉 (shuì jiào) and 觉得 (juéde)

Day 4

Focus:

Describe how well someone can do with regard to their hobbies.

Grammar & Vocabulary:

得，太 / 真

Phonetics:

得 neutral tone

Day 5: Review and Summative Assessment

Objectives:

Students will be able to:

- Find a language partner who shares the same interests or hobbies/activities (interpretive and interpersonal);

- Describe others' hobbies or favorite pastimes (presentational);

- Make plans for an outing with friends (interpersonal).

Teaching Materials and Resources:

- A video clip about picking a certain date for certain pastimes or hobbies

- Worksheets

- Allegro (快板)

Teaching Focus:

- Practice what students have learned throughout the whole unit.

Warm-up (7 minutes)

- Play an online audio or video clip of a song about picking a time and date for doing activities. For instance, http://www.youtube.com/watch?v=b0MklcpPt54

Activity 1 (Interpretive, interpersonal, and presentational, 45 minutes)

Pre-Activity

Help students review this unit by chanting a self-composed song (You may use 快板 to help students.)

> 周末、周末做什么？
>
> 看电影，看电视，
>
> 上网聊天儿，玩儿游戏。
>
> 周末、周末去哪里？
>
> 美术馆，电影院
>
> 去了音乐会又逛街。
>
> 周末、周末玩儿什么？
>
> 打篮球，打网球，
>
> 唱歌，跳舞，听京剧。
>
> 周末、周末你在哪儿？
>
> 健身房，朋友家
>
> 星巴客我找到你。

In-Activity: Look for a language partner

A group of Chinese students will come to study at your school for six months, and they are looking for language partners. By exchanging information, hopefully everyone will be able to find a suitable language exchange partner based on each other's common interests.

1. Oral work: Ask and answer the following questions. Present this to class after practice.

> 你叫什么名字？
>
> 你多大？
>
> 你喜欢吃什么？
>
> 你喜欢做什么？唱歌还是听音乐？打球还是跳舞？
>
> 你还喜欢做什么？
>
> 你周末常常做什么？看电视还是看电影？
>
> 你说中文／英文说得怎么样？
>
> 你觉得做什么很有意思？

2. Written work: Suppose the information below has been gathered about four students who are looking for language exchange partners. Please read each description carefully and write down answers to the following two questions. This is assigned as homework, but students can start working on it in class.

   1) If you are looking for a language exchange partner, which of the four would you choose and why?

2) Which one would you definitely not choose and why?

李欢

女，十九岁。英语说得很好，会说一点儿德语。喜欢运动、唱歌和跳舞，最喜欢打网球。周末常常听音乐、逛街。很喜欢旅游。中国菜、美国菜都喜欢吃。

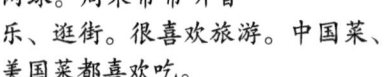

林朋

男，二十岁。会说一点儿英语。喜欢打篮球和乒乓球，篮球打得很好。也喜欢看电影，觉得看电视没有意思；有时候喜欢看书。周末常常打球、看电影。不喜欢吃美国菜。

王大卫

男，二十二岁。英语说得很好，也会说一点儿日语。喜欢打网球和太极拳，不喜欢踢足球。周末常常打网球、看书，有时候也下象棋。最喜欢吃的中国菜是麻婆豆腐，也喜欢吃美国菜。

白文英

女，二十二岁。日语说得很好，英语说得不太好。不喜欢运动，喜欢看书和看电视。周末常常在家看书、睡觉。很会做饭。最喜欢吃中国菜、日本菜。

Activity 2 (Interpersonal, 35 minutes)

Let's invite language partners to do something fun!

Scenario: You finally meet your language partner. Invite them to do something together.

1. You need to find out if the language partner is busy for the weekend or on a certain date.

2. After setting the date and time, invite your language partner to do something fun. If the first suggestion is rejected, please suggest an alternative.

3. It may take a few turns until you find a mutually agreeable activity. In your project, personal feelings and opinions need to be expressed about each suggested activity.

4. Work with your partner to practice this conversation in class and present it during the next class session for assessment.

Rubric for Assessing Speaking

Rating	Excellent 4	Good 3	Average 2	Below Average 1
Task Completion	Fully complete	Almost complete	Mostly complete	Barely or not complete
Comprehensibility	Fully comprehensible	Comprehensible	Mostly comprehensible	Barely or not comprehensible
Fluency	Fluent	Occasional pauses	Lots of pauses	Pauses most of the time
Pronunciation	Few errors	Sporadic errors	Several errors	Numerous errors
Accuracy (Grammar & Vocabulary)	Few errors	Sporadic errors	Several errors	Numerous errors
Volume	Clear and loud	Occasionally low volume	Low volume most of the time	Barely audible

Rubric for Assessing Writing

	Task Completion	Compre-hensibility	Level of Discourse	Vocabulary	Grammar
1	Not complete at all	Not comprehensible	Inadequate development: lacks examples, evidence, or supporting details	Inadequate word choice: rambling, inappropriate, incorrect	Inadequate structure: numerous errors
2	Minimal completion	Barely comprehensible	Minimal development: lacks examples, evidence, or supporting details	Minimal word choice: inadequate, incorrect	Minimal sentence structure: some incomplete sentences and errors
3	Less than partial completion	Partially comprehensible	Limited development: some use of examples or details	Limited word choice: 6 errors	Limited sentence structure: 6 errors

4	Partial completion	Mostly comprehensible	Adequate development: sufficient use of examples or details	Adequate word choice: 4 errors	Adequate sentence structure: 4 errors
5	Appropriate and adequate completion	Easily comprehensible	Effective development: clear use of examples or details	Effective use: 2 errors	Effective use: 2 errors
6	Superior completion: appropriate and with elaboration	Fully comprehensible	Exemplary development: strong use of examples or details	Exemplary word choice: vivid, specific, precise	Exemplary use: complete and correct with sentence variety

Zhiqun Song (宋智群) is an adjunct professor of Chinese at San Jacinto College, Houston, Texas. She received her Bachelor's degree in English Language and Literature from Hunan Normal University, and her Master's degree in Library and Information Science from the University of Iowa, Iowa City. She also received postgraduate training for Teaching English as a Second Language (ESL). She has worked as a librarian and an ESL teacher in the US. As an active STARTALK participant and a popular instructor with her students, Zhiqun Song has gained a wealth of insights about student-centered Chinese language instruction, and developed new skills that improve her teaching effectiveness.

Hobbies

Meiyao Wu-Gilbertson (吴玫瑶)

Grapevine High School and Colleyville High School, Grapevine-Colleyville ISD, Grapevine and Colleyville, Texas

Language Proficiency Level: Chinese 1/Novice High

Age Range: 13-18 (grades 8-12)

Class Size: 10-30 (suitable for different size classes)

Time Frame: 90 minutes per lesson, 5 lessons in total

Essential Questions:

- How can one's pastimes affect one's health and lifestyle?

- What social factors might affect one's choice of pastimes?

Unit Goals:

Develop students' abilities to discuss their hobbies, plan activities with friends, and extend and respond to invitations appropriately.

Standards: Based on the National Standards for Foreign Language Learning

- **Communication:**

    -Interpersonal (1.1)

    -Interpretive (1.2)

    -Presentational (1.3)

- **Connection:** Relate sporting pastimes with students' PE class, after-school activities, and competitions.

- **Comparison:** Compare and contrast activities: pastimes popular among older and younger generations; pastimes popular in China and the US; pastimes popular with men, women, or both; etc.

- **Culture:**

    -Practices of Culture (2.1) - Students learn and practice traditional Chinese hobbies, sports, and pastimes such as 打太极拳, 踢毽子, etc.

    -Products of Culture (2.2) - Equipment needed for practicing traditional Chinese hobbies such as 扯铃 / 抖空竹, 踢毽子, etc.

- **Community:**

    -Communities (5.1) - Students ask their friends/family about their hobbies. Students are encouraged to learn about Chinese pastimes outside the classroom, for example by taking 功夫, 太极拳 or 书法 lessons. Students are also encouraged to perform what they have learned in those lessons on special occasions in their community.

Unit Questions:

- Can students talk about their hobbies and ask about someone else's?

- Can students invite someone to do activities together?

- Can students accept or decline an invitation from a friend to do activities together?

- Can students talk about what activities they have done?

- Can students suggest other activities if their first suggestion doesn't work out?

- Can students find other people to do an activity with when their original invitee is not available?

- Can students plan an outing with friends or family?

Lesson Outlines:

- **Day 1:** What do you like to do? 你喜欢做什么？

- **Day 2:** What would you like to do? 你想做什么？

- **Day 3:** I only want to dance/I would like to dance the most (the least). 我只想跳舞。/我最（不）想跳舞。

- **Day 4:** Forget about it, I will find someone else... 算了，我去找别人……

- **Day 5:** How about we go to a movie? 我们去看电影，怎么样？

Learning Objectives:

Students will be able to:

Day 1

- Talk with others about hobbies by stating personal preferences (interpersonal);

- Discuss what activity one would like to do (interpersonal and presentational).

Day 2

- Invite others to activities or plan outings, such as seeing a movie or going shopping (interpersonal).

Day 3

- Appropriately accept an invitation for an outing (interpersonal);

- Appropriately decline an invitation for an outing (interpersonal).

Day 4

- Find someone else to hang out with when the first person is unavailable (interpersonal);

- Find a different activity to do when the first suggestion doesn't work out (interpersonal).

Day 5

- Ask and state if one likes or dislikes doing certain activities (interpersonal);

- Make plans and invite someone to an outing (interpersonal);

- Compare hobbies among different cultures and generations (interpersonal).

Day 1 (Sample Day): What Do You
Like to Do? 你喜欢做什么？

Learning Objectives:

Students will be able to:

- Talk with others about hobbies by stating personal preferences (interpersonal);

- Discuss what activity one would like to do (interpersonal and presentational).

Teaching Focus:

Grammar:

- 喜欢 vs. 想（想 - Modal Verb) + Verb (+ Object)

- (A-not-A) questions: 喜欢不喜欢，想不想

- Adverbs 也 and 都

- 去 + Verb: 去打球，去跳舞，去吃饭

- Basic Word Order: Subject + Adverbial Phrase (time) + Verb (+ Object)
  我周末喜欢看电影。/ 我中午想吃中国菜。/ 我明天想去逛街。/ 我星期
  五工作。

Vocabulary:

- Activities: 打球，踢球，唱歌，跳舞，听音乐，看书，看电视，etc.

Phonetics:

- Polyphonic characters:

  好 as in 爱好 (àihào) and 好看 (hǎokàn)

  乐 as in 音乐 (yīnyuè) and 快乐 (kuàilè)

Pinyin Spelling Rules:

- "iou" in 球 is spelled as "iu"

- "ü" in 去 and 羽 is spelled as "u"

- "üe" in 乐 is spelled as "ue"

Learning Difficulties/Teaching Focus:

- Students may have difficulty correctly positioning an adverb or an adverbial phrase in a sentence; both come before a verb.

Teaching Materials and Resources:

- Playing cards with authentic pictures of activities/hobbies on one side and Chinese characters on the other side

- Sports equipment for hobbies and pastimes: 棒球, 篮球, 网球, 足球, 橄榄球 (美式足球), 乒乓球 , 羽毛球 , 扯铃 , 毽子, etc.

- Video clips showing 太极 or 功夫 teaching or demonstration

- Pictures of activities, especially for those where the products cannot be easily found or brought in

- Paper, pens, and worksheets (for drill practice)

- PowerPoint slides that contain all teaching material for the Hobbies unit

- Short Chinese video clips about common American and Chinese hobbies and pastimes (shown when teaching the vocabulary)

- *Integrated Chinese* textbook (Level 1, Part 1) and other selected materials

Instructional Strategies:

Warm-up: Relate to One's Hobbies (10 minutes)

1. Think – Pair – Share: Ask each student to draw their hobbies on a piece of paper. Pair students up and have them ask their partner's hobbies based on each individual's drawing. Group two pairs together and ask the four group members to recap their findings. Ask each group to select a representative to report to the class about their group members' favorite hobbies. (Interpersonal and presentational)

2. Watch a clip about how Chinese people spend their spare time, then ask students the following questions:

   中国人喜欢做什么？/ 美国人喜欢做什么？/ 你喜欢做什么？

   中国人周末常常做什么？/ 美国人周末常常做什么？/ 你周末常常做什么？

Activity 1 (For Objectives 1 and 2, 20-25 minutes, interpersonal)

Purpose: To practice new words and expressions in contextualized sentences.

1. "A not A" question form

2. Basic Chinese word order involving time: subject + time + 喜欢 + verb (+ object), e.g., 我周末喜欢打球。

Pre-Activity

Project PowerPoint slides showing pictures of hobby-related vocabulary and have students repeat after teacher the pronunciation of 打球, 唱歌, 跳舞, 听音乐, 看书, 看电影, 看电视. Then introduce and have students practice pronouncing the sports word 球 by using real balls such as 棒球, 篮球, 网球, 足球, 美式足球, 乒乓球, 羽毛球.

1. After practicing the new vocabulary, ask students individually 你喜欢……吗？ Students answer with either 我喜欢…… or 我不喜欢…… based on their own situations.

2. Repeat Step 2, but using the "A not A" question form, such as 你喜欢不喜欢打球？

3. Teacher divides the class into two groups. Each group forms a line and the two lines face each other. Teacher projects pictures of hobby-related vocabulary.

   1) Students then ask and answer questions based on the individual pictures shown. For instance, if 唱歌 is shown, students from Line 1 ask their counterparts from Line 2 你喜欢唱歌吗？or 你喜欢不喜欢唱歌？The latter answer 我喜欢唱歌 or 我不喜欢唱歌 based on their own situations.

   2) After practicing all vocabulary with the help of the imagery shown in the pictures, Line 1 students remain in their positions while Line 2 students move down one spot to face a new partner and proceed with another round using the same visual cues, but changing 喜欢 to 想. For instance, 你想跳舞吗？

   3) For the next rotation, add time words like 周末 and some flexibility in choosing the auxiliary verbs. For instance, 你周末喜欢做什么？or 你周末想做什么？

Main Activity

1. Teacher asks a few pairs to do a Q & A session similar to what they did in the pre-activity. Teacher then asks the class from a third-person perspective: 他喜欢 ＿＿＿ 吗？ Teacher continues to call on individual students to assess their understanding and usage of the first, second, and third persons (我, 你, and 他).

2. Teacher asks students 你喜欢不喜欢＿＿＿？ and students answer: 我喜欢＿＿＿＿ or 我不喜欢＿＿＿＿。Teacher uses the teachable moment and asks students 他喜欢＿＿＿＿，你也喜欢＿＿＿＿吗？ or 他不喜欢＿＿＿＿，你也不喜欢＿＿＿＿ 吗？ to practice the use of 也.

3.. Teacher restates the facts to the whole class again: 他 (Student A) 喜欢＿＿ ＿＿＿，她 (Student B) 也喜欢＿＿＿＿ or 他 (Student A) 不喜欢＿＿＿＿，她 (Student B) 也不喜欢＿＿＿＿, then adding the fact: 他们都喜欢＿＿＿＿ or 他们都不喜欢＿＿＿＿。

4. Teacher polls students: those who like a certain activity (e.g., 喜欢打篮球) stand on one side of the classroom, and those who don't like that activity (e.g., 不喜欢打篮球) stand on the other side of the classroom.

5. Teacher points at Mary and asks the class: Mary 喜欢打篮球吗？ Students answer: Mary 喜欢打篮球。Teacher points at John and asks the class: John 也喜欢打篮球吗？ Students answer: John 也喜欢打篮球。Teacher then asks

the class: Mary 和 John 都喜欢打篮球吗？ Students answer: Mary 和 John
都喜欢打篮球。

6. Teacher repeats steps 4-5 and asks students about different activities and
pastimes to reinforce the use of 也 + verb and 都 + verb.

Post-Activity

1. After students are familiar with the usage of 也 and 都, teacher writes sentences
on the board.

(Choose one of the following to fill in the blank: 也 and 都)

Mary 喜欢打篮球。John _____ 喜欢打篮球。Mary 和 John _____ 喜欢打
篮球。

After students finish the task on the board, teacher then draws students'
attention to the positions of 也 + verb and 都 + verb in a sentence.

2. Teacher prompts students to ask Mary and John if they would like to play
basketball, or if they play often on weekends, since they like the sport: 你们周
末想不想打球？ or 你们周末常常打球吗？

Activity 2 (For Objective 2, 20-25 minutes)

Purpose: To practice the following language structures.

1. Basic Chinese word order involving time

Word Order in Chinese

Subject	Adverbial Phrase (time)	Verb	Object
王朋	周末	听	音乐
高文中	明天下午五点半	看	电影

2. "A not A" question form

Pre-Activity: Deck of Cards (For Objective 2)

1. Teacher first asks 你周末想做什么？, then uses the same set of picture slides
and asks students 你周末想不想 _____? Students may answer: 我周末想 __
____ or 我周末不想 _____ based on their own situations.

Students practice in pairs by using the form 你周末想不想 _____? Again, teacher selects a few pairs to present their dialogues in order to assess their understanding and usage.

2. Divide students into groups of three. Each group receives the same deck of teacher-made cards, with pictures on the front and Chinese sentences on the back, to practice speaking Chinese and reading Chinese characters (see Sample 1 below). The number of cards depends on how many vocabulary words were taught. The possible answers to the questions which are on the back include:

1) 我周末不想 _____。

2) 我也不想 _____。

3) 我周末想 _____。

Sample 1

Hobby Cards with Questions

Front (speaking practice)	Teacher needs to place an image of someone reading books (or any image of hobbies/ activities) HERE.	Teacher needs to place an image of a famous basketball player playing basketball (or any image of hobbies/activities) HERE.	Teacher needs to place an image of someone listening to music (or any image of hobbies/ activities) HERE.	Teacher needs to place an image of someone playing Chinese Yo-Yo (or any image of hobbies/activities) HERE.
Back (reading practice)	Q1: 你周末想 ____ 吗？ Q2: 你周末也（不）想____ 吗？ Q3: 你周末想不想 ____？ Q4: 你周末想做什么？	Q1: 你周末想 ____ 吗？ Q2: 你周末也（不）想____ 吗？ Q3: 你周末想不想 ____？ Q4: 你周末想做什么？	Q1: 你周末想 ____ 吗？ Q2: 你周末也（不）想____ 吗？ Q3: 你周末想不想 ____？ Q4: 你周末想做什么？	Q1: 你周末想 ____ 吗？ Q2: 你周末也（不）想____ 吗？ Q3: 你周末想不想 ____？ Q4: 你周末想做什么？

3. Place the deck of cards picture side down so that the questioner does not see the picture on the front. Student A picks a card and asks the question, filling in the blank with a hobby word: 你周末想_____吗？ Student B answers

according to the picture on the front of the card: 我想_____ or 我不想____
____。Student A continues to guess until the hobby word on the front of the
card is obtained or Student B uses the sentence 我周末想_____ to answer
the last question: 你周末想做什么？Students take turns until the cards are
finished.

Main Activity: Look for a Roommate (For Objectives 1 and 2, interpersonal and presentational)

1. Students are visiting Beijing for two months this summer, and are looking
   for roommates who have common interests. Students need to ask each other
   questions not only about their interests, but also basic personal information like
   name, age, etc. (interpersonal)

   Possible questions are:

   ● 请问，您贵姓？/ 请问，你叫什么名字？

   ● 你今年多大？/ 你今年几岁？

   ● 你（周末）喜欢做什么？/ 你（周末）喜欢打球吗？/ 你（周末）也
     喜欢看电影吗？

   ● 你周末想做什么？

2. After students find their roommates, they need to take turns introducing them
   to the class by stating what the two of them have in common: 我今年 17 岁，
   他今年也 17 岁，我们都 17 岁；我喜欢听音乐，他也喜欢听音乐，我们
   都喜欢听音乐，我们周末想去听音乐会, etc. (presentational)

Activity 3 (For Objective 2, 20-30 minutes, interpersonal and presentational)

Purpose: To practice the following language structures.

1. Basic Chinese word order involving time

2. 去 + Verb

Pre-Activity

Before moving on to the main activity, teacher asks students as a group first,
then lets students pair up and practice 你想去 + Verb (+ Object) + 吗？using
the vocabulary from Activities 1 and 2 above. Pay attention to students'

pronunciation of 去："ü" is pronounced like the "ü" in 女 (nǚ).

Main Activity

1. Teacher hands out an interview sheet (see Sample 2 below) and models how to conduct an interview.

Sample 2

Interview Sheet

Pair interview: 这个周末你想去看电影吗?

Instructions: Do a quick survey among your classmates. Walk around the classroom and poll five classmates asking if they would like to do the activities listed in the survey. Find out how many of them would like to do activities X, Y, or Z this weekend. After a quick tally, report your findings to the class.

Hobbies Survey

	Student #1	Student #2	Student #3	Student #4	Student #5
名字					
爱好	想（O） 不想（X）	想（O） 不想（X）	想（O） 不想（X）	想（O） 不想（X）	想（O） 不想（X）
看电影					
跑步					
游泳					
跳舞					
打篮球					
打棒球					
踢足球					

In your report, make sure you include the adverbs 也 and 都 and the conjunction 可是. For example, Henry 周末想去看电影，Alan 也想去看电影，他们都想去看电影，可是 Julio 和 Amy 不想去看电影，他们想去跳舞。

Note: 也, 可是, and 都 were previously introduced to students in Unit 2: Family.

Post-Activity: Writing (Presentational)

Word Order in Chinese

Subject	Adverbial (time, place, etc.)	Verb	Object
王朋	周末 / 常常	听	音乐
高文中	明天下午五点半	看	外国电影

1. Teacher models by writing one student's oral report on the board in Chinese characters.

2. Teacher then asks students to write down their own reports, based on their survey results.

3. After students finish writing, teacher pairs students up and has each pair check on one another's writing and help one another to make corrections.

4. Students continue to revise their written reports with peer support as teacher walks around checking on students' writing.

5. As a wrap-up, teacher can provide a fill-in-the-blank activity by writing sentences from students' reports on the board. Teacher again emphasizes the positions of 也 and 都 based on the sentences below.

   Instruction: Choose one of the following to fill in each blank: 也 , 都 , 可是

   1) Mary 星期六想去逛街也想去看电影，＿＿＿＿＿＿她不想去打网球。

   2) Alice 星期六想去打网球，想去看电影，＿＿＿＿＿＿她不想去打棒球，＿＿＿＿＿＿不想去游泳。

   3) Tim 和 John 星期六 ＿＿＿＿＿＿想去运动也都想去看电影，＿＿＿＿＿＿他们＿＿＿＿＿＿不想打乒乓球。

Student Reflection (Exit Ticket):

Teacher asks students to demonstrate one thing they learned today, such as describing their hobbies or weekend activities in a complete sentence, before leaving class. Teacher will set up tutoring times to work with those students who need help.

Homework Assignment:

Students write six complete and compound sentences based on their interview sheets from class. They need to combine their interview facts by using words such as 也，都，and 可是.

Teacher Self-Assessment:

- Have students reached the learning objectives?

- Did each activity transit smoothly to the next?

- Is there any teaching focus that needs to be reviewed the next day?

- Are the learning objectives too many or too few for students to handle based on the "i+1" theory?

Day 2: What Would You Like to Do? 你想做什么？

Teaching Focus:

Grammar:

- Tag questions with 好吗？ vs. 怎么样？

  我们周末去看电影，好吗？/ 我们星期六去跳舞，怎么样？

- Tag questions with 对吗？/ 对不对？and 你呢？

Vocabulary:

- 运动，有时候，请客，因为，所以，好久不见，不错

Phonetics:

The tone change for 好 as in 好久不见

Day 3: I Only Want to Dance/I Like to Dance the Most (the least) 我只想跳舞 / 我最（不）想跳舞

Teaching Focus:

Grammar:

- Superlatives 最 (Adverb) + Verb
- Verb + Object as a detachable compound

  唱歌 —唱英文歌 ; 跳舞 — 跳中国舞 ; 睡觉 — 睡午觉
- 只 (Adverb) + Verb + Object
- 觉得 + clause

Vocabulary:

- 上网 , 画画儿 , 聊天儿 , 玩儿游戏机 , 打电脑游戏 , 逛街 , 打乒乓球
- 有意思

Phonetics:

- Polyphonic character: 觉 as in 睡觉 (shuì jiào) and 觉得 (juéde)

Day 4: Forget about It, I Will Find Someone Else... 算了，我去找别人……

Teaching Focus:

Grammar:

- Auxiliary verbs 想 (would like to) vs. 要 (want to): 我想去打球/我要去打球。

- 太 (Adverb) + Adjective + 了 vs. 真 (Adverb) + Adjective

Vocabulary:

- 算了 , 找 , 别人

Phonetics:

- 得 neutral tone

Day 5: How about We Go to a Movie? 我们去看电影，怎么样?

Review and Summative Assessment:

Objectives:

Students will be able to:

- Find someone who shares the same interests (favorite hobbies or pastimes) (interpretive and interpersonal);

- Make plans and invite someone to an outing (interpersonal);

- Ask and state if one likes or dislikes doing certain activities (interpersonal);

- Describe one's hobbies or favorite pastimes (presentational);

- Compare hobbies across different ethnic groups and countries (interpretive and presentational);

Unit Theme: Hobbies

Can-Do Statements (Self-Assessment Rubric)

Interpretive		Interpersonal	Presentational	
Listening	Reading	Person-to-Person/ Communication	Speaking	Writing
I can understand basic statements about hobbies: what people like or dislike, inviting others to activities, accepting and declining invitations, and planning future outings.	I can understand short passages about hobbies: what people like or dislike, inviting others to activities, accepting and declining invitations, and planning future outings.	I can ask for and give information about hobbies: what people like or dislike, inviting others to activities, accepting and declining invitations, and planning future outings.	I can give an oral report about my hobbies: what I like or dislike, inviting others to activities, accepting and declining invitations, and planning future outings.	I can produce a written report about my hobbies: what I like or dislike, inviting others to activities, accepting and declining invitations, and planning future outings.

Meiyao Wu-Gilbertson (吴玫瑶) received her Master of Music degree and her teaching certificate from the University of Houston. She has completed graduate-level courses in Teaching Chinese as a Foreign Language (TCFL) at the University of Houston and the University of Virginia and attended workshops on Chinese language teaching in China and the US. She has designed the Chinese program curricula for two school districts in Texas and has taught Chinese at all levels, including courses for AP Chinese and IB Chinese.

Critique

Hobbies – Zhiqun Song
Hobbies – Meiyao Wu-Gilbertson

The theme "Hobbies" occurs in the curriculum of all language proficiency levels. Zhiqun Song and Meiyao Wu-Gilbertson present two designs aimed at slightly different proficiency levels and age groups. Song's design is based on the function of the language: what students can do when learning the Hobbies unit. Five well-thought questions cover the content scope and guide the design.

1. Can students talk about their favorite pastimes and ask about someone else's?

2. Can students invite someone to a weekend activity?

3. Can students comment on how well they do with their pastimes or hobbies?

4. Can students accept or decline an invitation to a weekend activity?

5. Can students find someone else to do activities with?

The instruction is implemented under the frame of Communicative Language Teaching with form-focused instruction. The design shows how syntactic structures such as word order and question forms are used in daily life situations; how language functions such as making suggestions and requesting opinions are used in context; and how vocabulary such as action and compound verbs are practiced in sentences and in discourse.

The instructional sequences of both designs are carefully planned and logically organized to enhance students' cognitive skills. Song's activities frequently start with learning vocabulary words in context. For example, in an initial warm-up activity of 老师说, students would easily comprehend hobby terms, particularly the Chinese verb compounds such as 打篮球, 踢足球, 跳舞, etc., conveyed through physical responses. After giving students a fair amount of relatively controlled but meaningful sentence practice, the design provides a variety of task-based activities and games such as using Information Gap to find out the missing information from partners, Think, Pair, and Share, interviews in the form of Inside-Outside Circles, All About Me, and looking for a language partner. These group activities enhance peer collaboration and facilitate differentiated learning. Activities are based on a contextual story with a plot, taken from the textbook. Therefore, students see the relevance and review what has been learned in class.

The final steps of the activities (such as post-activities) in Song's design provide not only formative assessment, but also open-ended communication and presentations that enable students to review and enrich their learning. Students' critical thinking skills are encouraged through problem-solving and information exchanges. Post-activities in Wu's design continue the main activity, extending it to cover new content or a new exercise. In this way, students review what they have just practiced, and their prior knowledge leads to new learning.

Similar to Song's instructional design, Wu presents clear step-by-step instruction to scaffold students' learning. For example, her instructional process starts with a simple sentence such as "你喜欢唱歌吗?" and moves to more complex sentences with time expressions, adverbs, and a different question form. Wu uses body language and entities in the classroom to create target-language input. Since the input is very much contextualized, it is easy for students to make sense and develop an accurate understanding of expressions and sentence structures, and consequently produce the language correctly (e.g., see Activity 1).

Both designs integrate Chinese culture into learning. Carefully chosen teaching aids and resources are provided to students, including Chinese culture products like 乒乓球, 羽毛球, 毽子 and culture practice such as 打太极拳. When introducing the vocabulary, Wu uses all kinds of real balls, such as 棒球, 篮球, 网球, 足球, 美式足球, 乒乓球, 羽毛球, to give students vivid images.

In the theme "Hobbies", one topic of conversation is how well a person can do a hobby, using an auxiliary verb such as 会 and the verbal structure "verb 得 adverb/adjective" to infer the manner and extent, This basic topic is absent in Wu's design. Song's design indeed includes 会 and 得 (Days 3 and 4), though it is important to provide the verbal structure in the grammar section and with a sample sentence, such as (我会打篮球，可是) 打得不太好.

With regard to the Exit Ticket in Wu's design "Teacher asks students to report one thing that they learned today" may need to be more concrete. Lastly, the function and usage of "Can-Do Statements (Self-Assessment Rubric)" is unaddressed in the text and thus remains unclear.

Theme 8
Family and Birthday

Family

Lili Liu (刘莉莉)
Pin Oak Middle School, Houston, Texas

Language Proficiency Level: Novice Intermediate

Age Range: 11-14 (Middle school, grades 6-9)

Class Size: 20-28 students

Time Frame: 90 minutes for each lesson, with 5 lessons in total

Essential Questions:

- How can our personal life experience with our own families be viewed as part of the community in which we live?

- How do diverse cultures contribute to and strengthen our communities?

Unit Goals:

To help students develop their ability to exchange information related to one's family in culturally appropriate language, and present information related to family.

Standards: Based on the National Standards for Foreign Language Learning

- **Communication:**

   -Interpersonal (1.1)

   -Interpretive (1.2)

   -Presentational (1.3)

- **Connection:** Social studies and math; use technology, the Internet and Web 2.0 tools to conduct research and complete an oral presentation assignment. (2.1)

- **Comparison & Culture:** Compare multiple perspectives related to family between Chinese and American cultures. (3.1) , (4.1) , (4.2)

Unit Questions:

- Can students ask someone's name in a culturally appropriate way?
- Can students ask and respond about one's age and nationality?
- Can students employ terms of kinship to name one's family members?
- Can students ask and say one's occupation?
- Can students create their own family trees and introduce a friend's family?

Lesson Outlines:

- **Day 1:** Hello! What is your name? 你好！你叫什么名字？
- **Day 2:** May I know your last name? How old are you? What is your nationality? 您贵姓？你多大？你是哪国人？
- **Day 3:** How many family members do you have? This is my dad. 你家有几口人？这是我爸爸。
- **Day 4:** What does your dad do? 你爸爸做什么工作？
- **Day 5:** My friend and his family 我的朋友和他的家人。

Learning Objectives:

Students will be able to:

Day 1

- Greet and exchange one's full name;

- Understand and use some simple classroom expressions (Note: this objective appears in the first five units of the first semester of Beginning Chinese);

- Identify the differences in the order of personal and family names between Chinese and Western cultures.

Day 2

- Ask for one's last name and full name;

- Inquire and respond about one's age;

- Inquire and respond about one's nationality.

Day 3

- Ask and answer one's age & nationality;

- Employ terms of kinship to name one's family members;

- Exchange information about each other's family.

Day 4

- Inquire about someone's occupation;

- Create one's family tree and describe the family members;

- Identify different preferences in addressing people between Chinese and American cultures.

Day 5

- Exchange information about family members, including age and occupation;

- Introduce someone's family;

- Gain knowledge of multi-generational households in traditional Chinese culture.

Day 5 (Sample Day)

Learning Objectives:

Students will be able to:

- Exchange information about family members, including age and occupation (interpersonal);

- Give an oral presentation introducing their favorite person's family, based on a prepared poster (presentational);

- Gain knowledge of multi-generational households in traditional Chinese culture (interpretive).

Teaching Focus:

Grammar:

- Question word for asking the number/amount of something: 几

- Placement of a measure word when there is number and a noun: 一个哥哥

- Word order when forming a question: 你家有几口人？你爸爸做什么工作？

Vocabulary:

- Professions: 商人, 老师, 运动员, 服务员, 医生, 护士, 工程师

- Related new word: 工作

- The usage of 二 vs. 两

Phonetics:

- Accuracy of tones

  (Note: Many students seem to have difficulty in pronouncing second and third tones. When introducing new words, have students say the new words with hand gestures. Make practicing second and third tones a routine in class.)

Learning Difficulties:

- Students may make mistakes when describing an object in the quantity of two. Instead of 两个哥哥, they might say 二个哥哥.

- They may also be confused about how to form questions in Chinese.

Teaching Materials and Resources:

- PowerPoint slides

- 快板 Allegro (Chinese bamboo clapping storytelling)

- Study guide for unit test

- Pictures of different families and occupations

- Sets of flashcards (occupations, nationalities, kinship terms)

- "Favorite person" poster created by students

- Printouts of different characters and information related to age, nationalities, and their family members

- Textbook: *Far East Chinese for Youth*《远东少年中文》

- http://quizlet.com (homework: readers needs to explore the website and create their own)

- http://clear.msu.edu (online speaking homework: same as Quizlet)

Instructional Strategies:

Warm-up (5 minutes)

Students, working in pairs, will play Tic-Tac-Toe or Connect Four (their choice). Students already learned how to ask about one's occupation on Day 4. The purpose of the warm-up is for students to review what they have learned in the previous class period. See Game Rules below.

1. Pass the game board and a set of flashcards to each group.

2. Students in each group will take turns flipping a flashcard and saying the correct words, phrases, or sentences in Chinese before they can mark their moves on the game board. Flashcards have pictures of people of different family relationships (expressed by kinship terms), occupations, and nationalities, such as 爸爸, 妈妈, 哥哥, 弟弟, 姐姐, 妹妹, 医生, 老师, 中国人, 美国人, as well as sentences in English for students to translate into Chinese, such as "How many people are there in your family?" and "What does your dad do? My dad is a teacher."

Tic-Tac-Toe Game Rules:

Prepare a 3 × 3 grid game board printout as shown below. Student 1 of each pair will draw a card from the pile and say in Chinese the picture, word, or sentence on the card. Then they can mark an "O" on the game board if they say it correctly. Student 2 will draw a card and say the picture word or sentences in Chinese correctly, then mark an "X" on the game board. If student can't say the sentence correctly, they will lose a turn. The objective is to have a row of three "Os" or "Xs" across the grid, horizontally, vertically, or diagonally.

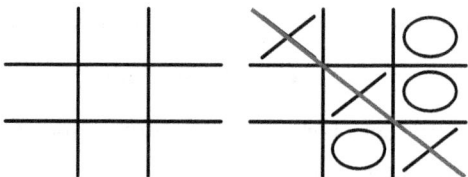

Connect 4 Game Rules: Create a table using the one below as an illustration. Teacher can use a blank table with vocabulary flashcards, or fill in the table with pictures, characters, words, and/or sentences in English, according to students' ability level.

四	九	三	五	九	三	二	七
八	三	二	十	四	六	八	五
二	七	九	七	三	九	二	八
十	九	四	八	五	八	九	十
五	六	十	二	四	七	六	二
十	九	七	九	六	七	八	九
八	二	八	八	五	十	二	六

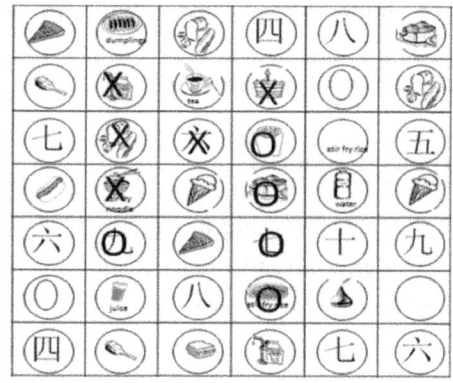

This game is usually played in pairs; however, group of three students can work as well. The objective of Connect 4 is to connect four boxes in a row, vertically or horizontally. To play, student 1 can start from any position in the game board as long as they can say whatever is in the box in Chinese. If they can say it correctly, they will mark the box with "O" or "X". Then student 2 will do the same, selecting a different box on the game board. To win the game, students also needs to stop their opponents from connecting four boxes.

Activity 1 快板——我的家 Allegro – My Family (For Objectives 1 and 3, 20 minutes)

Purpose: To develop students' knowledge and skills learned using traditional folk art, 快板 chanting.

Warm-up (5 minutes)

Play a short video clip or show pictures of Chinese family structure. Randomly call on students to see if they can identify any family members in the video. For example: 他家有几口人？他是谁？他是爷爷，奶奶 / 爸爸 / 妈妈……

Use PowerPoint or picture printouts of different Chinese families to briefly explain in English that three generations living together is not uncommon in traditional Chinese culture. (Readers can search on the Internet to obtain the video clip or images of Chinese families.)

Main Activity (10 minutes)

1. To model the chanting, teacher can use PowerPoint or give students a handout of the chant. Teacher will read the chant first and then have the whole class practice by repeating it after the teacher. See the modeling chart below.

2. T-S interaction: Teacher will chant (as Group 1) with a student (playing Group 2) to demonstrate the proper sequence on how to do the dialogues as 快板 allegro.

3. S-S group interaction: Divide students into two groups. Teacher can use PowerPoint or give students a handout of pictures of two different families. Assign one family to each group. Groups 1 and 2 will practice the chant as illustrated below. (Teacher can use family pictures of famous people found on the Internet to make the activity more interesting.)

Group 1	Group 2
他家、他家，有几口人？	他家、他家，有十口人。
十口人。他们是谁？	爸爸和妈妈，
	一个哥哥，两个弟弟，
	一个姐姐，一个妹妹，
	爷爷奶奶还有他。
	他爱他的家，他爱他的家。

Note: Reverse the group role and chant twice. To illustrate chanting, teacher will chant while clapping hands. For example, clap hands when saying the underlined character. Each clap is one beat.

4. S-S individual interaction: At the end of the activity, pass pictures of different families to each student. Students, in pairs, will exchange their assigned families' information by chanting.

Post-Activity (3-5 minutes) (Interpersonal)

Assessment: Teacher will call on students and their partners to check if the information exchanged is correct, e.g., ask student 1 how many family members in student 2's family. Then teacher will confirm with student 2 to check if student 1's answers are correct.

Activity 2: 他是谁？**Who is my new friend? (20 minutes)**

For Objective 1, interpersonal

Purpose: To review and get ready to complete the end of unit project.

Warm-up (5 minutes)

1. Using PowerPoint/family picture printout, teacher reviews sentence patterns by calling on students randomly and asking:

他叫什么名字？	他叫 × × ×
他是哪国人？	他是英国人 /……
他多大？	他三十五岁 /……
他家有几口人？	他家有四口人。他有一个哥哥 /……
他做什么工作？	他是运动员 /……

2. Pass pictures of different families to students. Teacher models the above sentence patterns with a student first, and then with the whole class. Then have students work in pairs, practicing the sentences using the given picture. Teacher circulates around the room to monitor students' progress.

Main Activity: 他是谁？ *Who is my new friend? (10 minutes)*

1. Pass personal data sheets and worksheets to students. (See the Sample Data Sheet and Worksheet below.) Students fill in the data sheet with fictional information. To make the activity move smoothly, teacher can project an image of the data sheet and explain to students what they need to fill in the sheet. Students will fill in the information with *pinyin* or Chinese characters, e.g., *pinyin* for occupations, Chinese characters for age and nationality, and total numbers of family and names in English.

2. Teacher will make the whole class fill in the information step by step. For example, teacher can say the following: "Let's fill in the information in the data sheet and each item is timed. For names, you can use famous person's name, your friend's name, or create a fun name." Teacher then says "请写名字" while using body gestures to help students understand the instruction, wait for 10 seconds, then says "停". Continue the same step until the whole class finishes filling in the information. The purpose of setting a time limit is to keep everyone on the same step.

3. Collect and shuffle the data sheets. Pass the shuffled data sheets to students.

4. Pair students up and have them tape the data sheets to each other's backs. Students need to find out the information about the person who is taped to their back by asking other students to get the information and fill it in on the worksheet. However, students can only ask one classmate one question at a time. In order to complete the task, they need to ask multiple classmates. Note that in this activity, students don't have fixed partners: they will walk around asking random students questions and answering questions in return. To answer the questions, student will look at the other student's back to find out the information. The purpose of this activity is to provide students the opportunity to move around and talk to different classmates. Taping information to students' backs makes the activity more interesting.

Student 1	Student 2
你好！	你好！
他叫什么名字？	他叫 ×××。
他是哪国人？	他是……国人。
他多大？	他……岁。
他家有几口人？	他家有……口人。
他做什么工作？	他是……。

5. At the end of the activity, put students in pairs. Students will take the data sheet from their partner's back and do peer checking. For example, after removing the data sheet from their partner, student 1 will ask student 2 " 他 叫 什 么 名 字？ "Student 2 will answer the question based on the information that he filled in the worksheet during the activity. Student 1 then checks the data sheet in his hand to see if student 2's answer is correct. Students will take turns checking each other's answers and use red pen to make any corrections. Teacher will collect both data sheet and worksheet and give a participation grade.

Sample Data Sheet

míngzì   niánjí   rìqī
名字：＿＿＿＿   年级：＿＿＿＿   日期：＿＿＿＿

Create a fictional person

Name:	Nationality:
Age:	Total number of family member:
Profession:	

Sample Worksheet

míngzi   niánlíng   rìqī
名字：＿＿＿＿   年龄：＿＿＿＿   日期：＿＿＿＿

Instructional strategies:

Find out your new friend's information. The sentence patterns below may help you form the questions.

You can only ask one classmate one question at a time. You will need to ask five different classmates questions to find out who the person is on your back. You will also need to look up the answer on other classmates' backs to answer questions asked by others.

Question	Response (look at your partner's back and answer)
Nǐ hǎo tā jiào shénme míngzi? 1 你 好，他 叫 什 么 名 字？	Nǐ hǎo tājiào 你 好，他 叫 ＿＿＿＿＿＿

Nǐ hǎo tā shì nǎ guó rén?
2 你 好，他 是 哪 国 人？

Nǐ hǎo tā shì ＿＿＿ guó rén.
你 好，他 是 ＿＿＿ 国 人。

Nǐ hǎo tā duō dà?
3 你 好，他 多 大？

Nǐ hǎo tā ＿＿＿ suì.
你 好，他 ＿＿＿ 岁。

Nǐ hǎo tā jiā yǒu jǐ kǒu rén?
4 你 好，他 家 有 几 口 人？

Nǐ hǎo tā jiā yǒu ＿＿＿ kǒu rén?
你 好，他 家 有 ＿＿＿ 口 人？

Nǐ hǎo tā zuò shénme gōngzuò?
5 你 好，他 做 什 么 工作？

Nǐ hǎo tāshì ＿＿＿.
你 好，他 是 ＿＿＿.

Name	Nationality	Age	Total # of family members	Profession

Teacher's note for main activity:

Taping the information to students' backs adds an element of the unknown to the activity. Having students ask one classmate one question at a time allows students to move around and gain the opportunity to talk to different students. Many schools now have double block class periods with 90 minutes per class, so in order to help students stay focused, it is important to design activities to allow them to move around.

Post-Activity (3 minutes)

Teacher will randomly call on a couple of pairs to check if students have completed the activity correctly. For example, teacher can ask student 1 " 你 的 朋友叫什么名字？" and then ask student 2 " 他说得对不对？" Teacher can also call on other students to recap what has been said. For example: "× × × 说什么?" Cross-checking keeps students on task, and teacher can make cross-checking part of the participation grade. For example, if a student is off task, teacher will take 5 points off from their weekly/biweekly participation grade. (Note: Grade deduction policy should be specified in the course syllabus and needs to be explained at the beginning of the school year.)

Activity 3: My Favorite Person's Poster Presentation (For Objective 2, presentational, 30 minutes)

Purpose: To practice the abilities of engaging in conversation and presenting information on topics related to family.

Warm-up (5 minutes)

Illustrate the critical elements that constitute a good oral presentation, such as eye contact, speaking volume, body language, and the opening statement. Teacher will model a bad oral presentation in Chinese and ask students for suggestions for improvement. For example, teacher says words or sentences with the wrong tones, incorrect grammar, and low volume, and has students point out what can be improved.

Project a family picture on the board. Show students the sentence patterns below and model the dialogue with one student. Students will then work in pairs to practice an oral presentation based on the picture projected.

> 大家好，我是 ×××。
>
> 他是加拿大人。
>
> 他二十二岁。他是运动员。
>
> 他家有四口人：
>
> 爸爸、妈妈、一个妹妹和他。
>
> 他爸爸五十八岁，是医生；
>
> 他妈妈五十五岁，是老师；
>
> 他妹妹二十岁，是学生；
>
> 他二十五岁，是运动员。

Main Activity (25 minutes)

1. Arrange students' posters, face down, on the tables across the room. (Note: The poster is the homework assignment that was due on Day 4. Teacher should arrange the posters before the class starts.)

2. Pass out worksheets containing a table for note-taking. Students will take turns giving oral presentations in front of the class. The rest of the class will take notes (See the sample note-taking worksheet below).

3. Teacher will show a blank worksheet first, explaining what information needs to be filled in.

   Note: Show student a completed worksheet first. If they have questions, they can raise their hands and ask the presenter " 再说一次 ". Remind students not to mention the names of their favorite persons, but include all other information in their presentation. (See narrative practiced during the warm-up section.)

4. After all the students have completed the presentation, teacher will flip the posters and the students will walk around to review the posters in the classroom. Students will try to identify each presenter's favorite person based on their notes.

Note-taking Worksheet

míngzi	niánlíng	rìqī
名字：_____	年龄：_____	日期：_____

Presenter's Name：			
Favorite Person's Name	Age	Nationality	Profession

Total Number of Family Members：			
Relation	Age	Nationality	Profession

Sample note-taking worksheet filled in by a student

míngzi	niánlíng	rìqī
名字：_____	年龄：_____	日期：_____

Presenter's Name: Mark S			
Favorite Person's Name	Age	Nationality	Profession
John	三十二	Fǎguórén 法国人	yīshēn 医生

315

Total Number of Family Members: 六			
bàba 爸爸	六十二	Same	gōngchéngshī 工程师
māma 妈妈	五十八	Same	méiyǒu 没有
gēge 哥哥	三十六	Same	yùndòngyuán 运动员
mèimei 妹妹	二十五	Same	lǎoshī 老师

Post-Activity (3 minutes)

Teacher calls on students randomly to check their understanding, e.g., teacher asks a student: "×××喜欢谁？他叫什么名字？他几岁？他做什么工作？" Then, confirm with ××× if the student's answers are correct.

To keep students on task, teacher can do cross-checking. For example, after asking one student a question, call on other students randomly and ask what has been said: "××× 说得对不对？" or "××× 说什么？" Teacher can make cross-checking part of the participation grade.

Assessment:

Formative:

Activity 1 - Interpersonal

Assign students to pairs for oral conversation based on what they have learned in class. Students demonstrate their abilities to engage in conversations and to exchange information about their own family members. The goal of formative assessment is to monitor student learning so teacher can provide ongoing feedback. Teacher uses the assessment to improve his/her teaching, not for grading.

Summative:

Activities 2 and 3 - Presentational and Interpersonal

Students demonstrate abilities in:

1) presenting information to audience on topics related to family;

2) understanding spoken language and writing down information in Chinese characters or *pinyin* related to the topics learned.

The goal of summative assessment is to evaluate student learning at the end of a learning unit. It is important at the beginning of the unit to provide students with rubrics specifying the criteria so they understand what is expected of them. Please see the sample rubrics at the end of the lesson plan.

Student Reflection:

Pass reflection slips to students. Students will write down what they have learned and their strategy to work on language difficulties. Teacher will review the reflections and share students' strategies in class. The purpose is to help the teacher understand each student's language difficulties and to evaluate the effectiveness of instruction. Students will write down their strategies in Chinese, and teacher should tell them that leaving the strategy part of the slip blank is acceptable if they can't figure one out. Sometimes, students can come up with interesting and helpful ideas; for example, a student once shared that " 早 is a 日 on top of 十 " and this helps her to remember 早上 is usually associated with early morning, earlier than 10 o'clock. To encourage students, teachers may consider giving a small reward to the students whose strategies are shared in class.

Sample Reflection Slip:

Míngzi 名字：	Rìqī 日期：
Jīntiān wǒ xué le 今天 我 学 了：	
Nán dǒng dē zì / cí / jùzi 难 懂 的 字/词/句子：	
Wǒ dē fāngfǎ 我 的 方法 (Strategy)：	

Homework Assignments:

1. Go to http://quizlet.com to practice vocabulary learned.

2. Go to http://clear.msu.edu to complete online speaking assignment. (Students will describe a family photo shown on the website.)

3. Pass out study guide for the next class containing a list of vocabulary, grammar, and dialogue patterns for the next class day's unit test. Go through the study guide with students and answer the questions about the unit test.

Teacher Self-assessment:

What went well?

What would need more review in the next class?

Did the activities help students learn effectively?

What should be done differently?

Rubric for Assessing Speaking

	Excellent 4 points	Good 3 points	Average 2 points	Below Average 1 point
Task Completion	Fully complete	Almost complete	Mostly complete	Barely or not complete
Compre-hensibility	Easily comprehensible	Comprehensible	Mostly comprehensible	Barely or not comprehensible
Vocabulary	Miss 2	Miss 4	Miss 6	Miss 8
Grammar	Miss 1	Miss 3	Miss 5	Miss 7
Eye Contact	All the time	Most of the time	Occasionally	Little
Volume	Clear volume	Occasionally low volume	Mostly low volume	Very low volume

Rubric for Assessing Poster Presentation

	Excellent 4 points	Good 3 points	Average 2 points	Below Average 1 point
Pictures	4 or more pictures	3 pictures	2 pictures	1 picture
Design, Layout, and Neatness	Exceptionally attractive	Attractive	Acceptably attractive, but a little bit messy	Poorly designed and very messy
Vocabulary	Miss 2	Miss 4	Miss 6	Miss 8

Lili Liu (刘莉莉) is the Mandarin Chinese teacher at Pin Oak Middle School, Houston, Texas. In addition to teaching at a public school, she has been working as a coordinator and curriculum developer for the Rice University STARTALK Summer Chinese Immersion program since 2010. Her strength is the integration of technology, music, and games into her teaching, making learning a fun and engaging experience for her students.

Family

Dai-Hau Ruth Tang (唐代豪)
Round Rock High School/Cedar Ridge High School, Round Rock, Texas

Language Proficiency Level: Novice Intermediate

Age Range: 14-17 (high school students)

Class Size: 20-22 students

Time Frame: 90 minutes for each lesson, with 5 lessons in total

Essential Question:

What special significance do family and kinship terms carry in Chinese culture?

Unit Goals:

Students will be able to talk about family and family-related events, and also be aware of how Chinese culture influences kinship terms between the paternal and maternal sides of the family.

Standards: Based on the National Standards for Foreign Language Learning

- **Communication:**

  -Interpersonal (1.1)

-Interpretive (1.2)

-Presentational (1.3)

- **Connection**: Technology (3.1) Using Glogster (www.glogster.com), an electronic online poster, to introduce a celebrity's family.

- **Comparison:** Comparing the different connotations of "family" in Chinese (家 vs. 家人 vs. 家庭) and the students' own culture.

- **Culture:** The practice of culture, e.g., extended vs. core families (2.1); the products of culture, e.g., different terms for relatives on the paternal and maternal sides: 爷爷, 奶奶, 外公, 外婆; Chinese vs. English sibling terms.

- **Community:** Students will interview their parents about their families and report their results to the class in Chinese (5.1).

Unit Questions:

- Can students introduce their family to friends?

- Can students ask and answer questions regarding family members' occupations?

- Can students introduce their family to a Chinese pen pal by writing an email?

- Can students understand the cultural perspective behind kinship terms (e.g., father's side and mother's side)?

Lesson Outlines:

Day 1: Do you have brothers and sisters? 你有哥哥姐姐(弟弟 / 妹妹)吗?

Day 2: Look at a family photo 看看家人的照片

Day 3: My elder brother and I are both high school students. 我和我哥哥都是中学生。

Day 4: Introduce "My Family" to a Chinese pen pal by writing an email (including their ages, occupations, and information on both sides of the family, including grandparents).

Day 5: Introduce one's own family or favorite celebrity's family verbally and present it with Glogster (an online poster, see http://www.glogster.com) or a physical poster.

Learning Objectives:

Students will be able to:

Day 1

- Talk about their family members (interpersonal);

- Ask the number of members in each other's family (interpersonal);

- Draw a family tree by listening to a description of a family photo (interpretive).

Day 2

- Acquire the information needed to identify someone's family members when looking at that person's family photo (interpersonal);

- State the ownership of one's family photos, such as 这是我的照片 and 这张照片是我的 (interpersonal).

Day 3

- Talk about one's family members' occupations (interpersonal);

- Ask and clarify one's occupation (interpersonal);

- Introduce one's family, including grandparents (presentational).

Day 4

- Introduce one's family, including their grandparents' families, with information such as their ages, occupations, etc. to their Chinese pen pal (presentational);

- Draw a three-generation family tree with correctly labeled ages and occupations by listening to a description of a family (interpretive).

Day 5

- Use Glogster or a physical poster to introduce three generations of one's own family, a favorite celebrity's family, or an animated/fictional character's family by listing all kinship terms, ages, nationalities, and occupations (presentational).

Day 1 (Sample Day)

Learning Objectives:

Students will be able to:

- Talk about their family members (interpersonal);

- Ask the number of members in each other's family (interpersonal);

- Draw a family tree by listening to a description of a family photo (interpretive).

Teaching Focus:

Grammar:

- Number + measure word (MW) + noun 一个人, 三个弟弟, 四个学生 (老师)
  几 : replace the number with 几 to form a question 你家有几个人?

Vocabulary:

- Kinship terms: 爸爸, 妈妈, 哥哥, 姐姐, 弟弟, 妹妹

Phonetics:

- "ji" as in 几, 家, 姐

- "e" as in 哥, 个

- Tone changes for 一 and 不 : When followed by a 4th tone, 一 and 不 change
  to a 2nd tone, e.g., 一个, 不是

Learning Difficulties:

English-speaking students tend to leave out the measure word between a number and a noun, or between a demonstrative pronoun and a noun:

Number/Demonstrative pronoun + measure word + noun

Teaching Materials and Resources:

- Teacher's and students' family photos

- Markers and paper

- Celebrities' or animated/fictional figures' family photos – PPT slides or printouts (e.g., world leaders' families, TV or movie personalities' families)

- *Integrated Chinese* textbook and other selected materials

Instructional Strategies:

Sample Dialogue Input:

> A: 你家有几个人？
>
> B: 我家有四个人。
>
> A: 你有哥哥吗？
>
> B: 我没有哥哥，我有一个妹妹。你呢？
>
> A: 我也没有哥哥，我有一个姐姐。
>
> B: 你妈妈叫什么名字？
>
> A: 我妈妈叫 Michelle。
>
> B: 你爸爸呢？
>
> A: 他叫 George。

Warm-up (Interpersonal, 5 minutes)

Teacher reviews a previous unit: Unit 1, Greetings.

1. Teacher's demonstration:

   Teacher asks a better prepared student：你好，请问你姓什么？

   > Student: 我姓 ×。
   >
   > Teacher: 你叫什么名字？
   >
   > Student: 我叫 ×××。
   >
   > Teacher: 你是中国／韩国人吗？
   >
   > Student: 我不是中国／韩国人。我是美国人。

2. Teacher may toss a small stuffed animal (or anything soft and easily catchable) to a better prepared student - do the demonstration a couple of times.

3. Student-student (interpersonal): Students can toss the stuffed animal to one another and find out their classmates' names and nationalities.

4. 你好！请问你姓什么？你叫什么名字？你是 _____ 人吗？ (End with a guessing game to practice asking questions.)

Note: Teacher needs to make sure that students answer in complete sentences. If students' answers are too short, teacher needs to use hand signals to remind them; for example, pull out a long line with both hands to indicate a complete sentence.

Activity 1

Pre-Activity: Teaching Vocabulary (Teacher's demonstration without any English input, teacher-student, 10 minutes)

1. 家：

   1) Show PPT of a cartoon family photo in a house and say 家.

   2) Show a photo of a world leader's family in a house and say 甘迪家.

   3) Show another photo of a celebrity's family and say X 家.

   4) Show a photo of teacher's family in a house and say 唐老师家. (Switch these photos and let students practice saying the new terms.)

2. 有 / 没有：(to have/not have)

   1) Show a quarter to the class, then put your hands behind your back with the quarter in one hand.

   2) Lift one hand and say 有 with a question tone. Do not open the hand yet.

   3) Do the same thing with the other hand.

   4) Open the hand with the quarter in it and say 家.

   5) Repeat this game a couple of times so that students can get the sound and meaning of it.

   6) After students can say it well, open the empty hand and say 没有.

3. 个：

   1) Teacher points at one of her family members in a photo and says 一个人.

   2) Point at another one and say 一个人.

3) Point at a student and say 一个学生, point at three students and say 三个学生. Using different pictures, say 个, 一个老师, 一个中国人, 一个美国人.

Tip: I draw a semi-circle in the air between the number and the object to indicate the measure word as a bridge. It can be a very useful hint for students to remember to use a measure word between a number and a noun.

4) Explain the role of measure words as a bridge between a number and a noun.

4. 几：

1) Show the teacher's family photo and say 唐老师家有四个人.

2) Show a couple different photos and say X 家有 X 个人.

3) Show a world leader or celebrity's family photo.

Teacher asks "(celebrity's name) 家有几个人？" (Write a big question mark on the whiteboard when saying 几.)

Students answer "(celebrity's name) 家有五个人。"

4) Show a couple more celebrity family PowerPoint slides and ask "X 家有 X 个人？" "唐老师有几个学生？"

5) Practice several times.

In-Activity: Information Gap (Pair work, 14 minutes)

Instructional preparation:

Form two groups, A and B.

- Prepare sheets with eight different family images: sheets A & B for groups A and B, respectively.

- Group A needs to get the information missing from their sheet by asking Group B questions, and vice versa.

- If a student guesses it right on his/her first try, student from the other group will answer "对，很好。"

Information Gap (Sheet A)

Instructions for Group A: You have **Sheet A**. Find a friend with **Sheet B**, guess how many members are in a celebrity's family twice, then use 几 (jǐ) to ask "(celebrity's name) 家有几个人？（_____ jiā yǒu jǐ ge rén?)" . Write down the answer the student with **Sheet B** gives you, and do not show your sheet to your partner.

Please find the answer to the next question from another friend who has **Sheet B**.

Example:

A: (celebrity's name) 家有四个人吗？　　B: 不对。

A: (celebrity's name) 家有六个人吗？　　B: 不对。

A: (celebrity's name) 家有几个人？　　　B: (celebrity's name) 家有五个人。

(celebrity's name) 家 *(leave a blank here)*	A celebrity's family photo	(celebrity's name) 家 *(leave a blank here)*	A celebrity's family photo
A celebrity's family photo	(celebrity's name) 家 *(leave a blank here)*	A celebrity's family photo	(celebrity's name) 家 *(leave a blank here)*

Information Gap (Sheet B)

Instructions for Group B: You have **Sheet B**. Find a friend with **Sheet A**, guess how many members in a celebrity family twice, then use " 几 (jǐ)" to ask, "(celebrity's name) 家有几个人？（_____ jiā yǒu jǐ ge rén?)". Write down the answer the student with **Sheet A** gives you, and do not show your sheet to your partner.

Please find the answer to the next question from another friend who has **Sheet A**.

Example:

B: (celebrity's name) 家有三个人吗？　　A: 不对。

B: (celebrity's name) 家有四个人吗？　　A: 不对。

B: (celebrity's name) 家有几个人？　　　A: (celebrity's name) 家有五个人。

A celebrity's family photo	(celebrity's name) 家 *(leave a blank here)*	A celebrity's family photo	(celebrity's name) 家 *(leave a blank here)*
(celebrity's name) 家 *(leave a blank here)*	A celebrity's family photo	(celebrity's name) 家 *(leave a blank here)*	A celebrity's family photo

Tip for choosing celebrities: Choose celebrities known to the students, as long as they do not know the number of the celebrity's family members.

1. Form two lines. Students from Group A stand in one line against the whiteboard. Students from Group B line up facing Group A.

2. Group A students ask questions according to the given sheet, then switch so that Group B asks questions from their sheet. Teacher will time each round for 1 minute and 30 seconds (1.5 minutes / picture × 8 pictures = 12 minutes). Then ask the leftmost Group B student to go to the right end of the line while the rest of Group B steps to the left and starts the process again with a different partner.

Post-Activity (Formative assessment, presentational)

At the end, ask a few students to the front and introduce four families.

Activity 2: 甘迪家有 X 个人。你家呢?

Warm-up (5 minutes)

Heart Attack Game (Student-student, game in groups of four)

1. Divide students into groups of four. Teacher prepares four sets of eight images (the same family images from Sheets A & B above) and cuts out each family image for a total of 32 images. Shuffle them and put the pile in the middle of the desk, face down.

2. Moving clockwise, group members take turns flipping over the top card of the deck. Everyone has the chance to describe the family shown: "(celebrity's name) 家有 五 个人。"Whoever gets it right first gets the image card.

3. The one who gets the most cards wins.

Pre-Activity: Teacher's Demonstration (Teacher-student, student-student, 2 minutes)

1. The teacher says to student 1 " (Celebrity's name) 家有五个人。你家呢？ "

Student 1: "我家有四个人。"

2. The teacher asks student 2 "Obama 家有 四个人。你家呢？ "

Student 2: "我家也有四个人。"

3. Student 2 then asks student 3 "Yao Ming 家有三个人。你家呢？ "

4. Students practice among themselves a couple more times.

In-Activity: Think-Pair-Share (Interpretive and presentational, 5 minutes)

1. Think: Using the same images, students hold one up, first writing down information about the family shown, then their own. (*Pinyin* is acceptable.) "_____ 家有五个人。你家呢？ ""我家有四个人。"

2. Pair: Student shares their written notes with a partner for peer evaluation.

3. Share: Students divide into groups of four and share their information with the group.

Post-Activity (2 minutes)

Ask a couple of groups to do a presentation in front of the class. For example:

_____ 家有三个人。 _____ 家也有三个人。 _____ 家有四个人。我家有五个人。

Activity 3

Pre-Activity: Reviewing Vocabulary (Teacher-student, teacher's demonstration, 5 minutes)

Kinship terms: 爸爸 , 妈妈 , 哥哥 , 姐姐 , 弟弟 , 妹妹

1. Project a family tree on the screen or draw one on the whiteboard (in advance) with ages in each shape. ○ stands for male, □ stands for female, and the eldest sibling is at the far left.

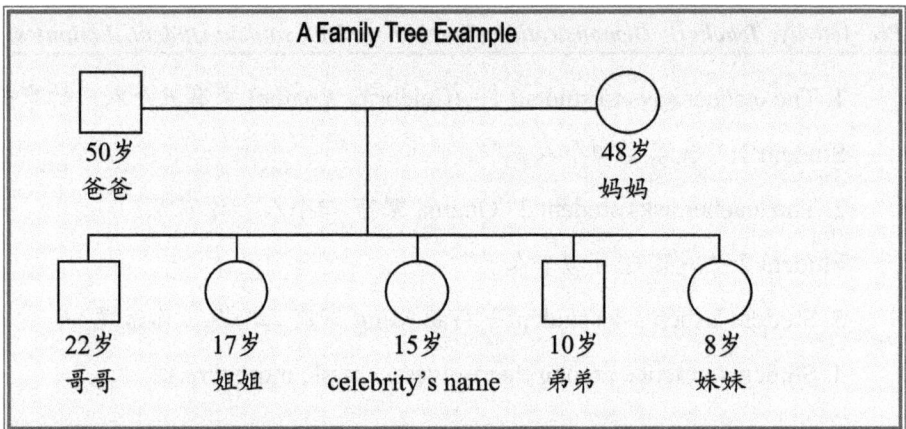

2. Teacher holds up a celebrity's picture and says "(celebrity's name) 家有七个人：爸爸，妈妈，哥哥，姐姐，弟弟，妹妹和她。"

3. Holding another celebrity family photo："＿＿＿ 家有五个人：爸爸，妈妈，弟弟，妹妹和她。"

4. Showing another celebrity's family photo on a PowerPoint slide, ask students to try to introduce the family, then have them practice more with other celebrities' family photos.

In-Activity: Inside-Outside Circle (Student-student pair work, interpersonal, 12 minutes)

1. Each student receives an image of a family.

2. Form an inside-outside circle: Students count off 1 and 2. Students with the number 1 are the inside ones, and students with the number 2 are outside ones, and those in each circle pair off facing each other.

3. The inside circle starts the conversation. Showing a celebrity's family picture or cartoon figures, the inside group uses all sibling terms to ask questions. If the answer is "Yes", ask how many siblings (see the dialogue below).

Dialogue sample:

The inside one asks, "＿＿＿ 有哥哥吗？" The outside one answers, "他没有哥哥。"

The inside one asks, "＿＿＿ 有姐姐吗？" The outside one answers, "他没有姐姐。"

The inside one asks, "＿＿＿ 有弟弟吗？" The outside one answers, "他有弟弟。"

The inside one asks, "他有几个弟弟？" The outside one answers, "他有一个弟弟。"

The inside one asks, "＿＿＿ 有妹妹吗？" The outside one answers, "他有妹妹。"

The inside one asks, "他有几个妹妹？" The outside one answers, "他有一个妹妹。"

---

4. Whenever teacher claps once, students switch roles, with the outside students showing a picture (e.g., another cartoon figure) and asking "_____ 有哥哥吗？" and the inside one answering. Follow the steps above; each round is 1.5 minutes.

5. Whenever teacher claps twice, the inside students move one step clockwise to face a new partner and start again, repeating the steps above.

6. Continue this cycle and practice it with four different classmates. (2 minutes × 4 = 8 minutes.)

Post-Activity (Presentational, formative assessment, 2 minutes)

1. Randomly ask three students to the front and give each of them a picture of a celebrity.

2. Ask them to introduce their celebrity's family by using 家, 有, 没有 and applicable kinship terms. For instance: _____ 家有五个人：爸爸，妈妈，一个弟弟，一个妹妹。他没有哥哥，也没有姐姐。

Activity 4: The Real Family

In-Activity: Family Interview Sheet (Student-student, interpersonal, 10 minutes)

Instructions to students:

1. Please interview three friends and ask whether they have brothers and/or sisters.

2. Write down the results on the sheet.

   Start the conversation with a greeting (see the following example). The teacher demonstrates it with a student first:

A: 你好！
B: 你好！
A: 我叫 _____。请问你叫什么名字？
B: 我叫 _____。
A: 请问你家有几个人？
B: 我家有四个人。你家呢？
A: 我家有七个人。你有哥哥吗？
B: 我没有哥哥，我有姐姐。你呢？你有哥哥姐姐吗？
A: 我没有哥哥，也没有姐姐。我有一个弟弟，三个妹妹。

Family Interview Sheet

Interview three friends and note down their answers. You will introduce them later.

	同学名字 tóngxué míngzi	几个哥哥 gēge	几个姐姐 jiějie	几个弟弟 dìdi	几个妹妹 mèimei
1					
2					
3					

Post-Activity (Presentational, formative assessment, 2 minutes)

Teacher asks 2-3 students to present their friends' information to class, using all sibling terms（哥哥, 姐姐, 弟弟, 妹妹）and 家, 几个, 有, 没有.

Activity 5: Draw an Imaginary Family Tree

Instructional Input (2 minutes)

Teacher draws a simple family tree and explain to students what this tree means, using the explanation from "A Family Tree Example" in Activity 3. Ask students to be aware of what a square or a circle symbolizes, and the position of the eldest children (on the far left).

In-Activity (Student-student, individual work to small group work, 5 minutes)

1. Ask students if they know any friends or celebrities who have a big family (at least five members).

2. Have each student draw a family tree for that big family, including the numbers of family members and siblings. *Note: Most students have only one or two siblings and seldom get the chance to use all kinship terms, which is why this activity was designed.*

3. Form students into groups of three. Each student takes turns describing this family tree by using 家, 有, 没有 to their group members.

4. Check the tree. (Peer evaluation)

Post-Activity (Student-student, interpretive, formative assessment, 2 minutes)

Teacher asks one or two students to the front to give a family narrative. The other students need to draw the family trees accordingly.

Homework:

Ask your parents about their family members, and if possible, ask the questions in Chinese. *Note: This is another way for students to practice speaking Chinese at home. They can explain to their parents what the Chinese words mean. The parents only need to give answers in English.*

Bring the data back to class and be ready to introduce your father's and mother's families to friends. (Community)

Possible questions:

- 你有哥哥吗？你有几个哥哥？他叫什么名字？他多大？
- 你有姐姐吗？你有几个姐姐？她叫什么名字？她多大？
- 你有弟弟吗？你有几个弟弟？他叫什么名字？他多大？
- 你有妹妹吗？你有几个妹妹？她叫什么名字？她多大？

Closure: (4 minutes)

Exit ticket: Teacher shows a celebrity's family photo, and students need to answer teacher's questions accordingly.

Teacher Self-assessment:

- What went well?
- What needs more review during the next class?
- Did the activities help students learn effectively?
- What should be done differently?

Day 2

Teaching Focus:

Ask for information to identify someone's family members.

Grammar:

- 这张照片是谁的？ → 这张照片是我的。

- 这是我弟弟。那是王先生的儿子。

- 二 vs. 两　两 + MW + noun　两个学生, 两个美国人, 两张照片

- S + # + 岁　他几岁？ → 他十岁。

- 他上几年级？ → 他上四年级。

Vocabulary:

- 两, 岁, 年级, 这, 那, 张, 我的, 照片, 男孩子, 女孩子, 谁

- Kinship terms: 爷爷, 奶奶, 外公, 外婆, 儿子, 女儿

Phonetics:

- "ui" as in 岁

- "zh" as in 这, 张, 照

- "po" as in 婆

- "ü" as in 女

Family Project Assignment: Part I

- Please use Glogster/A4 paper to draw your own or your favorite celebrity's family tree.

- List the ages, kinship terms, and nationalities of family members. (See the family tree example from Day 1, Activity 3.)

Day 3

Teaching Focus:

Talk about/clarify family members' occupations.

Grammar:

Adverbs 也 and 都

- 都 + verB: 爸爸和妈妈都是老师。哥哥和我都是中学生。

- 也 + verB: 我姓王，他也姓王。

Vocabulary:

- 做，工作，律师，医生，大学，大学生，中学，中学生，小学，小学生，英文，不工作，没工作

- Students can ask teacher the Chinese names of family members' occupations they have not yet learned.

Phonetics:

- "z" as in 做，作

- "ü" as in 律，学

- "ui" as in 退

- "iu" as in 休

Family Project Assignment: Part II

- Please use Glogster/A4 paper to draw the father's side of your own or your favorite celebrity's family tree.

- List the ages, kinship terms, nationalities, and occupations of family members. (See the family tree example from Day 1, Activity 3.)

Day 4

Teaching Focus:

Introduce one's family members' ages and occupations to a friend.

Grammar:

- Review: Number + MW + object 两个姐姐 , 一个弟弟

- Review how to use 几 to ask a question: 你家有几个人？我家有六个人。

Vocabulary:

- The order of siblings: use 大 , 二 , 三 ＋ sibling terms: 大哥 , 二哥 , 大妹 , 二妹

- Review all vocabulary, especially 有 , 没有 (not 不有) , 几 , 谁 , 谁的

- Measure words: 个 , 张

Phonetics:

- Review tone changes for 一 and 不 : 一个 , 不是

Family Project Assignment: Part III

- Please use Glogster/A4 paper to draw the mother's side of your own or your favorite celebrity's family tree.

- List the ages, kinship terms, nationalities, and occupations of family members. (See the family tree example from Day 1, Activity 3.)

- Send the Glogster link to the teacher through Edmodo, or bring a physical poster to class next time. (Technology)

- **Note:** Edmodo is a free educational platform, similar to Facebook but with a more secure, classroom use-only environment. More details can be found at http://www.edmodo.com.

Day 5: Review and Performance-based Assessment

Objectives:

- Introduce three generations of student's own or a favorite celebrity's family, including kinship terms, ages, nationalities, and occupations, using Glogster or a physical poster. (Presentational)

Teaching Materials and Resources:

- Laptop
- Glogster
- Overhead projector
- Poster (if laptop is unavailable)

Teaching Focus:

Review and reinforce what students have learned through the whole unit.

Sample Activity:

Pre-Activity: Preparation for Family Project performance (15-20 minutes)

1. Glogster presenters: Check if students sent the link to the teacher through Edmodo.

2. Physical poster presenters: Ask students to combine all the three family trees – immediate family, father's side, and/or mother's side – together on a physical poster.

In-Activity: Performance-based Assessment (Presentational, 60-70 minutes)

1. Students present their Glogster posters to introduce their own or favorite celebrity's three-generation family.

   Note on the family project: This assignment can be assigned on day 2, and students can start working on the project on days 3 & 4.

2. The rest of the students will draw the family tree while they listen during the presentation. (Interpretive)

3. The final product should resemble the example below, which was written by one of my students and orally presented in class.

X 家有六个人：爸爸，妈妈，两个姐姐，一个妹妹和他。他没有哥哥也没有弟弟。他爸爸四十五岁，妈妈三十八岁，大姐十九岁，二姐十六岁，妹妹九岁。他十五岁。他们是美国人。

他爸爸是公司经理，妈妈是护士。大姐是大学生，二姐和他都是中学生。他妹妹是小学生。他爸爸家有五个人，爸爸有一个姐姐，一个弟弟，没有哥哥，也没有妹妹。

Then continue introducing the celebrity's mother's side family.

Formative Assessment Rubric for Speaking

Category	5 Well Done	4 Good	3 Acceptable	2 Needs Improvement
Required Vocabulary	Used all	Missing 1	Missing 2	Missing 3 or more
Grammar	No errors	Few errors	Some errors	Many errors
Pronunciation	Near native	Intelligible with some mistakes	Intelligible with many mistakes	Unintelligible
Fluency	Smooth	Occasional hesitation	Some unnatural pauses	Many unnatural pauses
Task Completion	All done	Missing 1 part	Missing 2 parts	Missing 3 parts

Presentation Rubric (for Performance Activity)

Category	5 points	4 points	3 points	2 points
Comprehensibility	Fully comprehensible: requires no interpretation on listener's part	Very comprehensible: requires minimal interpretation on listener's part	Quite comprehensible: requires some interpretation on listener's part	Incomprehensible: barely comprehensible to the listener

Grammar Points	A couple of errors	Some errors	Many errors that do not obscuring meaning	Numerous errors that obscure meaning
Fluency	Smooth	Occasional hesitation	Some unnatural pauses	Many unnatural pauses
Pronunciation	Near native	Intelligible with some mistakes	Intelligible with many mistakes	Unintelligible
Required Vocabulary	Used all	Missing 1	Missing 2	Missing 3 or more

Writing Rubric

	Task Completion	Comprehensibility	Level of Discourse	Vocabulary	Grammar
6	Superior completion of the task: appropriate and with elaboration	Fully comprehensible	Exemplary development: strong use of examples or details	Exemplary word choice: vivid, specific, precise	Exemplary use: complete and correct with sentence variety
5	Appropriate and adequate completion of the task	Easily comprehensible	Effective development: clear use of examples or details	Effective use: 2 errors	Effective use: 2 errors
4	Partial completion of the task	Mostly comprehensible	Adequate development: sufficient use of examples or details	Adequate word choice: 4 errors	Adequate sentence structure: 4 errors
3	Less than partial completion of the task	Partially comprehensible	Limited development: Some use of examples or details	Limited word choice: 6 errors	Limited sentence structure: 6 errors

2	Minimal completion of the task	Barely comprehensible	Minimal development/ response: lacks examples or details	Minimal word choice: inadequate, incorrect	Minimal sentence structure: some incomplete sentences and errors
1	Not complete at all	Incomprehensible	Inadequate development: lacks examples or details	Inadequate word choice: rambling, inappropriate, incorrect	Inadequate structure: numerous incomplete sentences

Dai-Hau Ruth Tang (唐代豪) received her B.A. degree from Providence College with a major in Chinese Literature and a minor in Western Languages and Literature. She later obtained her Master's Degrees in Marriage, Family and Child Counseling and in Religion in the United States. She started teaching Mandarin Chinese as a second language in 2004, and now teaches at Round Rock High School/Cedar Ridge High School in Round Rock, Texas. She teaches all levels of Chinese language courses, including Pre-AP and AP Chinese. She attended STARTALK Chinese language teachers, training at the University of Houston and the University of Nebraska in the past few years, and was an instructor for the 2013 Rice University STARTALK Student Program.

Birthday (in Family)

Heidi Steele (施海蒂)
Peninsula School District, Gig Harbor, Washington

Language Proficiency Level: Novice

Age Range: 14-18 (high school, grades 9-12)

Class Size: 16-33 students

Time Frame:

Fourteen class sessions, each 55 minutes long (with possible extensions for longer class periods)

Essential Questions:

- How do you talk about family in Chinese, and what are some characteristics of family configurations in China?

- How do you talk about birthdays in Chinese, including asking about age, and how are birthdays typically celebrated in China?

Unit Questions:

- How do you describe who is in your family?

- What are family configurations like in China?

- How do you ask someone how many people are in their family?

- How do you ask someone when his/her birthday is, and how do you tell someone your own birthday?

- How do Chinese celebrate birthdays?

- How do you ask someone their age?

Lesson Outlines:

Day 1: The terms for family members (爸爸, 妈妈, 哥哥, 姐姐, 妹妹, 弟弟)

Day 2: Extended family (culture lesson)

Days 3 and 4: Activities on measure words

Day 5: How many people are there in your family, and who are they? 你家有几口人？我家有……

Day 6: Family pets 宠物

Day 7: Introduce family members (This is..., that is...) 这是我（的）……，那是我（的）……

Days 8 and 9: Activities on "whose/ 谁的 ": 那只小狗是谁的？这张照片是谁的？ Measure word for photographs, this/that photograph… 这张照片是……

Day 10: Occupations of family members

Day 11: Inclusive and exclusive sentences 都是, 都不是, 都有, 都没有

Day 12: Birthdays 你的生日是几月几号？我的生日是……

Day 13: Ask ages 你几岁？你今年多大？您多大岁数？

Day 14: Closure

Learning Objectives:

Students will be able to:

Days 1 and 2

- Talk about immediate family members;
- Recognize the characters for immediate family members;
- Tell their classmates if they have extended family members who are important to them.

Days 3, 4, and 5

- Demonstrate knowledge of when measure words are needed;
- Give examples of a few common measure words and the nouns they are used with;
- Specify the family members (e.g., two elder sisters, two younger brothers, etc.) they are talking about;
- Ask and tell how many people there are in their family;
- Tell someone who is in their family.

Days 6 and 7

- Name their household pets;
- Talk about their pets with the correct measure words;
- Introduce their family members, including pets, by using the possessive marker 的 .

Days 8 and 9

- Talk about photographs using the measure word 张 ;
- Talk about the ownership of photographs;
- Ask and answer "whose" questions using 谁的 to talk about people or objects.

Days 10 and 11

- Talk about the occupations of teacher, doctor, and attorney;
- State the occupations of their parents (based on a list previously compiled by the teacher);

- Describe their family members by making inclusive and exclusive statements using 都 .

Days 12 and 13

- Ask and tell someone when their birthday is;
- Fill in a birthdate form (extension activity);
- Tell someone their age;
- Use appropriate language to ask the age of a child, peer, and older person.

Day 14 (Closure)

- Use language related to family in conversation with native speakers.

Day 12 (Sample Day)

Learning Objectives:

Students will be able to:

- Ask and tell someone when their birthday is;
- Fill it in on a form (extension activity).

Learning Difficulties/Teaching Focus:

- Students may have trouble with the pronunciation of 月 and 日 .
- The syntax of the question 你的生日是几月几号? may pose a challenge because it is so different from the English "When is your birthday?"

Teaching Materials and Resources:

- Teaching station computer with Excel, screen, and overhead projector
- Puppets (optional)

- A document camera (for extension activity)

Instructional Strategies:

Greeting (1 minute)

Open the class with your traditional start (大家好, 老师好, and so on). Draw your students' attention to the learning goals for this class period, which you have already written on the board or posted in your customary place.

- I can ask and answer questions about the date (review).

- I can ask and answer questions about birthdays.

- I can read and write the characters for birthday (生日).

If you plan to add the extension activity described in this chapter, add the following:

- I can recognize the word for "birthdate" (出生日期) and fill in this field on Chinese forms.

Note: *You don't have to have a separate learning goal for every activity. Some activities, such as Activity 3 below, are meant to reinforce material students have just learned and/or learned in previous lessons. Others are meant to launch new learning, but will not wrap up until a future lesson. Activity 4 is an example of this.*

Warm-Up (10 minutes, target language)

Learning Objective:

Students review for fluency, pronunciation, tones, and syntax in asking and answering questions about dates. (This lesson assumes that students have already been introduced to dates and days of the week.)

Display a Chinese language calendar on the classroom screen that shows the current week with the current day highlighted. You can use the Calendar App on a Mac or iPad, the Calendar program on a Windows computer, and so on.

The Calendar App on a Mac with the Current Day Highlighted

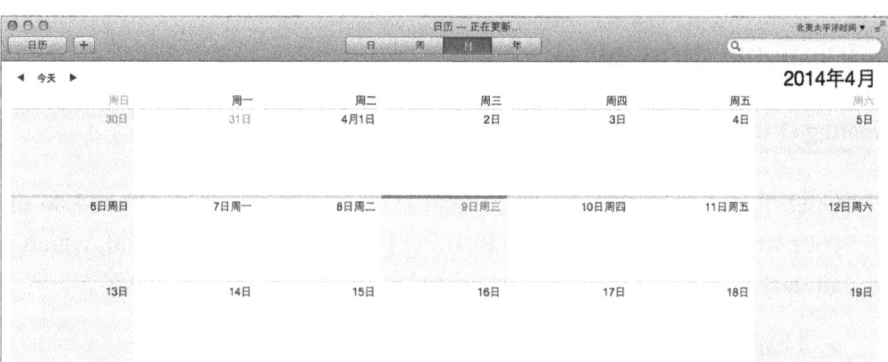

1. Warm-up: Ask students to read the calendar by saying "今天是四月九号，昨天是四月八号" while the teacher points the date.

2. Then ask one or two quick questions, such as 明天是几月几号？后天是几月几号？to refresh the students' memories before you begin the chant described below. (If you have not yet taught 周 as a more formal alternative to 星期 in days of the week and your calendar application refers to weeks this way, point out this form now. By the same token, point out 日 as a formal alternative to 号 if your students haven't learned this yet.)

3. Use the *Month and Date* body percussion chant (view video at http://www. heidisteele.net) to review how to ask and answer questions about the date and to do a quick formative assessment of how well the students have learned these sentence structures, such as "今天是几月几号？今天是四月九号。明天是几月几号？明天是四月十号", and so on. Begin by demonstrating the chant a few times, then lead the students in the body percussion only. Once they have learned the movements, demonstrate the body percussion and the chant together, including both the questions and the answers. When you demonstrate, include one silent sequence of the pattern after each question and answer. (During the "rest" sequences, students have an opportunity to hear the upcoming phrase in their heads, which will help them to internalize it as a musical phrase.)

4. Next, repeat the chant, but this time you ask the questions and the students respond with the answers. Again, give one "rest" sequence in between each speaking phrase. Adjust as needed, repeating phrases the students find more difficult.

5. Finally, split the class into groups A and B. Have the two groups stand up

facing one another. Lead Group A in asking the questions and Group B in answering. You can point to each date on the calendar projected on the screen so the students know whether to ask about today, tomorrow, yesterday (今天, 明天, 昨天). While one half of the group chants, the other half keeps performing the body percussion.

Rationale: *Using rhythmic chants that include body percussion activates the brain in multiple ways at the same time – language, music, rhythm, and large body movement are all included. These activities help students enter an engaged state that is conducive to learning. Just as songs get "stuck in your head," phrases that are taught with rhythm and movement attached can be accessed as complete "musical phrases" later on. This type of practice also improves tones and fluency because the phrases are remembered as complete units. They are fun, too!*

Activity 1 (15 minutes)

Learning Objective:

Students are able to ask and answer the question "When is your birthday?" (你的 生日是几月几号？)

As you transit into this activity, sing a phrase or two of《祝你生日快乐》and emphasize the word 生日 as you sing. Then quickly show a photograph (or series of photographs), such as birthday cakes, birthday hats, and so on. Look for very simple, uncluttered, and funny pictures to engage the students. You can look for images that include the words 生日 or 生日快乐 . Point to the image(s) and say 生日 . Alternatively, you could bring an actual birthday party hat, birthday candles, and so on into class.

Rationale: *By using photographs and/or props, you can teach the word 生日 completely in the target language.*

1. Using two puppets, have one puppet ask the other one:

   A: 你的生日是几月几号？

   B: 我的生日是____月____号, 你呢？

   A: 我的生日是____月____号。

   (If you don't have puppets handy, you can just use your hands or switch roles yourself.)

2. Do it again, but this time, pause after the puppet asks, "你的生日是……" and

gesture to the class to finish the sentence with 几月几号 .

Answer with: 我的生日是____月____号 , and pause again to have students fill in 你呢?

Answer with 我的生日是____月____号。

3. Finally, do it one more time, but write the birthdays you want to use in the dialogue on the board in characters, and then start the dialogue, gesturing to the students to fill in the entire conversation, using the dates you put on the board.

Rationale: *Beginning Chinese 1 students are at the Novice Low to Novice Mid level. They are learning to say short formulaic and memorized phrases. By slowly dropping out more and more of each phrase and asking students to fill it in, you are helping them develop the ability to hear the language in their mind without needing to hear it spoken out loud. In turn, this will make the phrases available to them in authentic settings with native speakers.*

4. Now have the students ask each other their birthdays in pairs first, and then in a chain, so that each student is asked by one other student. (For example, if students are sitting in a semi-circle, each student can ask the student to their right. Or if they are in rows, they can ask the student sitting in front of them, snaking from one column to the next.) Ask them to write down their classmates' answers. (They'll need this for the next activity.) As students are talking, roam around the room to do formative assessments.

Rationale: *By having all the students talking at once, you increase the amount of speaking time for all the students during class.*

Activity 2 (15 minutes)

Learning Objective:

Students review how to make inclusive statements using 都 (from Day 11) in the context of learning to talk about birthdays.

Display the Birth Month spreadsheet on the screen (available for download on http://www.heidisteele.net). Ask one student to volunteer to come up to the front of the classroom and input data. Each student reports the month of the birthday of the student whom they asked in the previous activity (她 / 他____月过生日). As they report, the volunteer tabulates the number of students who have birthdays in each month by entering numbers in the 生日人数 row of the spreadsheet. The chart and 总数 cell will update automatically. (If your students haven't learned 过 yet, simply write it in on the board with *pinyin* and the English "to celebrate," and refer to it as needed until students understand its use.)

Blank Birth Month Chart

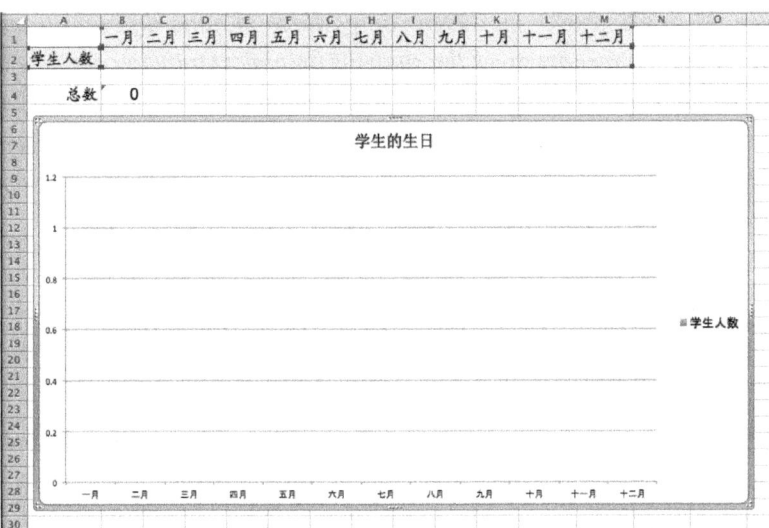

Filled-in Birth Month Chart

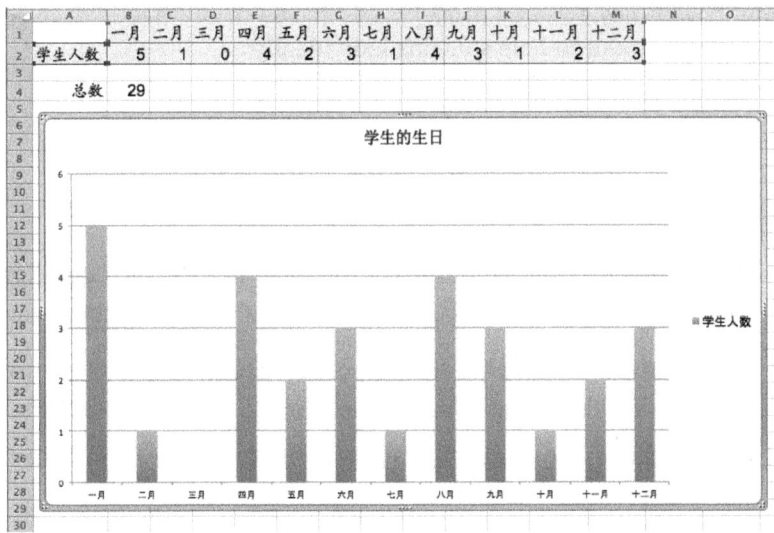

Once the data are input, ask 谁 × 月过生日？请站起来。Then ask them to answer "我们都 × 月过生日。" Depending on time and on the vocabulary your students already know, you can also extend this activity by asking questions such

349

as 几个同学十二月过生日？哪个月有五个人过生日？ As the students engage in dialogue with you about the chart, you can do a quick formative assessment, as well as help students with pronunciation, tones, and so on.

Rationale: *Reviewing the 都 V structure in a new linguistic situation is important since 都 in Chinese is an adverb only, which is quite different from the English "all." Creating a chart gives the students an opportunity to complete a meaningful task while using the language they are studying. Having a student input the data takes the focus off of the teacher. Finally, when students report information about a classmate instead of themselves, they practice talking about someone in the third person, an important linguistic skill.*

Activity 3 (5 minutes)

Learning Objective:

Students learn the meanings of 生 and 日 as well as the correct stroke order for writing them. In addition, they review the names of the strokes.

Refer to 生日 on the board. First, have the students trace the character with their fingers in the air, saying the names of the strokes (撇，横，横，竖，横) as they draw. Second, ask students to write " 生日 " a few times in their notebooks while you roam the room to help students individually.

Activity 4 (10 minutes)

Learning Objective:

- Students reflect on the birthdays role play in their own cultures in order to prepare them to explore the ways Chinese view and celebrate birthdays.

- They also learn to value and respect their own heritage – a critical part of laying a healthy foundation for respecting the heritage of others.

1. Give students five minutes to discuss the following questions in small groups of three or four. They can speak in English if necessary.

   1) How are birthdays typically celebrated in your culture? 你怎么过生日？(请朋友到我家，吃蛋糕。)

   2) Are birthdays more focused on kids, adults, or old people, and why? In

which culture?

3) What do we usually eat on birthday？过生日我们常常吃什么？(吃蛋糕)
What about Chinese people? 中国人呢?

4) What do we usually do on birthday？过生日我们常常做什么呢？(请朋友
去你的生日晚会。) 中国人呢?

2. Have the groups briefly share their findings, paying close attention to traditions other than the dominant Western ones in order to make sure all students feel seen.

3. As a homework assignment (done in English if necessary) in preparation for the next class, ask the students to find answers for these same questions about how birthdays are celebrated in China. Tell students to expect variation between rural/traditional and urban/modern areas.

Rationale: *Students discuss in small groups so that they learn more about each other. The students take ownership of their learning by thinking of other possible questions they may have.*

Closure (5 minutes, target language):

Ask students to tell you their birthdays in a complete sentence by writing the sentence on a card (我的生日是 × 月 × 号) and handing it to you as their "exit card" on the way out of class.

Rationale: *You can use the exit cards to assess the students' ability to form a syntactically correct sentence, as well as to assess the accuracy of their characters.*

Day 12 Extension:

Learning Objective:

● Students will understand that 出生日期 refers to their birthdate, not their birthday, so they must include the year.

● Students will also understand that because dates go from large to small, the year will come first, before the month and the date.

1. Tell students what your birthday (生日) is, and then write 出生日期：× 年 × 月 × 日······on the board.

2. If the students appear to need another example, write the birthdates of your siblings or celebrities as well.

3. Ask one or two students to write their birthdates on the board using ＃年＃月 ＃日 .

4. Ask them to guess the meaning of 出生 and 日期 .

5. Divide the class into groups and give each group one screen capture of a form that contains a field for birthdate. Ask the students to keep it face down (see examples below – you don't have to include the entire form).

The top portion of a school enrollment form that includes a 出生日期 field.

1. When you say start (开始!), each group flips over their form, finds the 出生日期 field, and fills it out correctly with the birthdate of one of the members of the group. The first group to raise their hands and say 好了! wins. (You can pass out a little prize if you like.)

2. Give each group a few more minutes to talk about what kind of form they think they might be looking at, such as 这是要上学的, 这是医院的.

3. Have each group bring their form up to the front and put it under the document camera. Have one of the students in the group point out the 出生日期 field and read the birthdate their group filled in.

Rationale: *Competitions are engaging for students and promote teamwork. Working with authentic materials is critical for preparing our students to function in environments in which they are only able to understand a portion of the language input around them. They must strengthen their ability to make inferences based on a wide variety of contextual and language-based clues, and they have to learn to relax even though they don't understand everything.*

Performance-based Assessment:

At the end of the Family unit, each student can create a presentation introducing their family using VoiceThread (http://voicethread.com).

The following instructions are an example of what you might give your students.

Instructions for Family unit VoiceThread:

1. Include at least five photographs, each on a separate VoiceThread slide. You do not need to include all the family members. You may include photographs of friends and pets.

2. Create a written and recorded (voice) comment about each photograph. These comments should not be the same.

3. As you make your recorded comments, use the VoiceThread pencil tool to draw attention to the person (or animal) in the photograph that you are talking about. You might draw a circle around something, draw an arrow pointing to it, and so on.

4. Speak in and write in complete sentences.

5. Make sure that your presentation includes information about how many people are in your family and who they are, as well as the occupations of one or two people. In addition, refer to at least one person's (or pet's) age, and to at least one person's (or pet's) birthday.

6. In at least a couple of places, talk about the photographs themselves by using the measure word 张 : "this photograph...", "that photograph...".

Rubric for Assessing the Students' VoiceThread Presentations

	Insufficient	Approaching	Proficient	Exceeds
Content (as Outlined in Instructions)	Includes almost none of the required content	Includes some of the required content	Includes all of the required content	Includes all of the required content as well as additional details
Speaking: Fluency	No recorded comments, or extremely halting speech	Speaks with very frequent pauses	Speaks smoothly with a few pauses	Speaks smoothly throughout presentation
Speaking: Pronunciation and Tones	No recorded comments, or incomprehensible pronunciation and/or no tones	Frequently hard to understand because of mispronounced words and incorrect tones	Can understand with some effort, although there are some problems with pronunciation and tones	Easy to understand because pronunciation and tones are almost all correct
Speaking: Grammar	No recorded comments, or grammar mostly incorrect	Frequent grammatical errors affect comprehensibility	Grammar is correct, with the exception of one or two small errors	Grammar is correct
Writing: Accuracy	No written comments, or filled with so many errors that text is not comprehensible	Some text is readable, but there are frequent typos	Only one or two typos	There are no typos
Writing: Grammar	No written comments, or grammar completely scrambled	Some text is grammatically correct, but there are frequent grammatical errors	Only one or two grammatical errors	Easy to understand because all grammar is correct

Note: *The "Proficient" level is based on the Novice Mid level of the ACTFL proficiency scale. Students are speaking in phrases at this level, but should also be able to produce formulaic sentences.*

354

Closure Activity for the Unit (Day 14)

A great way to wrap up this unit is to invite two or more native Chinese speakers to come to your class to converse with your students in an informal way about families. For tips on how to effectively design lessons that include native speaker visitors to your classroom, please see http://www.heidisteele.net.

Heidi Steele (施海蒂) began her study of Chinese in middle school, inspired by great-aunts who taught English in China during the 1930s and 1940s. She later earned a Master's degree in Chinese/English Translation and Interpretation from the Monterey Institute of International Studies. Since 2005, she has been teaching secondary Chinese in the Peninsula School District, WA, and coordinating a Confucius Classroom program that includes a two-way student exchange program with a partner school in China based on cultural and language immersion. In addition to her work with students, she mentors guest teachers from China for the College Board.

Critique

Family – Lili Liu
Family – Dai-Hau Ruth Tang
Birthday (in Family) – Heidi Steele

Three authors, Lili Liu, Dai-Hau Ruth Tang, and Heidi Steele, have written on the theme *Family and Birthday*. The targeted proficiency level is novice, though Lili Liu's students are younger than the other two groups. The authors provide work on the selection of instructional focus, varied activities, continuous assessments, and reflections on learning and teaching. Learning is made easy by well-structured instruction that progresses from simple language exercises to more complex communication. For example, when determining teaching focus at the beginning of the design, Liu pinpoints the facts that noun classifiers (几口人？ 两个哥哥) and Wh-questions can be confusing. Learning difficulty determines where the instructional focus should be. Consequently, a series of activities that require three communicative modes is carefully organized for students to create questions and carry out conversations in context. The special question forms and noun classifiers are repeatedly practiced in meaningful contexts in both "Family" designs. One vivid example is Activity 2 (他是谁？Who is my new friend?) in Liu's design, which requires students to investigate the person "on his/her back" by asking different students questions in order to find out the identity of this classmate or new friend.

356

The three authors divide their activities into a few steps to scaffold learning. For example, in both Liu's and Tang's designs, in addition to warm-up activities, each activity contains pre-, main-, and post-activity components. Activities start with instructional input and interaction between the teacher and students and gradually move to students' pair or group work. Main and post-activities should flow smoothly, thanks to the facilitating instructional processes of the warm-up and pre-activities. For example, Activity 3 of Tang's design starts with an innovatively designed Family Tree Example. The activity continues with a class conversation about a celebrity's family based on the picture provided, and then between two students in the format of Inside and Outside Circles. When students are asked to present the celebrity's family during the final step, they will able to do so successfully, since they have practiced at least four times with different partners. The family tree diagram is used continuously in Activity 5 and the unit project. It is worth noting that the activities designed by all three authors are diverse in format, style, and content, and all have clear teaching procedures.

Both formative and summative assessments provide valuable learning experience. All the three authors have arranged constant formative assessments into activities, mostly group work, in which every student is given one more opportunity to learn from peers. In the post-activity (as in Liu's and Tang's design) or last activity (as in Steele's design), the teacher frequently calls on students to present their work in front of the class. By calling on students who did well in the main activities, the teacher carefully avoids intimidating students who are still in the learning process and rewards those who have mastered the skills. In this way, the designs integrate differentiated instruction to accommodate students' varied needs and styles.

Another highlight is the reflections on learning and teaching. In Liu's design, at the end of the class sessions, students are given a carefully designed Reflection Slip, which covers learning outcomes (a positive reinforcement and review), what is not easy to learn, and the learning strategies that students bring to class and use in their task performance. Strategies are the most fundamental skills that students need to develop because they foster autonomous learning. In both Liu's and Tang's designs, teacher self-assessment is used as a mechanism to immediately reflect on one's teaching and think of alternatives for improvement. In Steele's design, rationales are constantly provided, evidence that the teacher knows what she is doing and reflects on her teaching for improvement.

All the three authors provide useful teaching techniques and tips throughout the designs. They include how to creatively use double block class periods (90 minutes) to keep all the students engaged and on-task (Liu's design), how to encourage students to say longer and complete sentences (Tang's design), and how chanting in context makes learning fun with rhythm and beats (Liu's and Steele's designs). In Steele's design, the example of helping students learn "the 都 V structure" demonstrates that it may not be useful for a teacher just to tell students that the Chinese adverb 都 is not equivalent to the English word "all" (although the translation in the dictionary and the textbook often state so). Instead, the teacher creates a context in which students understand the usage of 都 by using it to complete the task of finding out whose birthdays are all in a particular month.

Steele's design has two unique features. First, the topic "Birthday" is under the frame of Family, where the unit theme starts. It ends with birthday, which is an interesting way to implicitly introduce how Chinese culture views the relationship between the individual and the family. Second, Steele's design is especially valuable to new teachers who have little experience in teaching Chinese as a second language. The design provides many helpful details, notes, and the rationales underlying the activities and instructional steps.

In Liu's design, the third objective for the Sample Day, "Gain knowledge of multi-generational households in traditional Chinese culture" is practiced little in class. This objective could be fulfilled as a homework assignment in which students read a passage in English at home. In Steele's design, the learning objective of "how are birthdays typically celebrated in China?" presents a similar challenge. The objective is beyond the novice proficiency level, and consequently Activity 4 in Steele's design is largely in English. The validity of spending 10 minutes in English on the Chinese culture of celebrating birthdays in class is questionable. The homework assignment in Tang's design is unique and interesting. If the parents are committed to their child's learning, they may even learn a little Chinese language from their child's oral homework, and therefore the impact of such homework is invaluable. However, if parents are too busy to share time with their child, this homework would be difficult to do. In Steele's design, learning objectives such as "Name their household pets" and "Talk about their pets with the correct measure words" seem to be more discrete activities at the vocabulary level than objectives.

Index